CRITICAL PRAISE F
ON DEMOCRACY

"This lucid book goes beyond ... by now familiar exegesis of the current economic crisis to examine the ways in which the organization of the American economy shapes democratic politics. With flair and brilliance, Joshua Cohen and Joel Rogers examine both the constraints and the possibilities which delimit the future of the American political economy."

—Frances Fox Piven,
Coauthor, *The New Class War*

"The facts alone are worth the price of admission . . . the best extant statement of what's wrong with America—progressive diagnosis and progressive prescription—in the tradition of Debs and F.D.R., through the lens of the leading political philosophers of our time. This book transcends the divisions of the American Left, all the way to Marx and F.D.R., from George McGovern to Abbie Hoffman—it puts it all together."

—Duncan Kennedy,
Professor of Law,
Harvard Law School

"This is a spare, shrewd look at American politics, and a hopeful one. The authors think there's a light at the end of the tunnel. I hope they're right."

—James Ridgeway,
Columnist, *The Village Voice*

PENGUIN BOOKS

ON DEMOCRACY

Joshua Cohen is an Assistant Professor of philosophy and political science at M.I.T.

Joel Rogers is an Assistant Professor of political science at the Newark campus of Rutgers University.

ON
<u>DEMOCRACY</u>

JOSHUA COHEN and
JOEL ROGERS

PENGUIN BOOKS

Penguin Books Ltd, Harmondsworth,
Middlesex, England
Penguin Books, 40 West 23rd Street,
New York, New York 10010, U.S.A.
Penguin Books Australia Ltd, Ringwood,
Victoria, Australia
Penguin Books Canada Limited, 2801 John Street,
Markham, Ontario, Canada L3R 1B4
Penguin Books (N.Z.) Ltd, 182–190 Wairau Road,
Auckland 10, New Zealand

First published 1983

LIBRARY OF CONGRESS CATALOGING IN PUBLICATION DATA
Cohen, Joshua, 1951–
   On democracy.
   Bibliography: p.
   Includes index.
   1. United States—Politics and government—1981–
2. United States—Economic policy—1981–
3. United States—Social policy—1980–
I. Rogers, Joel, 1952–   . II. Title.
JK271.C715   1983   361.6'1'0973   83-12163
ISBN 0 14 00.6781 7

Printed in the United States of America by
R. R. Donnelley & Sons Company, Harrisonburg, Virginia
Set in Primer

CONTENTS

ACKNOWLEDGMENTS

Many people helped us write this book.

An earlier draft benefited from the comments of a large number of friends and colleagues. We thank them all, but wish particularly to acknowledge the extensive remarks provided by David Abraham, Suzanne Berger, Myriam Bienenstock, Robert Brenner, Stephen Bronner, Noam Chomsky, Robert Cohen, Colleen Dunlavy, Ellen Eisen, Gerald Epstein, Andreas Eshete, Steve Fraser, Jeff Frieden, Colin Greer, David Hills, Marcia Homiak, Mark Kesselman, Duane Lockard, Charles Noble, Claus Offe, Daniel Osherson, Frances Fox Piven, John Rawls, Sarah Siskind, Alan Stone, and Pheroze Wadia.

At Penguin Books, Martha Kinney offered consistently useful criticisms at each stage of the developing manuscript, along with the editorial enthusiasm and humor needed to make that manuscript a book, and Anne-Marie Demetz was unusually tolerant of our many questions and requests.

Signal debts are owed Adam Przeworski, whose work greatly influenced our discussion of capitalist democracy; John Rawls, whose influence on our discussion of the idea and practice of democratic association is apparent; and Noam Chomsky, whose exemplary political courage and uncompromising commitment to reason significantly inspired the essay.

More broadly, we are indebted to a tradition of thought, initiated by Jean-Jacques Rousseau and Karl Marx, which has critically explored the relationship between capitalism and democracy. Despite our many disagreements with parts of that tradition, it remains the source of our deepest intellectual and political obligations. In writing *On Democracy* we were once again reminded of that fact.

Joshua Cohen
Joel Rogers

ON
DEMOCRACY

1. OPENING

These are dark times. Against the ominous backdrop of domestic economic turmoil, high unemployment, looming trade wars, and global financial disorder, each day brings news of fresh political disaster. The powers of the American state are now deployed in a massive business offensive. Its basic elements are painfully clear. Drastic cutbacks in social spending. Rampant environmental destruction. Regressive revisions of the tax system. Loosened constraints on corporate power. Ubiquitous assaults on organized labor. Sharply increased weapons spending. Escalating threats of intervention abroad.

Together these initiatives promise a profound reduction in the living standards of millions of Americans, and a quantum leap in the militarization and business dominance of national life. Cynically advanced as expressions of the popular will, they constitute a direct attack on the norms of democratic culture. Ceaselessly promoted as a new mandate, they betray a system of conventional politics that thrives on the fragmentation and manipulation of political demand. Advertised as a strategy of general welfare, they seek to detach the exercise of private power from any significant public constraint, and claim an ever mounting pile-up of victims as their own.

But this onslaught of privilege moves forward on shifting grounds. Among the general population, supply-side optimism has been overtaken by confusion and fear. Among corporate elites, a sustained attack on working people and the poor has failed to resolve long-standing conflicts between protectionists and free traders, sunrise sectors and sunset firms, small businesses and multinational giants, core industries and commercial banks.

Something is wrong in American society, and something more than Reaganism is now at stake in national politics. Something is falling down and breaking apart, and it will not be relieved or explained away by endless recollections of the "national interest," ill-starred bouts of bipartisan consensus, or limitless smiles from party leaders. Everywhere there are sounds of intractable conflict over basic issues of public policy, from the direction of trade and industrial growth to the cost of credit and national defense. Everywhere there are signs of social decomposition and decay, from disintegrating neighborhoods and violent schools to pervasive crime and child abuse. The economy stagnates. The polity languishes. The once celebrated civic culture turns inward and now eats itself alive.

Prompted by political crisis, bitter struggles have erupted to control this country's future. The stakes are very high, but who will finally win or lose remains uncertain, and finally it is this uncertainty that defines the current moment. Even more than the anguish it has occasioned, the contingency of the present period is its overriding feature. Although years of economic decline and political immobility have laid bare the deep structures of American life, no one knows how they will be reordered, or if they can be reordered at all. The future is open.

Even the tedious self-congratulation of those who rule has been momentarily interrupted by the battles now underway. Faced with a potential explosion of anger from a population whose support they require, but whose mobilization they fear, the elites now fighting to dominate the state have abandoned the pretense of disinterest. Politics has again become mundane. Attempts at coalition-building proliferate. Debates and programs of action abound. Think tanks and policy research institutes steadily multiply. New corporate political action committees and private newsletters are born each day. Reaganism is only one strategy. There are many others.

But if those who occupy the commanding heights of private power are mobilizing their forces, those who live beneath them are in startling disarray. Massive discontent with politics-as-usual has not crystallized into insurgency. There is no fighting in the streets, no broad-based political or cultural challenge from below, no serious contestation of those forces and arrangements of authority that have generated the present tumult and its pain. Trade unions are in decline. The poor are in retreat. Independent political institutions are virtually extinct at the national level. The leadership of both major parties seems irretrievably hostaged to private interest.

Nor has any democratic left consolidated itself as a source of opposition and strategic action. During the past decade, most of those who participated in the popular movements of the 1960s and early 1970s have either withdrawn entirely from overt political action, or retired to the noisy silence of sectarianism, or practiced a loosely conceived and rarely successful "coalition politics" based on the short-term issue coordination of otherwise competing groups. Largely irrelevant to the central movements of power in American society, the left has joined the rest of the population in a communion of impoverishment, bereft of any shared structure through which it can articulate political demand.

Amid this fragmentation, opposition persists, but its effective expression is commonly denied. Millions march against the threat of war, but that threat grows steadily larger. Neighborhoods organize against corporate flight, but capital takes its business elsewhere. The language of racism and sexism is argued into extinction, but their grotesque practice endures. Struggle is baffled by defeat. Uncertainty forestalls brave action. There are many cries of resistance. There is no common voice.

This is the grim political world we now inhabit. It is a world in which broad attacks on poor and working people persist amid intense rivalry among business factions, a world in which the deep disintegration of mass political organization conceals both the logic of oppression and the process of its reversal. This is the world in which we wish to intervene. We who are committed to democracy believe it can and must be changed from a system chained to the whims of private power to one

which liberates in its very structure the strengths and imagi-
nations of all its members. As democrats we are therefore
committed to the transformation of politics in the United States.

Such commitments are neither the conclusion of some
pretended "science" of history, nor another article of ground-
less faith. They are based on an argument about the structure
of American society, the corruption it breeds, the dangers it
now harbors, and the possibilities of its transformation in a
direction more in keeping with essential human capacities.
This argument proceeds from the first principle of modern
politics, that the power of capital is directly dependent upon
divisions among the working population, to the claim that that
population has a clear basis for unity of action. It is above all
an argument about democracy, the idea that free and equal
persons should together control the conditions of their own
association. Democracy is neither an ephemeral dream nor a
dusty collection of legal rights, but a form of social organization
and political practice which can define a unified movement out
of the present morass. Running like a black thread through all
the present atrocities of private power and the state is an insis-
tent attack on this basic idea of human freedom. This book
attempts to answer that attack.

But because our answer is political, how it can begin is by
no means clear. It may be, as we will argue, that a determined
movement of opposition is needed at this time, and that the
possibilities and appeal of a genuinely democratic ordering of
social life can provide a unifying ideal for such a movement.
But we cannot begin there. For that ideal to be widely shared
there must at least be some agreement about what a democratic political order requires, and before those requirements
can be identified there must be a way to distinguish them from
that which now passes under the name of democracy. Drawing
that distinction in turn requires an analysis of the present
structure of power in this country. But such analyses are always
difficult and never fully successful, and because of their difficulty and uncertain benefit, many are understandably reluc-
tant to give them much patience or time.

So an initial act of persuasion is called for, some indication
of the importance of thinking seriously about these matters in
the first place. And that act of persuasion cannot itself rely on
an appeal to those specific political views whose clarification
and support comprise one burden of the subsequent analysis.
This last constraint is a particularly important one in the United
States, in part because traditions of collective political action
seem so remote in general, in part because of the acute problems of fragmentation that mark the present period. But in the
absence of clear traditions or clearly marked alternatives, any
first step in the argument will seem to move too far too fast.
There is always a problem of beginning, and as public frustration grows, so too do the dimensions of that problem. There are
always ways of closing off political discussion. More difficult is
finding a way to open and sustain one.

But present circumstances may themselves provide an answer
here, and that answer may indicate both the reasons for going
forward in thought and the need to consider going forward in
action. Things are now so strange and bad in America, so at
odds with conventional conceptions of this country and what it
stands for, that a bare listing of the most obvious symptoms of
the current crisis may itself provide an opening. The power of
such a listing does not depend on prior political agreement, nor
even on agreement that political action is required at this time.
But it does inevitably rely on a capacity for moral concern and
judgment, and on the recognition that such concern might not
be satisfied with merely naming this world. It might lead us to
wish to change it.

2. SYMPTOMS

For millions of Americans, faith in the inevitability of a better future has been shattered by the growing disorders of national life. Here we present a catalogue of those disorders. Organized by familiar classifications, and stated in the conventional terms of public debate, this catalogue may indicate some of the sources of the confusion, anger, and even despair now felt so widely in the United States. We stress again that it is not our purpose in this chapter to provide an analysis of American politics. Nor do we aim at a complete or even impartial description of the American social order. Rather, our purpose here is to present some basic facts about contemporary life in the United States, and in so doing to suggest the need for serious analysis of that life.

ECONOMY

Take your pick. Despite current fluctuations and mixed signals, on almost any standard measure the American economy has some serious problems. Consider employment and growth. In 1982 U.S. industrial plant operated at an average of only 69.8 percent of capacity, the lowest figure on records that go back to 1948.[1] Real gross national product (GNP) fell 1.8 percent during the year, the sharpest drop since 1946.[2] The average official unemployment rate was 9.7 percent, the highest yearly rate since 1941.[3] Nearly one out of every four workers was unemployed at some point during 1982.[4] By the end of the year the official jobless rolls included 12 million Americans, or fully

10.8 percent of the total workforce.[5] But that official measure did not include the 1.8 million "discouraged" workers who were estimated to have left the labor force before the December count, or the more than 6.5 million who had accepted part-time solutions to their quest for full-time work.[6] Unemployment is not only increasing, but also lasts longer. In 1980 the average duration of official unemployment was 11.9 weeks.[7] In 1981 it was 13.7 weeks.[8] By December 1982 the average had grown to 18 weeks, the highest average since the Great Depression.[9] While the 1982 unemployment figures are especially bad, average American unemployment rates have been increasing for decades. In the 1950s the average rate was 4.5 percent, in the 1960s it was 4.8 percent, in the 1970s it was 6.2 percent.[10] Thus far in the 1980s it has been 8.2 percent, and most estimates see that average increasing in the next few years.[11]

There are other measures of economic turmoil. Consider bankruptcy. In 1982 there were 25,364 reported business failures in the United States.[12] This represents a 50 percent increase over 1981 failure rates, and is more than double the rate of failure recorded in 1975, the peak period of the 1973–75 recession.[13] The 1982 rate of 89 recorded business failures per 10,000 firms may be compared with the average annual 1950s rate of 41.8 failures per 10,000 firms, the 1960s rate of 52.1 failures per 10,000, or the 1970s rate of 35.6 failures per 10,000.[14] Higher than any level achieved in the last 50 years, and 40 percent higher than any average annual rate ever achieved since World War II, the 1982 rate of business failure comes close to the 100 failures per 10,000 firms rate recorded in 1933 in the middle of the Great Depression.[15]

Consider money and banking. Double-digit interest rates have become a new fact of life for most Americans, as have $150-billion-plus federal budget deficits. Correcting for inflation, interest rates have been running several times the levels they maintained, with very rare disruptions, for close to 200 years.[16] In 1982, an estimated 50 percent of corporate cash flow went to debt service, and bank failures were on the rise.[17] In 1981,

for the first time since the Great Depression, total interest
payments exceeded corporate profits as a percentage of national
income. In 1982 the gap widened even further.[18] In the first
half of 1982, there were 22 bank failures.[19] For the first time
since World War II top ten banks posted three-month losses.[20]
In 1981 some 80 percent of savings and loan associations and
mutual savings banks experienced losses.[21] International bank
debt appears dangerously overextended.[22] At the end of 1982
non-oil-exporting developing countries owed $242 billion to
private lenders.[23] U.S. banks held 39 percent of that debt.[24]
The exposure of American banks in Latin America is a particular source of concern. To Mexico alone, in 1982 the nine
largest American banks had loans amounting to 45 percent of
their capital.[25] To Brazil alone, they had loans amounting to 42
percent of their capital.[26] Recent polls indicate that 90 percent
of Americans are "concerned" about the stability of U.S. financial institutions.[27]

Consider the performance of key economic sectors. In 1982
raw steel output dropped to its lowest level since 1946.[28] Automobile output dropped to its lowest level since 1958.[29] "Indefinite layoffs" of auto workers reached record levels in excess of
250,000.[30] Machine tool orders fell 49.1 percent in 1982, and
have dropped nearly 75 percent since 1979.[31] Housing starts
fell to a 36-year low.[32] Unemployment in the construction trades
averaged 20 percent during 1982.[33] By the end of 1982, factory
output had dropped to its lowest level since the beginning of
1977.[34] Of course at least one sector was still hiring. In fiscal
1982, military manpower requirements were easily satisfied by
the more than 327,000 new recruits who joined the armed
forces.[35] The Department of Defense added more than 70,000
new civilian employees in the first year and a half of the Reagan
presidency.[36] In 1982 military reenlistment rates jumped to
their highest level since 1964.[37]

Consider trade. Between 1970 and 1980, the United States
share of world manufactured exports declined 23 percent.[38] In
1982, the merchandise trade deficit set a yearly record.[39] In
part reflecting the declining competitiveness of American

manufacturing in international markets, foreign producers have captured 90 percent of the U.S. cutlery market, 45.5 percent of textile machinery, 28 percent of machine tools, and more than 20 percent of the highly protected domestic steel market.[40] Over the 1970 to 1980 period the foreign share of U.S. markets in autos jumped from 8 to 20 percent, in consumer electronics from 10 to 50 percent.[41] Japan, which controls 70 percent of the world market for 64K random access memory (RAM) chips, has also surged to claim 70 percent of the U.S. 64K market.[42] The overall "penetration" of the U.S. economy by imports increased 30 percent between 1973 and 1981 alone.[43]

Consider investment. Fixed capital spending is sharply off. Real capital spending dropped almost 5 percent in 1982, and direct foreign investment in the American economy fell 49 percent in the first half of the year.[44] In the public sector, deteriorating levels of government support for public works have accelerated the decay of an already rotting infrastructure.[45] Between 1965 and 1980 public capital investment dropped by 30 percent, falling from 3.6 percent of GNP to less than 1.7 percent.[46] This level of spending will not be adequate to repair the 45 percent of American highway bridges that are deficient or obsolete, provides less than a third of the cash needed to maintain the nonurban highway system at present levels of service, and falls well short of the estimated $230 billion now needed to maintain crumbling sewers and water mains.[47]

Not surprisingly, such general economic deterioration shows up finally in aggregate measures of long-term economic growth. During the 1960s the average American annual growth rate of real GNP per full-time worker was 2.1 percent.[48] During the 1970s the average was only 1.2 percent.[49] During the 1980 to 1982 period the rate of growth has averaged just under zero percent per year.[50]

STANDARD OF LIVING

It is commonly said that the American standard of living is the highest in the world. Measured by per capita gross domestic product (GDP), so it once was.[51] But among the industrialized nations of the Organization for Economic Cooperation and Development (OECD), in 1980 it ranked 11th, behind that of Switzerland, Denmark, Sweden, West Germany, Iceland, Norway, Belgium, Luxembourg, the Netherlands, and France.[52] This basic measure may be regarded as inadequate on a variety of grounds. It is limited to goods and services traded in international markets, and is highly sensitive to exchange rate variations. But by other measures as well, the quality of American life is at odds with popular conceptions.

Consider health. Virtually unique among advanced industrial states in having no program of national medical insurance, the United States spends nearly 10 percent of its GNP on health care.[53] Health care costs have risen steadily, and faster than almost all other commonly consumed goods.[54] Between 1950 and 1970 the Consumer Price Index (CPI) increased 62 percent, but medical care costs increased 125 percent.[55] In 1982 the 11 percent annual increase in medical care costs was higher than any other inflation factor measured in the CPI.[56] Between 1971 and 1981 the cost of an average hospital stay tripled, from $670 to $2,119.[57] This high level of expenditure notwithstanding, U.S. performance in such standard health measures as infant mortality and life expectancy, while showing improvements in absolute terms, remains far worse than many other countries. The United States ranks 20th in the world in male life expectancy, 11th in female life expectancy, and 22nd in infant mortality.[58] In Washington, D.C., the infant death rate is almost twice the national average, and higher than the infant mortality rates of a number of developing countries, including Barbados, Jamaica, Costa Rica, and Cuba.[59]

Consider air pollution. Between the close of World War II

and the beginning of the 1970s, smog levels in cities increased an estimated 1,000 percent.[60] Measured by emissions of carbon monoxide, hydrocarbons, and nitrogen oxide, the levels of air pollution in the United States are significantly higher than those of most of its major industrial rivals.[61] Consider noise pollution. Each day approximately 20 million Americans are exposed to noise levels permanently damaging to their hearing.[62]

Consider housing. By the end of 1982, the average purchase price for a home reached $78,500.[63] The average new home cost $97,200.[64] In 1950 approximately 70 percent of all American families could afford to buy a house. By 1980 first-time purchase of a home was impossible for all but about 20 percent of the population.[65] Many who have homes fear that they will soon lose them. In 1982 some 66 percent of current homeowners and farmowners expressed the fear that they would lose their homes or farms in the next year as a consequence of failing to meet mortgage payments.[66] There are grounds for such fear. Payment delinquency rates and mortgage foreclosures reached record levels in 1982. Between the first half of 1979 and the first half of 1982, delinquency rates nearly doubled and foreclosure rates more than tripled. Over the same period, the unpaid balances on foreclosed mortgages jumped from $321 million to $1.317 billion.[67] Of course one can always try rental housing, but here too the pressures are growing. The proportion of renters paying more than 25 percent of their income for rent increased from one-third in 1950 to more than half in 1979.[68] Many Americans simply cannot afford any housing at all. Estimates of national homelessness range between 500,000 and 4 million.[69]

Consider worker benefits. Measured in vacation time, sick leave, accident compensation, job retraining programs, and insurance against job loss, the United States lags far behind the rest of the industrialized West.[70]

Consider occupational safety and health. Reported industrial accidents more than doubled between 1965 and 1979.[71] There are now more than 5 million in the United States each year.[72] In 1980 alone, 2.2 million such accidents brought "disabling injuries," of which 80,000 were permanently disabling.[73] Fatal workplace accidents claim approximately 13,000 lives per year.[74] Deaths from job-related diseases run to more than 100,000 per year, and there are roughly 400,000 new cases of job-related disease each year.[75] More than 13,000 toxic chemicals are regularly handled by workers in industry. Exposure standards exist for only about 400 of them.[76] Almost 2 million Americans are severely or partially disabled from an occupational disease.[77] Only 5 percent of the severely disabled receive workers' compensation.[78] In 1978 it was estimated that the Occupational Safety and Health Administration (OSHA) inspected establishments with more than 250 workers on the average of once every four years.[79] Establishments with fewer than 25 workers, which employ 24 percent of the labor force, were inspected on the average of once every 125 years.[80] OSHA enforcement has since declined under the Reagan administration. Estimates of 1982 (fiscal year) enforcement, as compared to 1980 (fiscal year), indicate a 55 percent decline in inspections in response to employee complaints, an 86 percent decline in follow-up inspections, and a 77 percent decline in penalties imposed for violations of the Occupational Safety and Health Act.[81] President Reagan has described his own conception of the proper role of the agency: "My idea of an OSHA would be if government set up an agency that would do research and study how things could be improved, and industry could go to it and say, we have a problem here and seem to lose more people by accidents in this particular function. Would you look at our plant, and then come back and give us a survey?"[82]

Consider environmental hazards. There are some 180,000 contaminated ponds, pits, and lagoons in the United States, 90 percent of which present potential threats of ground-water contamination.[83] In 1980 alone there were 146,000 recorded violations of safe drinking water standards.[84] There are an additional 12,000 to 50,000 toxic waste dumps, many leaking poisonous chemicals into the water supply.[85] Some 90 percent of the 125 billion pounds of hazardous wastes dumped into the environment each year are disposed of improperly.[86] For a task

of toxic-waste supervision estimated to require the full-time
labor of at least 400 trained personnel, the EPA supports the
equivalent of 2.6 employees.[87] Asbestos exposure alone will kill
scores of Americans. Direct occupational exposures will claim
an estimated 8,000 to 10,000 lives a year for the next 25 years
from asbestos-related cancers or complications associated with
asbestosis.[88] An estimated 2 to 6 million students are still
attending schools with asbestos surfaces in student areas, while
100,000 to 300,000 teachers are exposed to the same asbestos.[89] The hazards have been known for some time. In 1935
the president of the major asbestos manufacturer Raybestos-
Manhattan told the general attorney for Johns-Manville, another
major asbestos producer: "I think the less said about asbestos,
the better off we are." The Johns-Manville attorney concurred
in this judgment: "I quite agree with you that our interests are
best served by having asbestosis receive the minimum of
publicity."[90]

Consider social spending. As a percentage of GNP, social
spending in the United States is less than half what it is in
West Germany and Sweden, and is also exceeded by spending
in the Netherlands, France, the United Kingdom, Japan, and
virtually all other advanced industrial states.[91] Between 1950
and 1977 the annual rate of growth of government transfer
payments was smaller in the United States than in Austria,
Canada, Denmark, Finland, France, Germany, Greece, the
Netherlands, Sweden, and Switzerland.[92] This already weak
relative position will deteriorate sharply as a result of the ongoing cuts in real social spending by the Reagan administration.
Those cuts are very nearly comprehensive, covering programs
ranging from black lung payments to disabled coal miners and
food stamps for low-income households to federal retirement
and disability benefits, aid to families with dependent children,
school lunches, unemployment insurance, CETA jobs and
training programs, and Medicaid.[93]

Consider crime. On the average, death by homicide is eight
to nine times more likely in the United States than in other
advanced industrial states.[94] It is more than two and one-half

times more likely than in Finland, the second most murderous country in the OECD.[95] The probability of being murdered for nonwhite men in the United States is one in 28, almost six times as great as the probability for white men.[96] Between 1972 and 1981 the number of reported crimes increased 61.1 percent, while the official crime rate increased more than 46 percent.[97] There was a 74 percent increase in the number of reported rapes in the same period.[98] In all, 13,290,300 murders, rapes, robberies, aggravated assaults, burglaries, larceny-thefts, motor vehicle thefts, and arsons were recorded in 1981.[99] Between 1977 and 1981 there were almost 61 million such crimes reported in the U.S.[100] Some 52 percent of all robberies are committed on the street. The number of reported street robberies increased by two-thirds between 1977 and 1981.[101] If one was born in and remains a resident of a major American city, one's chances of death by murder are greater than the threat of death in combat experienced by American soldiers in World War II.[102]

Consider punishment. As its prison population increases at record rates, it has been estimated that the United States already has a larger percentage of its citizens behind bars than any other nation except the Soviet Union and South Africa.[103] Between 1971 and 1981 the proportion of the American population in prison increased 60 percent, from 96 per 100,000 to 154 per 100,000.[104] In the first half of 1982 the prison population increased 6.9 percent, equivalent to an annual rate of 14.3 percent, 2 percent higher than any previous annual increase on records that go back to 1926.[105] Since 1974 the number of women in prison has increased by more than 100 percent, the number of men by roughly 70 percent.[106]

Consider other indicators of violence and insecurity. A new handgun is sold every 13 seconds in the United States.[107] These guns are frequently used to kill people. In 1981 half the murders in the United States were committed with handguns, 27 each day.[108] While 29 Americans were killed each day in 1979 with handguns, 8 people were killed all year with handguns in Great Britain, 34 all year in Switzerland, 21 in Sweden, 52 in Canada,

8 in Israel, and 42 in West Germany.[109] Those who can afford it hire others to protect them. By 1978 the private security business had grown to a $5 billion industry, with a growth rate of 10–15 percent per year.[110] The gross receipts of Pinkerton's increased more than fivefold between 1965 and 1975.[111] By the end of the 1970s there were 45,000 police officers in California and 50,000 private guards, while New York City had 30,000 public officers and 75,000–100,000 private protection agents.[112]

Different people respond to social stress in different ways. Each percentage point increase in the unemployment rate is for example associated with 318 additional suicides, a 2 percent increase in the mortality rate, a 5–6 percent increase in homicides, a 5 percent rise in imprisonments, a 3–4 percent increase in first admissions to mental hospitals, and a 5–6 percent increase in infant mortality rates.[113]

Consider drug abuse. There are now approximately 13 million alcoholics and problem drinkers in the United States.[114] In 1979 some 20 percent of the teenagers in Massachusetts between 14 and 19 years old had an alcohol-abuse problem.[115] One-third of the American people say that alcohol abuse has caused problems in their family, and 81 percent consider it a major national problem.[116] There are now somewhere between 450,000 and 600,000 heroin addicts in the United States.[117] In New York City the addict population grew 50 percent between 1978 and 1980 alone.[118] Roughly one in every 40 residents of that city is a heroin addict, and municipal authorities report some 6,000 cases of heroin overdose each year and an 80 percent increase in deaths from overdose over the 1978–80 period.[119]

Consider killing. During the 1970s the suicide rate in the United States increased 10 percent and death by homicide and legal intervention jumped 36 percent.[120] Between 1950 and 1978 the suicide rate for 15- to 24-year-old Americans increased 276 percent.[121] Together, suicide and homicide are now the sixth leading cause of death in America.[122]

Finally, consider income. Real median family income fell by 3.5 percent in 1981, dropping back to its 1968 level.[123] The real disposable income of the average American worker has declined to its 1956 level.[124] Government calculations for 1980 for an average family of four subsisting on an average family income and living, as most Americans do, in a city, indicate that the budget could provide amenities at the level of one toaster every 33 years, one family meal out every five weeks, one man's suit every four years, five record albums per year for domestic entertainment, five movies per adult per year, and one sixpack of beer every two weeks.[125] The budget allows for zero savings above this level of consumption.[126]

WEALTH AND INCOME DISTRIBUTION

Living conditions in the United States are strikingly unequal. The lowest fifth of the population receives a smaller percentage of total after-tax income in the United States than in Japan, Sweden, Australia, the Netherlands, West Germany, the United Kingdom, Norway, Canada, and France.[127] Nor is there any tendency toward a reduction in inequality. The gap in real income level between the bottom quintile of families and the top five percent has nearly doubled over the past 30 years.[128] Between 1950 and 1977 the percentage of families receiving less than half the median national income actually increased.[129] In 1951 the bottom 20 percent of American families received 5.0 percent of gross national income, while the top 20 percent received 41.6 percent.[130] In 1981 the bottom 20 percent received the same 5.0 percent share while the top 20 percent captured a 41.9 percent share.[131]

The percentage of wealth held by the top 1 to 2 percent of the population is greater here than in most industrial states.[132] In the "people's capitalism" that is said to describe the U.S. system, the top 0.5 percent of the households own approximately 50 percent of all corporate stock and 52 percent of the bonds, while approximately 85 percent own no stock at all.[133] In 1972 the share of net worth held by the top 0.5 percent of

American families was roughly 20 percent, unchanged from the 1945 share.[134]

Poverty remains widespread.[135] The official incidence of poverty increased in 1981 to 14 percent of American house-holds—31.8 million people—as 2.2 million more Americans joined the ranks of the poor.[136] End-of-the-year 1982 poverty levels were projected to reach highs last reached in the period prior to the War on Poverty.[137] One in every seven Americans, and more than one in every five children under the age of six, lives in poverty.[138] The poverty rate for black Americans is three times the rate for white Americans.[139] More than one-third of the black population and more than one-quarter of the Hispanic population live below the poverty line.[140] For black Americans under 18, the poverty rate is 43.0 percent, for Hispanics, 34.7 percent. In 1981, even before the major Reagan cuts, more than 40 percent of the families living below the poverty line received no food stamps, Medicaid, housing subsidies, or low-price school lunches.[141] Almost 60 percent received no food stamps, 50 percent no Medicaid.[142] By government estimates, the diet of those living at the official poverty level is so deficient that it is suitable only for "temporary or emergency use."[143]

Inequalities persist within the workforce itself. Consider gender-based and gender-compounded inequality. Earnings for women working full time are less than 60 percent of full-time earnings for men, down from 65 percent in 1955 to 59.5 percent in 1981.[144] Full-time black women workers earn 53 percent of what men earn, and Hispanic women only 44 percent.[145] In 1980, the mean annual income of women with four years of college was $14,908, or only 56.5 percent of the $26,381 mean annual income of men with four years of college, 81.4 percent of the $18,309 earned by men with four years of high school, and 96 percent of the average earnings of men with only one to three years of high school.[146] Among full-time working women in 1980, one in three earned less than $7,000.[147] Of those families officially classified as poor, nearly 50 percent are headed by women.[148] In 1981 52.9 percent of the families headed by a black woman with no husband were living under the poverty line, while 27.4 percent of the families headed by a white woman with no husband were officially poor.[149] Of the elderly poor, 72 percent are women, and the poverty rate for elderly women is twice as high as the poverty rate for elderly men.[150] In 1980, 82 percent of elderly black women not living with relatives were classified as below or near poverty.[151]

Among men, black and Hispanic men earn only about 80 percent of what white men of the same age and same level of education earn.[152] Access to comparable jobs is itself largely blocked. More than 60 percent of black men and 50 percent of all Hispanic men are clustered in low-paying job classifications.[153]

Unemployment liabilities are also distributed unevenly across gender and racial lines. A cumulative measure of the differentiated impact of unemployment shows such unemployment inequality doubling between 1951 and 1981.[154] At the end of 1982 the unemployment rate among blacks was 20.8 percent, more than double the 9.7 percent for whites.[155] Among black teenagers the rate was 49.5 percent, more than double the 24.5 percent for teenagers generally.[156] The income gap between white and black families has actually widened slightly since 1970, as black median family income dropped from 66 percent to 65 percent of white median family income.[157]

The stratification that permeates American life is now widely recognized. Only one-quarter of the working population still thinks that doing their work well will lead to an offer of a better job.[158]

THE POLITICAL PROCESS

The vitality of democratic political systems is conventionally measured by the degree and scope of the electoral activity of their citizens. By this measure, the U.S. political system is in deep decay, and ranks among the least democratic of those states holding reasonably regular and reasonably free elections.[159] U.S. voter turnout is below that in Australia, Austria, Belgium, Canada, Denmark, Finland, France, West Germany, Iceland, Ireland, Israel, Italy, Japan, Luxembourg, the Netherlands, New Zealand, Norway, Sweden, Switzerland, and the United Kingdom, among others.[160]

Nearly half the eligible electorate in the United States no longer votes even in presidential elections.[161] On election day in 1980, the 53.2 percent turnout was the third lowest in American history, higher only than the 1920 and 1924 elections that followed the abrupt swelling of the eligibility rolls resulting from the enfranchisement of women.[162] In winning the victory that continues to be labeled a "mandate" and a "landslide" by the national press, Ronald Reagan gained a smaller percentage of the eligible electorate than did Wendell Willkie in his decisive 1940 loss to Roosevelt.[163]

Turnout rates for "off-year" congressional elections are even lower. In 1982 only 35.7 percent of the eligible electorate voted.[164] The off-year turnout rate has not been above 40 percent since 1970.[165] It has been more than 60 years since an off-year election drew more than 50 percent of the eligible voters to the polls.[166]

There are of course other measures against which democratic systems may be evaluated. Consider equality of participation. Working class voting turnouts in the United States are roughly 30 percent lower than middle class turnouts.[167] Black Americans vote roughly 20 percent less often than whites.[168]

Consider public trust and confidence in major institutions. Over the 1966–78 period, the share of the population expressing "a great deal of confidence" in the military dropped from 62 to 29 percent; in major corporations, from 55 to 22 percent; in the Congress, from 42 to 10 percent (up from a 1976 low of 9 percent); in the executive branch, from 41 to 14 percent; in organized labor, which had much less far to fall in public esteem, from 22 to 15 percent.[169] The average for nine such major institutions fell from 43 to 25 percent over the same period.[170]

Public distrust of government is especially noteworthy. In 1964 the belief that "government is run for the benefit of all"

was held by 64 percent of the population.[171] By 1980 this belief
was shared by only 23 percent of the American people.[172] In
1966 only 26 percent of the population agreed that the "people
running the country don't really care what happens to you."[173]
By 1977, 60 percent agreed.[174] In 1964 fully 76 percent of the
population thought that government could be trusted to do
what is right "most of the time" or "all of the time."[175] By 1980
a mere 26 percent thought so.[176] A 1976 poll indicated that
only 10–13 percent of the American population thought that
the government "will actually be able to do" something about
the most pressing problems facing the country.[177] In 1980 78
percent of the American people, and 87 percent of those between
18 and 24 years old, believed that there were senators or representatives who won election by using illegal or unethical
means.[178] Forty percent of the people thought that this was
true of at least one-fifth of the members of Congress.[179]

Consider the role of private wealth in the electoral process.
Annual outlays for corporate and trade association institutional
advertising ran in excess of $400 million per year during the
mid-1970s.[180] In the late 1970s, their outlays for advocacy
advertising and other grassroots lobbying were estimated to
run to $1 billion per year.[181] Corporate and trade association
political action committees (PACs) spent more than $50 million
on the 1982 off-year elections alone.[182] Of the 3,500 PACs,
1,497 are corporate and 613 represent trade associations.[183]
The realtors' PAC alone spent $2.1 million in 1982.[184] Oil and
gas interests have 196 PACs representing them.[185] By the end
of July 1982 they had contributed $4.3 million to congressional
candidates for the 1982 elections.[186] PAC cash is targeted carefully. Figures for July 1982 showed members of the influential
House Energy and Commerce Committee collecting $2.9
million, the Ways and Means Committee $2.1 million, the Judi-
ciary Committee $1.2 million, and the Foreign Affairs Commit-
tee coming in with just under $1.1 million.[187] Such spending
levels leave an imprint on political outcomes. In 1978, the bigger
spender in campaigns for either the House or Senate was the
winner more than 80 percent of the time.[188] In 1980, corpora-

tions won in 11 of the 14 ballot initiatives in which their spending significantly exceeded the spending of their opponents.[189] In 1982, of the 33 winners in Senate races, 27 had outspent their opponents, and in five out of the six races won with less than 4 percent of the vote, the winner spent at least twice as much as the loser.[190]

Consider the strength of nonbusiness institutions outside the formal political arena. Union membership as a percentage of the total labor force declined during the 1950s, 1960s, and 1970s.[191] It now stands at roughly 20 percent of the labor force, lower than unionization rates in Australia, Belgium, France, Japan, the Netherlands, West Germany, and the United Kingdom.[192] Measured in absolute numbers, between 1968 and 1978 total union membership increased only 2 million, while the workforce swelled by 20 million.[193] Such declining strength is reflected in the pattern of industrial relations. Employers are becoming more aggressive. Between fiscal years 1970 and 1980, unfair labor practice complaints issued by the National Labor Relations Board against employers increased more than 250 percent.[194] Union militancy, by contrast, is declining. Wage and benefit increases in contracts signed in 1982 reached a record low on records kept since 1967.[195] Strike incidence in 1982 reached its lowest level since World War II.[196]

DEFENSE AND FOREIGN POLICY

The 1983 budget proposes the biggest peacetime military buildup in American history. Between 1984 and 1988 the Reagan administration plans to authorize expenditures of more than $1.8 trillion for defense.[197] The proposed buildup would result in an increase in defense outlays of more than 70 percent in uninflated (real) dollars over the 1981–88 period, and raise direct military spending to 7.4 percent of GNP by 1987, up from 5.4 percent in 1981.[198] It would push real defense outlays to 30 percent above peak expenditure levels during the Vietnam War.[199] If approved, by 1988 military spending will consume more than 35 percent of total federal outlays, up from 22.2 percent in 1981.[200] Military bands received more support in the administration's 1982 budget than the National Endowment for the Arts.[201]

Cost overruns are familiar in the defense sector: $13 billion on the XM-1 tank through 1981, $26.4 billion on the F-18, $4.7 billion on the UH-60A helicopter, and $33 billion on the Trident and F16 together.[202] Thus, for these few major weapons systems, over a short period, there were cost overruns totalling $77 billion. If spent otherwise, the sum is large enough to wipe out poverty for all Americans for four years.[203]

Strategic nuclear forces are certainly the most publicized elements of the planned military buildup. The United States now possesses roughly 9,000 "strategic" warheads. The Reagan program would push this to more than 14,500, more than 6,500 on submarines alone.[204] Even if they were not on special alert, the subs would be able to deliver a second strike of roughly 3,000 warheads carrying 750 equivalent megatons of explosive power, equal to nearly 14,000 Hiroshima bombs.[205]

But less than 20 percent of the funds in the five-year program are to be spent on Trident submarines, MX missiles, cruise missiles, and other nuclear forces.[206] The largest component will buy a huge expansion in munitions, an expanded "600 ship" Navy, a Rapid Deployment Force, and in general, the kinds of "conventional" forces needed to maintain continuity with U.S. foreign policy of the last thirty years.[207]

On almost any objective measure, that foreign policy has been an exceptionally aggressive and violent one. Consider the U.S.-sponsored coups in Iran (1953), Guatemala (1954), Brazil (1964), Chile (1973), and the current attempts to overthrow the government of Nicaragua, one of at least ten covert operations currently underway.[208] Or consider the efforts to assassinate foreign leaders, including eight officially acknowledged attempts to kill Fidel Castro.[209]

Consider the U.S.-sponsored Bay of Pigs operation against Cuba (1961), and its outright invasions of Lebanon (1958), Vietnam (1962), the Dominican Republic (1965), and Cambodia (1970). Or consider the less visible but more constant use of military "force without war" on 215 occasions between 1946 and 1975, including 19 incidents involving the deployment of nuclear weapons.[210]

Consider the use of "conventional" air power in Indochina: 539,129 tons of U.S. bombs dropped on Cambodia, 257,000 tons during a single six-month period, 18,000 tons of U.S. bombs dropped on North Vietnam during Christmas week 1972 alone, in the single most intensive conventional bombing in history; a total of 7 million tons of U.S. bombs dropped on the countries of Indochina during the course of American "involvement" there, roughly 90 times the 160,000 tons dropped on Japan in all of World War II, equal to 720 bombs of the sort dropped on Hiroshima on 6 August 1945.[211]

Consider the sustained support during the 1970s, through military aid, advisers, or the supply of torture equipment, to authoritarian regimes in Argentina, Bolivia, Brazil, Chile, Colombia, the Dominican Republic, El Salvador, Ethiopia, Greece, Guatemala, Haiti, Indonesia, Iran, Laos, Morocco, Nicaragua, Pakistan, Paraguay, Peru, the Philippines, Portugal, Saudi Arabia, South Korea, South Vietnam, Spain, Tunisia, Turkey, and Uruguay.[212]

Consider the policies of the current administration, which the human-rights organizations Americas Watch, Helsinki Watch, and the Lawyers Committee for International Human Rights have jointly described as having "cheapened the currency of human rights by invoking its principles to criticize governments it perceives as hostile to the United States and by denying or justifying abuses by governments it perceives as friendly to the United States."[213] The judgment may be clarified through a few examples.

Consider Pakistan. In 1981 the Reagan administration proposed a six-year aid package of $3.2 billion for Pakistan. In 1982 they asked for a 348 percent increase in military aid and assistance for fiscal 1983.[214] The martial law regime of President Zia ul-Haq banned all political and trade union activities in 1981, ended the independence of the judiciary, and has been accused by Amnesty International of "a consistent pattern of gross violations of human rights."[215] When President Zia came to Washington in December 1982, his meeting with President Reagan was noted for its "openness and warmth," although "torture is systematically practised in Pakistan."[216]

Consider Turkey. Turkey is the third largest recipient of military and related assistance from the United States, and was marked by the Reagan administration for a 16.6 percent increase for 1983.[217] Throughout 1981 and most of 1982 Turkey was under martial law. Almost 30,000 political prisoners were officially acknowledged in November 1981.[218] The new constitution makes the current military ruler president for seven years, and permits the president to declare martial law or emergency rule at any time, suspending already highly restricted civil liberties.[219] Familiar methods of electric shock, burning with cigarettes, beating of soles of feet, and violent attacks on sexual organs have been used to torture prisoners.[220] The prime minister of Turkey was one of the stars of the administration-sponsored extravaganza, "Let Poland be Poland."[221]

Consider Guatemala. With the help of the Reagan Commerce Department, the government of Guatemala was able to buy jeeps, trucks, and helicopters for military use in 1981, although "torture and murder were part of a deliberate and long-standing program of the Guatemalan government."[222] Survivors of the counter-insurgency operation by the Guatemalan government's "security forces" described one brutal episode. They had been "beaten and kicked, burnt with cigarettes, subjected to mock executions and near-garotting, and hooded with rubber hoods impregnated with chemicals by *kaibiles* [special counter-insurgency troops]." Captives were "interrogated about support they might have given to guerrillas. Rubber 'gloves' were placed over the hands, testicles, throats and breasts of some of the captives, and set alight, burning down to the bone in some cases before they eventually burnt themselves out."[223] The present government of General Rios Montt came to power in March 1982, suspended the constitution, abolished the right to strike, assemble, demonstrate, or organize unions, and then declared a state of siege, suspending freedom of the press, habeas corpus, and other civil liberties.[224] Massacres in the countryside resulted in roughly 2,600 deaths in the first six months of the new regime.[225] There are now an estimated one million refugees either displaced within Guatemala or living in Mexico.[226] Recognizing Rios Montt as a "man of great integrity" who is "totally dedicated to democracy" but has been "getting a bad deal" and a "bum rap," President Reagan is pressing for renewed economic aid and military assistance to the current regime.[227]

Thus it goes. President Marcos of the Philippines presided over nine years of martial law, and then was told by Vice-President George Bush, "We love you, sir. . . . We love your adherence to democratic principles and democratic processes."[228] In Chile all political parties have been banned since the coup of 1973, detentions for political reasons increased in 1982, and electric shock treatment has become routine for political prisoners arrested under "state of emergency" and "state of perturbation" laws. An estimated 10,000 to 35,000 Chileans now live in exile.[229] Against this background, UN Ambassador Kirkpatrick has praised the Chilean regime for its "constitutionalism," and, in a reversal of previous U.S. policy, the Reagan administration has supported multilateral lending to Chile, while seeking to end a six-year-old arms embargo.[230]

Finally, consider the current administration's overall goals in military and foreign policy. According to Department of Defense policy statements, the United States must now develop the military force levels necessary to "prevail even under the conditions of a prolonged [nuclear] war," "meet the demands of a worldwide war, including concurrent reinforcement of Europe, deployment of Southwest Asia, and support in other potential areas of conflict," and "revitalize and enhance special-operations forces to project United States power where the use of conventional forces would be premature, inappropriate, or infeasible."[231]

POLITICAL CULTURE

Other aspects of American society are more difficult to measure and explore, but nevertheless provide important indicators of the strength of democratic process.

Consider corruption. In 1978 some 84 percent of the American population believed that corruption and payoffs were common among government officials.[232] The sources of this belief are not obscure. Between 1970 and 1981, federal convictions of local government officials increased 1,219 percent.[233] Altogether in 1981 some 436 government officials were convicted of federal crimes, up from 32 in 1970, 155 in 1975, and 303 in 1980.[234] Sometimes the people involved are central operatives in the political system. In the Watergate scandal alone, more than 75 individuals and corporations, including some of the biggest names in corporate America and a good portion of the White House staff, were found guilty of lying, spying, obstructing justice, tampering with the electoral process, or other violations of elementary morality and democratic values.[235] President Nixon of course was pardoned for his role in the affair, and appeared on national TV to claim: "I am not a crook."

But such officially recognized corruption may be less important than more everyday violations of democratic norms. Often people are simply lied to or otherwise manipulated in their opinions. Often the instruments of the state are turned against those Americans who choose to exercise their "protected" rights. Such actions may directly threaten and subvert the free expression of political belief, but they are difficult to chronicle. They are rarely discovered at the time of their occurrence, and many, it may be safely assumed, are never discovered at all. We must therefore be more anecdotal and less current in our presentation here.

Consider surveillance operations.[236] In the middle 1970s the Federal Bureau of Investigation (FBI) maintained intelligence files on an estimated 6.5 million individuals and groups.[237] In 1972 alone the Bureau opened 65,000 new files with internal or national security classifications.[238] In 1975 the FBI itself acknowledged spying on 1,100 organizations.[239] In 1976 the Bureau spent $7.4 million on political informers, more than twice its budget for organized crime informers.[240] Such large-scale operations were not limited to the FBI, however. The Central Intelligence Agency (CIA), for example, mounted a major domestic intelligence program against Americans opposed to the Vietnam War. Called Operation CHAOS, this CIA program included the development of files on roughly 10,000 U.S. citizens and more than a hundred groups, along with an index of more than 300,000 citizens and organizations.[241] The range of activities and individuals subjected to government surveillance has been extremely broad. Records on a single FBI informer based in Washington, D.C., during the late 1960s indicate his surveillance of The Academy of Political Science, the American University chapter of the Union of Radical Political Economists, the American Friends Service Committee, the American Civil Liberties Union, the Institute for Policy Studies, the Children's March for Survival, the D.C. Statehood Party, and Common Cause, among many other groups.[242] Popular entertainers, including rock star Jimi Hendrix and folksinger Joan Baez, were also objects of surveillance, and for ten years the FBI kept a file on Helen Keller.[243] Some sense of how the Bureau evaluated national security threats can be gained from a memo written by J. Edgar Hoover in the early 1970s on a new surveillance target, the "WLM." Hoover wrote that it was "absolutely essential that we conduct sufficient investigations to clearly establish the subversive ramifications of the WLM and to determine the potential for violence presented by the various groups connected with their movement as well as any possible threat they may represent to the internal security of the United States."[244] WLM was the FBI designation for the women's liberation movement.

Consider disruption. Between 1960 and 1966, before the development of mass resistance to the Vietnam War, the FBI burglarized the offices of the Socialist Workers' Party on the average of once every three weeks.[245] Almost 300 documented

actions were carried out against black activist groups by the
FBI's Counter Intelligence Program (COINTELPRO).[246]
COINTELPRO operations included a successful campaign to
promote violent confrontation between the Black Panther Party
and a group called United Slaves.[247] Such provocative activities
were not unusual. Of the 2,340 COINTELPRO operations
undertaken between 1956 and 1971, nearly one-third were
designed to disrupt the functioning of a single group or to
promote conflict between groups.[248] The FBI regularly attempted
to promote distrust within groups of political activists.[249] Sometimes it intervened directly in private relations. The Bureau
sent the following letter to the husband of a white woman
involved in a St. Louis–area civil rights group called ACTION:
"Look man I geuss your old lady dosen't get enougf at home or
she wouldn't be shucking and jiving with our Black Men in
ACTION, you dig? Like all she wants to intergrate is the bed
room and us Black Sisters aint gonna take no second best from
our men. So lay it on her, man—or get her the hell off Newstead.
[sic]"[250] The letter was signed "A Soul Sister."[251] A report filed
four months later by an FBI agent in St. Louis indicated that
the couple had separated and that the "matrimonial stress and
strain should cause her to function much less effectively in
ACTION." The report went on to say that: "While the letter
sent by the St. Louis Division was probably not the sole cause
of this separation, it certainly contributed very strongly."[252]

One of the largest single-target operations conducted by the
FBI was a massive campaign to discredit Martin Luther King.
The campaign included taping King's conversations, including
conversations in bed, and then playing the tapes for such major
national figures as Lyndon Johnson.[253] FBI objectives were
described clearly by William Sullivan, the head of the Bureau's
Domestic Intelligence Division: "Martin Luther King must, at
some propitious point in the future, be revealed to the people
of this country and to his Negro followers as being what he
actually is—a fraud, demagogue and scoundrel. When the true
facts concerning his activities are presented, such should be
enough, if handled properly, to take him off his pedestal and

reduce him completely in influence. When this is done, and it can and will be done, obviously much confusion will reign. . . . The Negroes will be left without a national leader of sufficiently compelling personality to steer them in the proper direction. This is what could happen, but need not happen if the right kind of national Negro leader could at this time be gradually developed so as to overshadow Dr. King and be in the position to assume the role of leadership of the Negro people when King has been completely discredited."[254] Sullivan later remarked, "I'm very proud of this memorandum, one of the best memoranda I ever wrote. I think here I was showing some concern for the country."[255] Sullivan planned to replace the "completely discredited" Martin Luther King with Samuel Pierce, the Reagan administration Secretary of Housing and Urban Development, who in 1982 was accused of racism by other blacks in the government.[256]

Consider lying. Deception and manipulation are routinely employed in the formation of public opinion. In several cases the stakes were particularly high. More than 20 years ago, for example, a claimed "missile gap" between the United States and the U.S.S.R. served as the justification for the major buildup of U.S. strategic nuclear forces that marked the early 1960s.[257] Many argued at the time that a continuation of then current trends would lead to U.S. strategic inferiority to the U.S.S.R. It was claimed that by 1960 the Soviet Union would have 500 Intercontinental Ballistic Missiles (ICBMs), while the United States would have only 30, and that by 1963 the Soviet Union would have a 2,000-to-130 advantage in ICBMs.[258] In fact, the Soviet Union had no operational ICBMs until 1961, when they had a force of only four.[259] Even leaving aside U.S. superiority in long-range bombers and submarines, by the end of 1961 the United States had a six-to-one ICBM advantage, and by 1963 an eight-to-one advantage.[260] The Kennedy administration knew the actual missile levels by early 1961, but tried to keep this knowledge out of the public domain until approval was secured for a program to build 1,000 ICBMs.[261]

The Gulf of Tonkin resolution, which provided congressional

authorization to escalate the U.S. invasion of Vietnam, was based on an almost entirely fabricated "incident."[262] "For all I know, our navy was shooting at whales out there," President Johnson declared in private.[263] Delighted with the lack of opposition to passing the resolution, Johnson told a reporter, "I didn't just screw Ho Chi Minh, I cut his pecker off."[264] While continuing to campaign on a "peace" platform dedicated to limiting U.S. involvement in Vietnam, the Johnson administration was at the same time developing plans to escalate American commitment to the war.[265]

In 1970 President Nixon ordered the director of the CIA to prevent democratically elected Chilean leader Salvador Allende from taking office by spending "10 million dollars, more if necessary," and by trying to "make the economy scream."[266] Reflecting the views of the chief executive, the CIA cabled its Santiago station: "Parliamentary legerdemain has been discarded. Military solution is objective."[267] Efforts against the economy included seeking ways to drive down the price of copper on the world market, bringing "maximum feasible influence to bear in international financial institutions to limit credit or other financing assistance to Chile," and virtually eliminating American development assistance.[268] By 1971 the Santiago station was busy making lists of who would have to be arrested after a military coup and what government facilities would have to be occupied immediately, all as part of a program "to stimulate the military coup groups into a strong unified movement against the government."[269] Reflecting sensitivity to possible public opposition if such activities were acknowledged, a secret administration document of the period urged that this program of coup-plotting, disinformation, and economic warfare be pursued "within the context of a publicly cool and correct posture toward Chile."[270]

But opinion formation through deception is not limited to foreign policy maneuvers, nor is it a thing of the past. In the fall of 1981, Office of Management and Budget (OMB) Director David Stockman told an interviewer that the Reagan administration's supply-side tax cuts were sold through lying, and that the budget estimates he prepared for lobbying Congress were a sham.[271] But now even exposed lying is apparently politically acceptable. While the story got headlines, Stockman remains director of OMB and a major economic spokesperson for the administration's new tax plans. Nor were Stockman's phony numbers an isolated aberration. Growth and unemployment projections contained in the administration's 1982 midyear economic report were so obviously inaccurate that Treasury Secretary Regan announced that while he might be "dumb," he was not so "stupid" as to try to defend the figures.[272]

But aside from such obvious cases, it is difficult to judge the present scope of government deception. Much of the needed documentation is not yet available, and indeed it may never beome available if the present administration has its way. A 1982 executive order on classification already makes it far easier for the government to keep information from the public. Prior to the executive order, federal classifiers were compelled to point to an "identifiable" harm to national security to justify secrecy classification. Now any unspecified "damage" can serve as ground for such classification, and the "public interest in access to government information" is no longer officially recognized as even one of the factors to be weighed before classifying.[273] A second executive order permits domestic covert operations by the CIA, allows both the FBI and the CIA to "infiltrate" domestic organizations, and permits the FBI to "influence" them.[274] The recent Agent Identities Law makes it a crime to reveal the name of any covert intelligence agent, even if the namer of names never had any access to classified information and relied exclusively on published sources.[275] Finally, the administration has proposed weakening the Freedom of Information Act, under which information about such government activities as CIA mind-control research, CIA collaboration with the United Fruit Company in the 1954 Guatemala coup, FBI COINTELPRO operations against U.S. citizens, the secret bombing of Cambodia, and government lying about the dangers of atomic testing in the 1950s first became available to the public, and upon which we have indirectly relied for much of the information presented here.[276]

And so things are, now and in America. In place of economic well-being, high and persistent unemployment. In place of equality, privilege. In place of popular will, demobilization and decay. In place of commitment to democratic process abroad, support for brutal regimes created by American policy itself. In place of public reason at home, surveillance, manipulation, and deceit. Common expectations routinely disappointed. Conventional norms routinely violated. And commonly following upon this disappointment and violation are yet additional symptoms of the current disorder. Pervasive cynicism. Intellectual frustration. Political immobility.

In presenting this list of symptoms we have attempted to provide an opening for discussion. If that attempt has been successful, how should the discussion now proceed?

One strategy would be to add further facts to the list already here. Another would be to add a list of explanations to the present list of facts. But our own argument will pursue a different course. The sheer pervasiveness of these many symptoms suggests that some more coherent structure underlies their patterns and governs their appearance. It is to this structure of social power that we now turn.

3. STRUCTURE

How can one make sense of something as complex as a social system? There are so many different aspects of such systems, and no clear way of deciding in advance which are important and which are not. Here again there is a problem of beginning. In considering the basic structure of the American system we will begin by abstracting from many of its most distinctive features. Some of these features, like the famous American devotion to canned beer and professional football, are obviously peripheral to the basic operation of its political and economic order. But other particularities of the United States are just as obviously important. The impact of America's international role on the shape of its domestic politics, the relative absence of collectivist traditions in what was the world's first liberal demo-cratic state, and the relative weakness of organized labor in the United States are all distinctive features which are crucial to the operation of this exceptional system. While they will even-tually be included in our account, here too we wish initially to abstract from such details. Before considering the United States in its exceptionalism, in other words, we wish to consider it in its ordinariness. The most profound characteristics of the American system, we will argue, are provided by its structure as a capitalist democracy, a structure it shares with virtually all of the world's most advanced industrial states. We order our analysis first by considering this structure as a framework for domestic politics, and then by considering it at the level of international relations. But before that analysis begins, it may be helpful to offer a preliminary word about the nature and limits of such an approach.

In one respect our procedure here is uncontroversial. All theoretical enterprises proceed by initially abstracting from certain aspects of a system and focusing on others. This is as true of discussions of political order as it is of investigations of human language, the structure of the brain, or the formation of spiral galaxies. Depth and simplicity of explanation are gained by isolating certain features of such phenomena and pursuing the logic of their operation before considering any particular instance of that operation.

But our judgment that the central features of the American system are provided by its structure as a capitalist democracy *is* controversial. Some alternative approaches focus on certain shared values that mark American society and culture, that the United States is "conceived in liberty," for example, or that it is "dedicated to the proposition that all men are created equal," or more generally, that it is committed to a mix of liberty and equality in varying proportions in the relations among its citizens. Other approaches focus on the existence of free markets and electoral competition, and the nature of the choices made within such markets and formal political arenas. In our view, however, these values and acts of individual choice are themselves best understood against the background of a framework of economic and political relations between people, relations designated by the term "capitalist democracy." While the values and choices are in a way more evident and obvious features of American social order, we argue that these background economic and political relations significantly shape and limit the choices open to individuals, as well as the interpretations and consequences of those choices. They therefore provide a more appropriate place to begin.

Of course one always loses something on such an approach. After abstracting from the distinctive features of a particular system, one cannot expect to account for everything about its functioning. Since the basic framework of capitalist democracy is shared by many states, it cannot for example account for the often quite important differences among capitalist democracies. And no general theory of capitalist democracy will be able to "explain" the many symptoms of American disorder enumerated in the last chapter. But such limitations are less important than they may first appear. Understanding the framework of a social order is in some ways analogous to knowing the rules of a game. Such basic knowledge does not impart mastery of all the details. Knowing the rules of chess, for example, will not tell you what distinguishes different styles of opening, be they "hypermodern" or more "classical" in approach. On the other hand, there is no hope of understanding *any* opening strategy if you do not have a basic grasp of how the game itself is played. Likewise, the ultimate test of our claim about the centrality of capitalist democracy is not an ability to predict tomorrow's unemployment rate, or who will win the next presidential election, but the capacity of this approach to illuminate the broader and more enduring operations of American politics. And whether it succeeds in doing so can only be judged after the framework of capitalist democracy has itself been presented.[1]

To describe the American system as a capitalist democracy is in part to indicate the presence within a single social order of private property, labor markets, and private control of investment decisions on the one hand, and such formal organizations of political expression as political parties and regular elections on the other. But the nature of capitalist democracy is not captured by merely listing these forms of economic and political organization. Capitalist democracy is not a system in which a capitalist economy persists alongside a democratic political system, each unaffected by the other. Nor is it a system in which capitalism and democracy are only temporarily joined in an unstable structure of inner antagonism, each striving to forsake the other. Capitalist democracy is neither just capitalism, nor just democracy, nor just some combination of the two that does not change its component parts. Indeed even to think of such separate "parts" is to miss the vital integrity of the system.

Capitalist democracy is different from plain capitalism, since workers possess political rights. Along with rights of speech and association, they can vote, join or form political parties, and engage in a number of other actions in the political arena which can influence the behavior of capital by influencing state policies. By using their vote, for example, workers can promote politicians committed to maintaining higher levels of employment, or punish those who are not so committed. The legality of such political action reduces its cost and thereby increases its likelihood. But the presence of political rights can also enhance the ability of workers to engage in forms of opposition outside the arenas of formal politics. It can, for example, enhance their ability to form trade unions or other secondary organizations from which to press further political demands.* While no gain is guaranteed, everything else being equal, capitalist democracy's provision of political rights creates more favorable conditions for the material gain of workers than do other kinds of capitalist regimes, such as fascism or bureaucratic authoritarianism.

But if capitalist democracy is not just capitalism, still less is it just democracy. In a capitalist democracy the exercise of political rights is constrained in two important ways. In the first place, the political rights granted to all citizens, workers among others, are formal or procedural, and not substantive. That is, they do not take into account in their own form and application the inequalities in the distribution of resources, characteristic of capitalism, which decisively affect the exercise of political rights and importantly limit their power of expression. Both an unemployed worker and a millionaire owner of a major television station enjoy the same formal right of free speech, but their power to express and give substance to that

---

*To underscore this common interaction between the exercise of explicitly political liberties such as suffrage and the exercise of classic associational and expressive liberties such as the liberties of assembly and speech, we shall refer to all such universal formal liberties as "political rights."

right are radically different. We will return to this "resource constraint" below.

But before considering in detail the role played by the resource constraint in the normal course of politics, a second constraint needs to be introduced. Capitalist democracy does not only rest on the material inequalities that limit the effective expression of the formal rights it guarantees. Capitalist democracy also tends to direct the exercise of political rights toward the satisfaction of certain interests. This structuring of political demand, or what we shall call the "demand constraint," is crucial to the process of consent. The problem highlighted by the demand constraint might be put this way. It is clear that within capitalist democracies there are profound underlying structural inequalities that shape the normal course of politics. What is less clear is how that normal course is possible at all. How is it that politics in a capitalist democracy can proceed at all without the underlying inequalities themselves becoming a central object of political conflict? Why do people consent? This is a central question for anyone whose interest in understanding capitalist democracy is informed by a desire to transform it.

Two answers to the question of consent are familiar. According to the first sort of account, determined opposition to capitalist democracy is stifled by force or fear in anticipation of the use of force. People go along because they know that if they did not go along they would be beaten up or killed. The second sort of account relies upon some kind of mass delusion as the explanation of consent, although there is much disagreement about the precise source of that delusion. Sometimes it is said to derive from "false consciousness," sometimes just from an innate inability to understand. Many may find these explanations satisfactory in themselves. Others may think that there is no alternative account that is not simply an apologetic rationalization for existing inequality.

Finding neither explanation adequate, we wish to offer a nonapologetic alternative. The central thesis of this alternative is that capitalist democracy is in some measure capable of satisfying the interests encouraged by capitalist democracy itself, namely, interests in short-term material gain. Capitalist democracy is capable of satisfying the standards of rational calculation encouraged by its structure. To observe this is to note again that capitalist democracy is a system. It rewards and thereby promotes certain sorts of interests and patterns of behavior based on those interests, and given those interests and patterns of behavior it is capable of providing satisfaction. Though fear and delusion no doubt play a role, consent is based on narrowly defined calculations of private advantage, calculations which together comprise a norm of "economic rationality."

Specifying a social norm in this way should not be confused with more ambitious claims about human motivation, a point we shall return to later. To say that economic rationality is especially important within capitalist democracy is not to say that it is the only interest that people have in general, or that it is the only motivation ever expressed or acted upon within capitalist democracy, or that reasoning about action is in principle limited to calculations of material gain. It is merely to claim that calculation of economic interest has a special importance in capitalist democracy because it is especially encouraged by the system, and its pursuit tends to reproduce that system over time.

To develop this thesis about interests, and explore the workings of the demand constraint, we will consider two points: (1) how capitalist democracy tends to reduce political conflict to conflict over short-term material advantage; and (2) the concomitant difficulties associated with any attempt to move out of this system to a materially more satisfying form of social organization.

Capitalism is a form of economic organization in which profit provides the motive for investment and investment decisions are preeminently the decisions of competing units of capital. Capitalists earn profits by, among other things, hiring labor at wages that permit the extraction of profit. Those whom they hire typically have no other assets than their ability to work.

As a result of their control of investment, the satisfaction of the interests of capitalists is a necessary condition for the satisfaction of all other interests within the system. This is not a polemical remark but a straightforward point about the logic of interest satisfaction within a capitalist structure. Failing to satisfy the interests of capitalists means failing to secure them adequate profits. But if profits are insufficient, there will be no investment. If there is no investment, then there is no production or employment. If there is no production or employment, then workers whose principal resource is their capacity to produce starve to death. This is the famous "bottom line." It might be objected that this conclusion is too harsh, since modern capitalist democracies protect workers against such a fate through the provision of unemployment insurance and other assistance programs. But such an objection misses the mark. All such welfare measures are themselves dependent upon tax revenues, and if people are not working those revenues soon begin to dry up. There must be production for employment. There must be investment for production. And there must be an expectation of profit for investment. The requirement of profitable accumulation is not eliminated by the "welfare state."

Under capitalism, therefore, the welfare of workers remains structurally secondary to the welfare of capitalists, and the well-being of workers depends directly on the decisions of capitalists. The interests of capitalists appear as general interests of the society as a whole, the interests of everyone else appear as merely particular, or "special."[2]

In fact, the dependence of workers on capitalists runs even deeper. As the source of funds for investment, profits are the social form characteristic of capitalism in which present resources are withheld for future production. But for wage earners this form of withholding or "saving" provides no guarantee of future benefit or return. While present profits are a necessary condition for future well-being, they are not a sufficient condition. Material uncertainty remains in the society, since investment decisions remain out of the reach of social control. Profits can be consumed, used for financial speculation, diverted to rare coins, race horses and antique cars, or used for productive investment outside the economy from which they were extracted. And even if profits are reinvested in some form in the domestic economy, such investment does not per se guarantee material improvement to wage earners. Profits made in Factory A can be diverted to a new Factory B within the same economy, but employing different workers. Or profits made in Factory A can be used to automate Factory A completely, throwing workers out of work.

There is then a characteristic economic rationality to the actions of workers specifically encouraged by capitalism. In the face of material uncertainties arising from continued dependence on the labor market under conditions of the private control of investment, it makes sense for workers to struggle to increase their wages.

As indicated earlier, in a capitalist democracy, workers' struggles to improve their material position are aided by the existence of political rights. Given the potential material benefit deriving from the exercise of such rights, and given the pervasive material uncertainty for workers characteristic of capitalism, it makes sense that workers' use of political rights be directed toward the achievement of material ends. The structure of capitalist democracy thus effectively encourages the reduction of politics to striving over material gain. In addition to acting outside the framework of formal politics, workers can take action *within* that framework aimed either at improving their material position directly or enhancing their capacity to make and enforce material demands in other arenas. Workers can vote for social programs such as Social Security, unemployment insurance, or Medicaid and Medicare to protect themselves from poverty and the extremities of unemployment. They can rally around more ambitious programs of economic stabilization, such as the Humphrey-Hawkins Bill or various full employment acts, or they can press for the passage of laws easing the constraint on their own organization, such as the Wagner Act that legalized the formation of trade unions. What a capitalist democracy provides are specifically political means whereby workers can try to capture some of the benefits of past "savings," and thus generally reduce their material uncertainty. But material uncertainty remains. Indeed, to say that material uncertainty over the future is never eliminated in a capitalist democracy is really only to restate a defining characteristic of that system. For future uncertainty to be eliminated (leaving aside the uncertainty of nature), workers would have to control investment themselves. Such control violates the very definition of capitalism as a form of economic organization in which investment decisions are preeminently the decisions of competing capitals. The reproduction of capitalist democracy reconstitutes material uncertainty, and thus reconstitutes the conditions that encourage the reduction of political demand to the defense or promotion of material interests.

It might be objected that we have simply begged the question of consent by neglecting the most important possibility of all, namely, that workers might use their political rights to contest the basic structure of capitalist democracy. Workers might exercise their rights of association and suffrage by forming political parties and voting for programs that call for the transformation of the entire social order. They might demand the construction of a society that was not defined by conditions structuring demand toward the overcoming of material uncertainty. Given the structure of capitalist democracy, it may be economically rational to use political rights for short-term material gain. But in what sense is it rational to consent to that basic structure itself, and not pursue transformative struggle?

Thinking through the conditions of demand formation within capitalist democracy reveals the obstacles to such collective action. Capitalist democracy encourages economic calculation through the generation of conditions of material uncertainty. But economic calculation leads rationally to a rejection of more radical longer-term struggles against capitalism itself. Short-term material improvement is the preferred aim of materially based conflict within a capitalist democracy because of the different requirements and competing logics of short-term pursuits and longer-term struggles, and the rational pursuit of material advantage within capitalist democracy thus leads to a less radical and less global pursuit of short-term material gain.

Why this is the case might be clarified by considering the dimensions of short-term as against longer-term struggles. Short-term struggles are relatively easy to coordinate. One can even engage in them all by oneself. One can try to get a raise or a promotion by flattering the boss, or working late in the evening, or discreetly suggesting that someone is not doing his or her job as well as "someone else" might. Short-term struggles are often recognized and licensed by the state, as in enabling legislation for the formation of trade unions as bargaining representatives for workers, or penalties imposed on employers for failing to bargain with those representatives. In addition to relative ease of coordination and potential for official recognition, short-term struggles always have the advantage of relative clarity of aims. While there might be debate and sharp disagreement about *how much* to demand, there is not the same problem of determining *what sorts* of demands to make, as is commonly the case in longer-term struggles.[3] This is true even for militant short-term struggles to alter the conditions under which material benefits are bargained for within a capitalist democracy, as in struggles to organize unions or to form a party of labor. Even in these cases, the scope of debate is reduced by the fact that the more basic organization of political and economic arenas is held fixed, and the relative clarity of purpose facilitates the struggle.

Where successful, the cumulative effect of short-term struggles can be materially very satisfying. Some people say that capitalism cannot improve workers' material well-being. This is simply not true. It is often the case that individual workers do better than they have done in the past. And this can be the case even if not all workers are better off. Even during times of recession, some people get raises. Even if wages overall are dropping, it may be the case that a strong union can get better wages for its members. Having encouraged the reduction of political conflict to struggle over material interest, capitalist democracy provides many avenues to and examples of short-term satisfaction of those interests. In so doing, capitalist democracy more specifically encourages the reduction of politics to striving for *short-term* material gain.

It might still be argued that while it is rational for individual workers to try to improve their position within capitalist democracy, the only way for all workers to improve their material position steadily would be by struggling together to overthrow capitalism. This may indeed be true, but at almost any given point it is also true that it would be economically irrational for individual workers to engage in such a struggle. In contemplating the costs of such a long-term fight, individual workers face a familiar problem of collective action. Far from there being an "invisible hand" that guides their individually rational choices to the best collective outcome, the structure in which they find themselves yields less than optimal social results from their isolated but economically rational decisions. While we reserve a more complete exploration of this point about collective action for our discussion of the "resource constraint," a few observations on the problem are directly pertinent here.

In considering social struggle, individual workers lack information about how other workers will behave. Other workers or groups of workers may choose not to join the struggle, or they may abandon it at a later point. Undertaking a long-term battle against capitalism under such conditions of uncertainty means that individual workers do not know how great their personal burden of the costs of that struggle will be. It therefore makes sense for individuals to try to get as much as they can for themselves in the short run before even contemplating cooperation with others in the longer term. But the achievement of short-run material satisfaction often makes it irrational to engage in more radical struggle, since that struggle is by definition directed against those institutions which provide one's current gain.

Thus the situation in which workers make their decisions leads them rationally, on the basis of material interest, to choose not to struggle against capitalism. The long-term production of consent within capitalist democracy is based on just such short-term decisions to consent to capitalist production. The system can provide workers with short-term material satisfaction, and workers participate in the system to assure that satisfaction. And even when, as is not infrequently the case, capitalism is failing to deliver material benefits, rational calculation does not mandate a longer-term transformative conflict. Individual workers may hope that the burdens of decline will not fall on them. They may calculate that protecting existing gains from further erosion is more likely to deliver benefits than engaging in a costly and in any case uncertain long-term effort. And if they are organized, their organizations, designed to deliver short-term benefits under better conditions, are likely to be ill-suited to the enterprise of radical transformation.

The integrity of capitalist democracy indicated by the demand constraint can be underscored by exploring the process of its disruption. Let us assume for the sake of argument that all workers solved their problems of information and coordination and came together to radically contest the system. What would happen? Assuming that such contestation was motivated exclusively by interests in short-term material gain, no transition to a more materially satisfying social order could be completed under democratic conditions. This may seem like an implausibly strong assertion, but it follows from the nature of collective action within capitalist democracy.

Fighting for total system transformation carries many costs. People often get killed. Internal resistance from capitalists is substantial. External pressures are often exerted by international lending agencies or hostile states. When the people of Chile elected a socialist government, President Nixon said he wanted to disrupt the internal workings of the Chilean state, drive down the price of copper on the world market, and generally crush Chile's economy. Helped along by many powerful people, he soon got his wish.

But let us again make an improbable assumption, this time that there is no violence, or internal subversion, or external subversion. Even in such a scenario, one cost that always accompanies a transition out of capitalist democracy is economic crisis. As workers try to change the basis of economic institutions from profit to something else, capitalists withdraw their capital. It makes sense for them to withdraw, since they can no longer be assured of making profits, and even if the state offers them guarantees, their future position is uncertain. But if investment stops, chaos results. Unemployment increases. Redistributional measures and state compensation of jobless workers must increase. Inflation then increases. Borrowing needs become greater, and yet more difficult to satisfy. Creditworthiness is impaired by the new weakness of the economy. The currency is debased on international markets, making debt payments more difficult to satisfy. And so on.

Consider what this means. Economic crisis means that short-term material interests suffer. But if support for the project of transition is motivated by short-term material interests, then at the point of economic crisis, support will begin to vanish. Within the coalition seeking transition, sharp splits will open if the appeal of that coalition is based on the satisfaction of short-term material interests. These splits and defections will become overwhelming long before a democratic transition can be completed. Under democratic conditions the transition will be halted or reversed.

It might be argued that workers would see their material gain in longer terms, but that is to forget that capitalist democracy ceaselessly structures the articulation and satisfaction of demand toward short-term gain. The point again underscores the status of capitalist democracy as a system.

The integrity and relative stability of capitalist democracy indicated by the demand constraint permits and encourages a more normal course of operation based on compromise between workers and capitalists.[4] The most general conditions of such compromise follow directly from the conditions of stability of capitalist democracy itself. Workers must "agree" not to enforce wage demands that preclude profits. Capitalists must "agree" to invest a sufficient share of profits to provide for future well-being. Of course, an important asymmetry remains between the concessions of the two classes. Workers are agreeing to something they are doing now, namely, restraining wages. Capitalists are agreeing to do something in the future, namely,

invest a sufficient share of profits. Uncertainty and conflict are
never fully eliminated, and any compromise therefore remains
an unstable one. But so long as the terms of a compromise are
kept, it permits the satisfaction of the material interests of both
workers and capitalists within the structural inequality that
defines capitalism.

Within the boundaries just described, there is a range of
possible outcomes pertaining to both the shares of product
distributed between capitalists and workers and to the direction of profit to productive investment. Both Sweden and the
United States are capitalist democracies, for example, but
Sweden is much more a "welfare state" than the United States,
and is currently experimenting with a variety of attempted
controls on the disposition of profits. In terms of both distribution and production, the Swedish and U.S. cases yield different
results. The range of possible outcomes within the boundary
conditions of capitalist democracy provides yet another source
of uncertainty and possible conflict within the system. At any
given point, the outcome achieved along this range is importantly determined by the relative power of workers and capitalists, including their degree and forms of organization and their
willingness to engage in conflict at all. In determining this
balance, the first constraint on the exercise of political rights,
the "resource constraint" mentioned earlier, figures prominently.[5]

We can begin our discussion of the resource constraint by
noting that the ability to take advantage of the formally equal
political rights characteristic of capitalist democracy is not only
a function of an individual's own resources. It also depends
upon the ability of large numbers of individuals who share
common interests to coordinate their actions in pursuit of those
interests. The ability to coordinate, however, requires more than
shared enthusiasm or convergent interests. Successful coordination commonly requires the expenditure of material resources
and the availability of strategic information. Everything else
being equal, coordination is easier to achieve for small groups
than for larger ones, and the likelihood of its occurrence varies
directly with the probability of its success.

On each of these dimensions, capitalists have advantages over workers. They have enormous fixed and liquid assets. They already know a great deal about their own operations, the conditions in their industry, and the economic situation more generally, all of which is information essential to their own economic performance, and all of which makes them relatively better informed and hence more efficient political actors. They operate as a relatively limited number of units, often of colossal size. Their importance to the economy guarantees their access to key decision-makers, including public officials and other capitalists, and together importance and access increase the likelihood that they will get what they want.

These advantages of assets, structurally based information, limited numbers, and access to key decision-makers are cumulative in their effect. The presence of accumulated reserves lowers the costs of political action. Good information makes the target of political action more clearly visible. Together, information and assets reduce both the need for and the relative cost of acquiring further resources. From this position of initial strength, coordination is further facilitated, made less costly, by the relatively limited number of actors involved. Importance to the economy and access to other decision-makers finally ensures that action will be given due regard. When capitalists are upset, they make a loud noise. When they walk, they make a booming sound. And when they need to talk to someone, someone answers the phone.

The operation of such cumulative processes cannot be detailed here. But some of their essential features may be highlighted by exploring a typical scenario of the interaction of workers and capitalists within a system of formal political equality. Let us begin with an accurate assumption of initial gross inequalities in resource distribution. Let us assume, too, on the basis of our discussion of the demand constraint, that actors within the political arena behave in economically rational ways. In deciding how to act they must consider not only the potential benefits of a course of action, but also both the likelihood of success and costs of the action, including the cost of foregoing *other* courses of action. Economic rationality dictates that an action should be undertaken if and only if the expected value of the benefits of the action exceeds the expected value of the full range of costs. What happens within such a system of political conflict?

Two problems will be examined here. The first is a problem of information; the second, of bargaining and coordination.

We can begin to explore the information problem by stating the obvious. Under the workings of formal representative democracy, political decisions are always made under conditions of uncertainty. Politicians do not have perfect information about the wishes of voters, even assuming that they want to represent them accurately, and voters do not have perfect information about the future behavior of politicians, or about the costs and benefits of the programs for which they stand, even assuming complete fidelity to articulated programs. Several things follow from this. The lack of information clouds the decision process, and the "transparency" necessary to fully efficient representative decision-making is not achieved. But this is especially true for those the scarcity of whose resources precludes their regular or easy acquisition of costly information.

Rational economic motivation applied to questions of information acquisition dictates that information should be acquired only if the marginal cost of that information is exceeded by the marginal benefits gained by action on that information. For most citizens, there is virtually no costly acquisition of political information that satisfies this condition. Policy choices rarely present the average citizen with opportunities for great personal gain, and the average citizen is in any case almost powerless to affect any policy choice alone. The small expected benefit, discounted by the ineffectiveness of personal action, is virtually always outweighed by the costs of acquiring relevant information. Citizens therefore choose, rationally, to limit their acquisition of information to that information which can be obtained at zero cost. They choose a strategy of "rational ignorance." Virtually the only information that satisfies the conditions of zero cost is that which is supplied "free" by advertisers, lobbyists, and the like. This information, however, is by no means objective. Its very supply derives from the interest private decision-makers with a large stake in the outcome of a particular decision have in trying to influence that decision in a direction beneficial to themselves.

The constraints voters place on their own acquisition of information, and the special interest that motivates the supply of "free" information by producer groups, result in distortions in the consideration of issues of public policy. It makes sense, for example, for the private individuals who will benefit from a taxpayer subsidy of a $37 billion Alaska natural gas pipeline to spend hundreds of thousands of dollars lobbying and advertising to influence that decision, but it makes no sense for any individual taxpayer to spend any amount of time or money acquiring the information needed to make a correct decision about the pipeline. In the same way, it makes sense for sugar growers to spend money lobbying for import restrictions on sugar, because for sugar growers that decision is of monumental importance, but it makes no sense for individual consumers of sugar to spend time or money acquiring information or organizing around the import question. For the average consumer, a small increase in the price of a pound of sugar is outweighed by the costs of acquiring information. If on the other hand there is another producer group with a very large stake in the price of sugar, for example the manufacturers of soft drinks, who purchase tons and tons of sugar each week, such information acquisition and organization does make sense. The same might be said of disputes between the construction industry and the makers of high-priced domestic steel, or between aluminum can manufacturers and bottle factory owners, or between savings and loan associations and commercial banks. Because of the many divisions among producers, such situations are common. It is often the case that different producer groups take turns bombarding the public with misleading information. This is called "national debate."

In a system of formal political equality, the information problem thus compounds economic inequality by guaranteeing a systematic bias in the information upon which public decisions are made. The bias is systematic in the sense that it is always weighted toward producers and against consumers, toward capitalists and against workers, and correspondingly affects the resulting decisions. It is worth noting again that such a bias is generated within this system *because* all the important actors—producer lobbyists and advertisers, politicians and voters—are behaving in economically rational ways. The information problem thus helps to generate further inequalities even without the additional impetus produced by the tremendous direct payoffs, bribes, campaign contributions, and backdoor pledges that place the stamp of private dominance on the American public arena. Once those additional practices are factored in, of course, the inequalities become greater still.

The second major aspect of the resource constraint concerns the process of group mobilization and bargaining. The bargaining of groups within the political system further compounds economic and political inequality because of the persistence of so-called free-rider problems. The free-rider problem is a problem of collective action. It arises from the existence of "public" or "collective" goods whose provision benefits all members of a group, and whose "consumption" by any member of the group does not preclude consumption by any other. Such goods are relatively common. A harbor lighthouse, for example, benefits all sailors navigating the harbor, and the fact that one sailor is helped by the lighthouse ("consumes" its benefits) does not mean that another cannot be helped as well. There is however a difficulty in providing for such collective goods, since individuals who are economically motivated have little or no incentive to contribute voluntarily to their provision. This is true even when the individuals would derive benefits from the goods. Not contributing ensures zero costs, but does not exclude receipt of the benefits that may be achieved through the contributions of others. One's own contribution, on the other hand, does not guarantee that the good will be made available. It thus ensures the presence of costs but not the receipt of benefits. Given a free choice, it makes sense to take a "free ride" on the backs of others.

Free-rider problems are important because collective goods are commonly the object of bargaining or struggle in the political system. The sugar import restrictions mentioned earlier provide one example of such group benefits. If import restrictions are imposed, they benefit all domestic sugar growers. Another example would be clean air. If clean air standards are enacted and enforced, everyone breathes easier. National defense, street lights, public parks, and public education are all similar goods in that consumption of the good by one person does not preclude consumption by another.

The examples indicate that collective goods comprise many of the most familiar objects of political concern, but they also underscore the fact that where collective goods are provided they are usually provided through the state. In the political arena, the free-rider problem most commonly and directly arises as a problem of mobilizing people to make demands upon the state for the provision of some particular collective good. It is here that there are significant differences between workers and capitalists. While the free-rider problem confronts all attempts to mobilize in pursuit of collective goods, the force of the problem depends on the size of the group, the resources available to those who wish to organize, the relative improvement brought about by the benefits struggled for, and the certainty of achieving those benefits through concerted action. If the group is small, it is easier to coordinate. If the benefits are large, there is more initial incentive to join in their pursuit. If the benefits are certain, the cost of achieving them can be allocated more rationally. If initial resources are high, then potential free riders can be coerced into joining the struggle or rewarded by others for not disrupting it. While any mobilization offers opportunities for participation, the participation of the rational economic actor may follow on receiving "an offer he couldn't refuse." In all these respects, capitalists have advantages over workers. They can more easily solve their free-rider problems.

If the information problem thus tends to distort public debate, the free-rider problem tends to bias the pattern of public expenditures and benefits. Everything else being equal, more specific benefits applicable to small groups of powerful actors are easier to organize for and extract from the state than benefits which will accrue to much larger groups in the political system. Everything else being equal, getting a tax writeoff for the ten largest oil companies is easier to organize and achieve than getting clean air for everyone, getting preferential trade treatment for the steel industry is easier than getting safe working conditions for the workers in that industry, getting a favorable antitrust decree for a particular class of firms is easier than getting restrictions on runaway shops.

This bias toward more specific expenditures and benefits has a differentiated impact on workers and capitalists. This is not only because capitalists can more readily solve their free-rider problems in the pursuit of more particular collective benefits, but because their greater initial resources enable them to compensate for the failure of the political system to provide adequate public goods. A rich person is less critically affected by the absence of decent public schools, or effective police protection, or attractive public recreational facilities than a poor person. Rich people can afford to send their children to private schools, or can hire bodyguards or private security forces, or purchase a private beach house or ski condo, all with a relatively small impact on overall resources. The poor person cannot. This difference in impact of the free-rider problem upon capitalists and upon workers compounds the structural inequality with which we began our discussion of the resource constraint. It closes the circle of those constraints.

But it closes another circle as well. Because the formal political system cannot fully redress initial inequalities, because it tends to reproduce and compound them over time, it continues to generate those conditions of material uncertainty that first lead individuals to accede to the reduction of politics to short-term material striving. This is where we began our discussion of the formation of political demand in a capitalist democracy, and we are led back to that starting point again. Along with all the other problems of resource inequality and organization, the free-rider problem effectively encourages individuals to find a personal way out. But that personal way out only reproduces on its own terms the short-term strivings for material satisfaction which give the free-rider problem force. The free-rider problem encourages the pursuit of particular material benefits by small groups or individuals. Need it be noted again that those are precisely the sorts of pursuits encouraged by capitalist democracy?

The free-rider problem again underscores the problem of motivation within capitalist democracy, a problem mentioned at the beginning of the discussion of the demand and resource constraints. We entered a caveat then about the consideration of motivation within those constraints. Having completed our discussion of the constraints, we return to that caveat now. At the time, we said that capitalist democracy encourages certain sorts of interests and patterns of behavior, precisely the sorts that lead to the reproduction of capitalist democracy. But we also observed that those interests and patterns do not exhaust all motivations that people have, nor even all motivations evident within a capitalist democracy. How are these points consistent? How is the acknowledgment of the diversity of human motivations compatible with our insistence on the central role of economic rationality in the operation of capitalist democracy?

The question of compatibility is important for at least two reasons. First, unless there is some way of acknowledging the presence of concerns other than those of short-term material gain, our account of human beings is manifestly implausible. The fact is simply too obvious to be dwelt upon that virtually all people are moved by any number of feelings, desires, and aspirations other than economic maximizing. But the question is important as well for the same reason that the question of consent is important. For those whose interest in understanding capitalist democracy is informed by a desire to transform it, the presence of powerful concerns other than short-term material striving is crucial. As our discussion of transition problems indicated, a democratic movement out of capitalist democracy is impossible in the absence of other such concerns.

But while the compatibility problem is of supreme importance, it is not so very difficult to solve. Everyday life and experience indicate innumerable ways in which diverse motivations are channeled or structured into patterns of behavior compatible with capitalist democracy. In developing this point we consider two sorts of structuring. One involves the pursuit of means to fixed and determinate ends, the other involves reasoning about the ends of actions themselves. Again, the aim of the discussion is not to provide a theory of human nature or a f·ill account of the springs of human action as expressed in capitalist democracy. The point rather is to show that the account of consent and stability offered earlier is not rooted in a perverse inattention to the familiar diversity of human motivation, and that it remains robust even in the face of motivational facts that do not fit with the basic account of economic rationality.

The first sort of structuring can be described as seeking money as a means to other things. Money is the "universal equivalent."[6] It can be exchanged for any other good, and other goods commonly cannot be had without it. Wishing to pursue other goods thus commonly leads to an interest in money. Consider a familiar situation. Let us make the safe assumption that parents love their children, that they want the "best of life" for their children, and that they recognize that the best of life costs money. Parents will then be led to struggle for money under the conditions of uncertainty characteristic of capitalist democracy. They may work longer and harder hours to get the savings needed to pay for college for their children, or to pay for dance lessons, music lessons, chemistry sets, or the rental of prom tuxedos and formal gowns. What motivates parents to work harder to acquire the money to pay for these many things is not greed, but love for their children. Or consider the example of those who want to write poetry. To write poetry they need peace and quiet, and time to take advantage of their peace and quiet. But to get peace, time, and quiet, they need money. "The spirit must become flesh."

These examples and countless others underscore a familiar point. The pursuit of nonmaterial concerns—the love of children, the love of poetry—is commonly conditional on the availability of material resources, and therefore conditional on conforming to the rules of those arenas in which such resources become available. This does not require greediness or any particular affection for the rules themselves. But within capitalist democracy, it does typically require dependence on labor markets, and such dependence binds the initial motivation to an interest in short-term material gain.

The second sort of structuring can be described as "institutionally constrained deliberation about ends." Even within a capitalist democracy it is of course possible to view social activity as other than merely a way to secure the material prerequisites of private satisfactions. Social activities can be valued for their own sake. They might be valued as expressing one's talents, enhancing the general welfare, or simply being the morally correct things to do. If such noninstrumental attachments motivate behavior within capitalist democracy, which they sometimes do, then our previous account of consent and stability is incomplete. Without addressing the question of the extent to which such attachments are operative in social activity, we can still explore how serious this incompleteness is.

Consider someone interested in finding a social outlet for his nonmaterial aspirations. Because those aspirations are themselves typically indefinite and unclear, such situations present a twofold problem. In addition to the task of finding an outlet for the aspirations there is the task of specifying the aspirations themselves in greater clarity and detail.[7] Both the finding and the specifying commonly take place through available institutions. If one wants to promote solidarity among working people, for example, one is commonly encouraged to work for a union, and to identify the promotion of solidarity with the achievement of higher wages for union members. If one wants recognition for a talent, one is commonly encouraged to make that talent commercially viable, and to identify the exercise and acknowledgment of that talent with its commercially viable form. If one wants to express love in a gift, one is commonly encouraged to make the gift an expensive one, and to identify gifts of love with expensive gifts. If one's love extends to one's country, one is commonly encouraged to fight in imperialist wars, and to identify patriotism with the willingness to fight in such wars. None of this is to say that all union officials have forsaken the ideals of solidarity, that those who use their talents commercially do not truly value those talents for their intrinsic merit, that there are no feelings of love between those who exchange expensive gifts, or that all patriots are imperialists. It is, however, to observe that if certain institutions contribute to the stability of an order, it is not surprising to find that those institutions come to exhaust the variety of institutional outlets available for the expression of interests. And if acting through those institutions is systematically rewarded and accorded respect, it is not surprising to find people realizing their aspirations through those outlets and coming to specify their aspirations in terms of them.

Finally, it might be asked why reasoning about means or ends should be so willing to accommodate the existing structures of social choice. What prevents people from judging the existing arenas of social activity as inadequate, confining, or even degrading? The answer is that many do judge them so. Alienation is not unfamiliar. And sometimes there is determined resistance to the structure of social opportunity and reward. But however familiar alienation is, consent and not resistance is the norm. Thus the original question persists. Why do people consent? But answering *that* question would simply require repeating everything we have said up to this point. Material uncertainty gives encouragement to beginning any activity with a small hoard of cash. The equivalent status of money recommends that the pursuit of nonmaterial aspirations begin with the pursuit of material means. The difficulty of coordinating more transformative struggles, together with the ability of capitalist democracy to "deliver the goods," encourages the search for private forms of satisfaction. Reasoning about ends is constrained by the existing models of social expression, and these are themselves existing models because they contribute to and are compatible with the continued existence of capitalist democracy.

To say that capitalist democracy is a system is not merely to claim that it is stable *on the assumption* of economic rationality. The claim to the status of a system also involves the strong claim that capitalist democracy can take many different people with diverse motivations and effectively bend them to engage in certain shared patterns of consensual behavior with which they will at least partly identify and which they find at least in some measure rewarding. At the level of individual acculturation, this is commonly called "growing up."

We argued earlier that the production of consent within capitalist democracy encourages a normal course of operation based on compromise between workers and capitalists. While the terms of such compromises are largely determined by the aggregate balance of power between workers and capitalists, the compromises are themselves organized through and enforced by the state. When the conditions of compromise are thus organized and enforced, the state is sometimes said to be performing its "legitimate functions," such as the "defense of national security," "the administration of justice," or "the promotion of the general welfare." But these functions are not universal or eternal, and they do not drop from the sky. The content and manner of their performance varies significantly over time. And often, as in the case of the "welfare function" assumed by modern states, there is enduring conflict over whether these functions are appropriate ends of state action at all. In fact the state's famous functions are more usefully thought of as arising from the requirements of compromise itself. Their terms and conditions mimic the terms and conditions of the compromise. In performing its functions, the state tirelessly reiterates the terms of the compromise just reached, and it does so on the basis of the distribution and mobilization of power that led to the enactment of that compromise. It expresses and enforces the compromise, and is itself the product of previous conflict and compromise. The state in a capitalist democracy may thus be thought of both as an outcome and an expression of material conflict. In any of its particular forms, themselves determined by the content of the compromise it is currently enforcing, the state holds together as a set of particular institutions and practices only so long as the compromise upon which it is founded holds together.

Upholding a compromise or organizing the terms of a new one is the central domestic condition of regime stability in a capitalist democracy. This may be seen as a threefold requirement. The state must provide conditions such that capitalists will continue to invest. It must make some sort of deal with labor such that the conditions of profitable accumulation are satisfied. And it must ensure broad consent to its own use of coercion in enforcing these agreements by demonstrating its own legitimacy.[8]

Aside from the legitimacy that derives from its "fair" enforcement of the existing compromise (the rule of law), state legitimacy is secured under capitalist democracy by winning elections. Electoral viability is determined through a system of party competition whose structure and content, like everything else within capitalist democracy, reflect the aggregate balance of power between workers and capitalists and their preferred methods of organization. The rules on party competition and financing, the number of parties, the methods of counting the ballots of voters in "winner take all" or proportional representation schemes, the commitment of the state to the registration of voters, and the enlistment of citizens in the actual processes of formal politics are all examples of such structure and content, which vary widely from regime to regime.

Satisfying this threefold requirement provides the framework for national politics within capitalist democracy. Through its institutions the state may facilitate the organization and continued viability of a democratic capitalist regime. But it is not by itself the decisive factor in ensuring the reproducibility of such a system. While the continued reorganization of the terms and conditions of relations between workers and capitalists requires and is achieved through the institutions of the state, those institutions do not themselves control the conditions of reorganization.

Such considerations of the nature and limitations of the state underscore the limitations of class compromise itself. Since the basic condition for compromise within the structure of class subordination that marks capitalist democracy is the satisfaction of the interests of capitalists in profitable accumulation, compromise is subject to disruption whenever the conditions of such accumulation are undermined. The conditions of profitable accumulation are several. Wages must not be too "high" and markets must clear. In addition, capitalists must keep their cost conditions competitive, that is, their productivity relative to other capitalists must be maintained. When these conditions are absent, there are profitability problems. And when there are profitability problems, symptoms of those problems appear in all arenas of a capitalist democracy, because all action within such orders is materially conditioned. While not all action is undertaken in pursuit of material advantage, all action depends on material resources. Profitability problems result in a shortfall of those resources for a variety of actors and institutions, including the state, and may result in the breakdown of a compromise, and its reordering. While such breakdowns occur within particular states, however, there is no reason to conclude from this that the problems from which they ensue can be explained solely in terms of conditions within the domestic system. Demand-side problems can arise on international markets, as when a recession or protectionist policies in another state restrict foreign demand. Supply-side problems can be posed by international competitors whose wages are significantly lower, or whose labor productivity is significantly higher. Such problems have become all the more frequent with the development of an increasingly integrated world economy. Understanding the conditions of profitable accumulation which underlie the domestic compromises of capitalist democracy thus requires looking beyond the domestic arena to consider international relations from the standpoint of a democratic capitalist state.

Capitalist democracies relate to other states through global markets, diplomacy, and the use of force. For any particular capitalist democracy, the basis of this relation is provided by the needs and interests of domestic actors, while the expression of these interests is constrained by the structure of international relations. Here we first examine the interests, and then consider the structure through which they are expressed.

The basic framework of foreign policy is set by the nature of the accord or compromise that the state is presently enforcing. Since the interests of workers are structurally subordinated within the domestic system to the interests of capitalists, it is reasonable to assume that the conduct of foreign affairs indicates the same hierarchy of interest satisfaction. Again, the interests of capitalists appear as general interests, while the interests of everyone else appear as particular. Indeed, it is commonly said that foreign affairs is conducted according to what is sometimes called "the national interest."

At the grossest level, the only shared interests of capitalists are in the preservation of capitalism and the taking of profits. The interests of capital are otherwise varied, not only because different capitalists are in competition with one another, but because they are differently situated in terms of their competitiveness at the international level. A summary but inadequate list of the different interests of different capitalists might include interests in raw materials for production, markets for selling their products, opportunities for profitable investment, and, where necessary, protection from foreign competition. But this list is inadequate, not only because it is too brief, but also because it fails to indicate the variations within the respective interest categories. The raw materials required by a rubber manufacturer are, for example, different from the raw materials required by steel producers, as are the sources of those materials.

While there are innumerable such differences among capitalists, some are more important than others. One such deeper difference between the needs of whole classes of firms arises from the fact that for technological, political, and economic reasons, capitalism does not operate uniformly on a global scale. There are countries that are not capitalist, there are industries that are limited to particular areas, there are markets that have not yet been created and filled, and there are barriers to the clearing of markets on a world scale. Such uneven development has many consequences, but a particularly important one for the conduct of foreign affairs is that different capitals themselves operate on different scales. Some capitalists operate largely within domestic markets, though their operations are affected by the existence of international competitors and by the need for imported materials. Other capitalists operate within both domestic and international markets. The needs and demands upon the state of these "domestic" and multinational capitals tend historically to diverge, and this divergence becomes especially marked under conditions of increasing global competition and the penetration of domestic markets by foreign firms. The American shoe industry, for example, is not competitive on global markets and does not operate extensively abroad. As a result, it demands different things from the state than do the giant oil companies with headquarters in the United States but with operations spanning the globe.

Such differences in needs among capitalists, even such deep and cross-cutting differences as those between domestic and multinational capital, are sometimes relatively insignificant to the conduct of foreign policy. There are halcyon periods of foreign policy "consensus," periods when the many different particular interests of at least the most powerful capitalist firms can be adequately satisfied within the existing framework of international relations. Sometimes, however, the differences in their interests are very significant indeed. And when they are, the organization of these differences and the pursuit of different foreign policy strategies become the objects of intense political competition. If for example one part of capital remains competitive in international markets, while another large part does not, one can expect sharp conflict over the proper relationship of the state to the operation of international markets, and the relative merits of free trade and protectionism.

Absent from the discussion of foreign policy thus far are the interests of workers. Again there are structural reasons for this, and again there are resource constraints. The structural reasons have to do with the motivational base of worker political action in capitalist democracy. The political action of workers is largely governed by the material uncertainty characteristic of capitalist democracy, and workers are led by that uncertainty rationally to limit their struggles to struggles for short-term material gain. Workers pursue gain on the basis of relatively limited information, and within the framework of established political institutions. Unless the operation of foreign states or foreign capital directly threatens the short-term material well-being of workers in a way which is recognized as a potential source of mobilization by those institutions, workers will tend to abstain from struggles over issues of foreign policy. When such operation does threaten their well-being in a way which is commonly recognized, then their interest will increase substantially. The resource constraint on the expression of such interests, however, is even more powerful in the area of foreign policy than it is in domestic policy. The general problems of information and coordination that constrain workers become almost fatal at the level of international affairs.

This generates an important asymmetry between workers and capitalists in their influence on foreign policy. While both workers and capitalists can operate within the domain of domestic politics to influence state action in foreign arenas, only capitalists routinely operate in and help to shape those foreign arenas themselves. Foreign policy thus reflects the class subordination that characterizes the domestic system, and within that class subordination the content and aims of foreign policy reflect the goals of dominant domestic actors.

The goals of foreign policy are pursued within the structure of interaction that governs relations between states. Like the domestic compromise or accord between capitalists and workers, this structure is commonly codified in law. But the operation of any system of rules is constrained at the international level by the absence of a clear mechanism to assure the legitimacy of any instrument of enforcement. There is no world government. As a result, the problems of wildcatting and "criminal" international behavior abound. Where nation-states cannot pursue their interests through peaceful negotiations or within the extremely fragile framework of international law, they commonly resort to coercive attempts to impose their will. Such coercive attempts can and often do include the use of physical force. There can be blockades, assassinations, and select bombings. Sometimes there is open invasion and outright war.

The ways in which international order can be disrupted are familiar. Much less straightforward are the conditions under which order can be secured at all. The parameters of international compromise and order are set by the condition that all actors who possess significant international power and who can therefore disrupt that order significantly must enjoy a comparably significant opportunity to express their interests within the framework of compromise. Like the domestic compromise, the regulation of such order is not governed by principles of justice or equity. If particular nation-states or particular capitals are powerless to affect the conditions of international order, their interests will not be represented. A weak country will not necessarily be accorded respect within the framework, even if that country is weak in part because of a previous history of colonial domination by a stronger country. If on the other hand a particular nation-state or particular group of capitals is all-powerful, then international order will consist merely in the unadorned expression of their interests.

As in the case of the domestic accord, a range of international orders and a variety of stable patterns of interaction between nation-states can be imagined within the limits just described. But the absence of a global political order poses special problems. Since there is no mechanism for consensual and legitimate use of force to ensure conditions of order, the costs of negotiating suitable rules of international interaction are extremely high. Historically, the problems both of arriving at the rules of international order and of enforcing those rules have been solved most effectively when a single nation-state was clearly dominant in international arenas. Under such arrangements, the dominant nation-state within the world system, or "hegemon," provides the conditions for more general order that permit the satisfaction within the limits of its dominance of the interests of all significant actors within the system. Typically this means that the currency of the dominant state is the dominant currency for international payments, and the military of the dominant state is the dominant enforcer of the conditions of international compromise.

Even an international arrangement featuring a hegemonic state is susceptible to instability, however. Like the domestic accord between capital and labor, there is always the possibility that the relative power of the parties to the accord or institutional arrangement can change over time. In the case of international arrangements, tendencies to such change are encouraged by three important problems. Each of these problems has implications for all actors within the international system, but each may be approached from the standpoint of the hegemonic power.

First, there is the problem of distributing enforcement costs. Within the domestic system, the compromise between workers and capitalists is codified in law and the enforcement of that compromise is paid for through a coercive system of taxation. In the international system, however, there is neither adequately codified law nor an officially recognized enforcer of the conditions of order. Under such circumstances, the barriers to achieving enforceable consensus on the distribution of enforcement costs among the parties to that order are prohibitively high. Under a solution to international disorder provided by the rise of a hegemonic power, a single state can emerge as de facto enforcer of the international compromise. The hegemon, which benefits most immediately from the international arrangement it dominates, itself pays the basic costs of enforcing that arrangement. But such internalized enforcement costs are high and may weaken the economic basis of the hegemonic power's dominance. Playing the role of policeman for the world brings many benefits, but it is also extremely expensive. Unless the benefits are both greater than the costs and effectively repatriated to the domestic regime that carries the burden of those costs, the costs of enforcement can constitute a serious drain on resources for that regime.

The second problem is one of differences in interest between capitalists and their "home" states. It is a famous fact of life within capitalist democracies that profits are often taken out of the domestic economy and invested elsewhere. It is said that "capital knows no country." But in the case of capitals based within the hegemonic power, this lack of knowledge often becomes extreme. The structure of international markets and exchange often leads capitalists within the hegemonic power to benefit from its dominant economic and military position by shifting investment to more profitable locations elsewhere. There are many reasons for such shifting of investment. If monetary arrangements benefit the currency of the hegemonic power, investing elsewhere may be cheaper than investing in the domestic economy. If other economies are subordinated in their own development to the hegemonic power, they may offer a more repressed and less expensive workforce, or protected markets for foreign accumulation. But whatever the reason, if profits are shifted too heavily abroad, the domestic economic sources of the hegemon's international dominance may be undermined. Such processes of disinvestment are often cumulative. As the relative attractiveness of domestic investment declines, there is less investment, which may make future domestic investment even less attractive.

The third problem is one of coercive threats. Within the domestic system, the dominant position of capitalists is importantly assured through a threat of exit. If capitalists do not get what they want out of workers or the state, they can take their business out of the domestic system. Workers know this, and often moderate their demands accordingly. Givebacks to firms suffering from foreign competition or threatening to go abroad are a newly classic example of such moderation. But for the hegemonic power within the world system, no such threat of exit is possible. There is nowhere else for it to go. While that power's accumulated strength permits it to disrupt the world system, it remains part of that system. Any strategy of disruption will bring severe costs to itself as well. An individual firm can leave a community to die as it seeks investment opportunities in another community within the domestic system or abroad. A hegemonic power cannot leave the world economy to die if it wishes to remain viable itself. The hegemon can exit from the world system, as hegemon, only through decline.

The three major problems of the hegemonic power all indicate correlate advantages for other states. They may benefit from the stability that derives from global order, but do not have to share fully in the costs of maintaining that stability. They may profit from the rise of investment in their own economies as profits are drained from the dominant state. And they may bargain more aggressively with the hegemonic power for particular concessions and gains, knowing that it cannot "walk away" from the bargaining table.

Thus, even if the rules of the international system are arranged in a way that perfectly reflects at the time of their enactment the dominance of a particular power, there are reasons to expect that the positions of different actors will change. There is a potential for gaps to develop between the actual distribution of power at any point and the distribution of power reflected in the rules in place at that point. The rules of the game may remain unchanged, even as the grounds upon which those rules were originally constructed are steadily eroded. As the relative power of the hegemon declines, the relative position of other economies proportionately grows. Then a game based on allegiance to rules of clear domination will find fewer players, or less happy ones.

Because of all the coordination problems already noted, gaps that develop within the international system are difficult to close. But difficulties in readjustment may lead to further widening gaps. There tends to be a multiplier effect on disorder. Under such conditions of growing disparity between a set of rules and corresponding privileges and the actual distribution of economic power within the international system, it is more rational for actors within that system to play away from the rules than by them. Given that it is rational for actors to maximize their gain with a minimum of risk, if they have the power to so maximize and are constrained only by allegiance to a set of rules governing their behavior, then it makes sense to reconsider and perhaps abandon that allegiance. But such reconsideration or abandonment makes behavior less predictable, and thus further undermines the stability of the international order. International instability and challenges to the original order would be expected in such a case. These have an additional and cumulative effect. With growing instability, the incentives of nation-states to resort to the use of coercion and force to settle their claims and advance particular interests would correspondingly grow.

At some point, growing instability and competition within the international system would thus come to affect the terms of the domestic accords of particular states. Our discussion of the international arena began from this point, and returning to it here underscores again the interdependence of domestic and international arrangements as they affect the politics of any particular capitalist democracy. Further understanding of that interdependence of course requires attention to specific accords and specific states. Since our chief concern is with the United States, in the next chapter we take up that more specific analysis by examining recent U.S. history through the structural framework presented thus far. The analysis considers the general institutional arrangements that shaped U.S. international and domestic relations during the period after World War II, and focuses chiefly on the disintegration of those arrangements in recent years. The discussion in the next chapter follows directly from our account of capitalist democracy's formal features. But because it deals with a specific set of accords and a specific process of decay, it may be useful to clarify that discussion further here. We do so first by exploring some of the characteristic problems of response and restructuring that accompany the breakdown of accords and then by giving initial notice to two of the distinctive features of the U.S. system that critically shape its current response.

We argued earlier that undermining the conditions of profitable accumulation has consequences throughout the domestic system of capitalist democracy, since all action is conditioned on the availability of material resources, and a shortfall in profits denies those resources to important actors within the system. One consequence of such accord breakdowns is a scrambling of the expectations of actors within the system and the erosion of the institutions whose legitimacy and force depends upon the satisfaction of those expectations. Workers accustomed to steady employment contracts may be surprised at employer demands for givebacks. Capitalists accustomed to political potency may be surprised that the state can no longer assure them foreign markets. As a variety of expectations are disappointed or overwhelmed by events, uncertainty and confusion ensue.

Because of this scrambling of expectations, periods of breakdown present important political opportunities along with their obvious dangers. Within a capitalist democracy the production of consent is centrally based on the capacity of the system to "deliver the goods." When those goods are not being delivered, when short-term material interests suffer, so does the legitimacy of capitalist democracy. Also important to the production of consent is the institutionally constrained deliberation about ends described in our discussion of motivation. That deliberation typically takes the form of shaping individual aspirations to the institutional outlets available. But if those outlets are themselves in decay, such deliberation may take more speculative forms. Both because the system is no longer delivering the material benefits it once did, and because the institutions of the system are no longer capable of absorbing and shaping nonmaterial interests the way they once did, periods of break-down therefore present challenges to the maintenance of consent.

Of course, there is no guarantee that such obstacles to the production of consent will provide the basis for radical action. How a person will respond depends both on how others respond and on his or her own willingness to act on interests and aspirations only partially satisfied by the institutions of capitalist democracy. As unemployment increases, employed and unemployed workers may join together to contest their common dependence on the uncertain operation of labor markets. But for all the reasons indicated in the discussion of the demand and resource constraints, they may also compete with each other more bitterly for the fewer remaining jobs. Similarly, traditional divisions among workers based on race, culture, and gender may be overcome during such periods, but they may also be heightened. Workers might join in attacks on their weakest colleagues in the labor force and participate in driving women, racial minorities, or immigrant workers out of labor markets in the hope of tightening those markets for themselves. As threats of war increase, workers in one state may come to see a shared interest in peace with workers in other countries, but they may alternatively come to see the expression of their short-term interests as lying in military adventurism and forceful attempts to shift the costs of breakdown onto workers in other systems. In short, periods of breakdown are always periods of great contingency for workers, not only because of the material deprivations that traditionally mark such periods, but because of the mounting and cross-cutting pressures on individuals and the uncertain direction of their individual and collective response. Put otherwise, periods of crisis manifestly heighten the importance of politics.

Persisting alongside the phenomena of breakdown and scrambling are attempts to end the crisis and restore the conditions of consent. This is of course the basic path of "re-adjustment," but such readjustment is neither painless nor automatic. During periods of breakdown, material rewards available within the system diminish. The operation of societies under such circumstances is sometimes analogized to "zero sum games" in which the gains by one party or group of parties require an exactly equal loss by others.[9] Since not everyone can gain at the same time, zero sum conditions highlight distributional conflict. One "solution" to such zero sum conflict is simply to force losses on weaker actors, and this is commonly attempted in periods of difficulty. The poor are typically attacked first, since they are usually the weakest actors within the system, and capitalists will typically attempt to force losses on workers.

Often, however, forcing losses on noncapitalists is simply not enough. Often profitability problems are caused or aggravated by problems of "overaccumulation," or the presence of large quantities of capital stock that cannot generate adequate return under competitive conditions. In such cases, restoring the conditions of profitable accumulation may require that capital-ists themselves, or at least some capitalists, take a substantial loss. But forcing losses on such powerful private actors is extremely difficult. It is seldom the case that the terms of an existing compromise specify the mechanisms whereby the rules or major parties benefiting from that compromise can be changed. More commonly, declining but still powerful private actors use the state to gain special benefits or restrictions on competition to prolong their life and protect the residual value of their assets. But such action prolongs and deepens the prob-lem of readjustment.

One "solution" in such situations is war and the outright destruction of overaccumulated capital stock. Another "solu-tion" is sustained economic crisis, during which bankruptcy does what political action did not. But both war and economic crisis of course carry enormous additional costs and may them-selves further threaten the stability of the regime, hastening the breakdown of the old order while limiting the ability to

organize a new one. An accord that facilitated profitable accumulation may thus come to constrain that accumulation, and
the process of restructuring may be blocked by the formidable
residual power of those who benefited centrally from the previous accord.

Within any given state, the actual working out of any of the
dynamics of accord development, disintegration, and restructuring depends crucially upon the relative power of workers
and capitalists within that state and upon its own location within
the hierarchy of states competing in the world economy. At the
beginning of our discussion of capitalist democracy we deliberately abstracted away from many of the particularities of the
American case with a view to seeing its general structure of
power and interest articulation. To be useful and plausible,
however, our general abstract account must now be filled in
and tied to the actual development of politics at the domestic
and international levels. As we begin to enrich our formal
account, there are again any number of contenders for pride of
place among the many particularities of the American system.
In a very preliminary fashion, here we note only two.

The first is that the terms at which class compromise is
struck in the United States indicate, even for capitalist democracies, unusually weak worker organization. This is highlighted by relatively low rates of unionization, general commitment to highly individualistic strategies of interest satisfaction,
the lower percentage of U.S. GNP directed to social spending
and other factors. But the most telling evidence is the exceptional lack within the American system of a political party which
is based on worker organizations, a party of labor. In the aggregate balance of power between workers and capitalists, workers within the United States have never reached the point of
forming a durable political party of their own to compete in the
electoral arena. In their political activity, they are forced to go
into alliance with one or another of the major capitalist parties,
a fact which powerfully restates within the political system
their structural subordination to capital. The second observa-

tion is that for a generation after World War II, the United States operated as the hegemonic power within the world system. During that period, its power was virtually uncontested, and a sustained period of global growth was achieved.

In the first decades after World War II, these and other peculiarities of the United States were embedded in a system of domestic and international accords. The dynamics of that system leave a distinctive legacy to the present period, a set of institutional arrangements and expectations which shape national response to the crisis to which we have continually alluded. Understanding the dynamics of the postwar period is thus crucial to understanding the patterns of political conflict which dominate the present. Those patterns, in turn, reflect the structural constraints characteristic of capitalist democracy which have provided a central focus of our discussion thus far, and exploring alternatives to the present disorders of American politics will eventually require reconsidering those constraints themselves. But in the meantime, our formal discussion enables us to specify the crisis itself, and now in its structural features rather than its merely symptomatic ones. The crisis may now be seen to consist in the breakup of the domestic and international accords which defined American life for more than a generation. Its dangerous momentum is provided by the search of participants in those accords to find another basis for the expression of their power. It is to this accumulating breakup and search for new ground that we now turn, but as we do so a final preliminary note is warranted.

In analyzing the breakup of the postwar accords, we wish both to deepen our formal account by considering some of the prominent historical details of a specific period, and to see if that account can usefully illuminate the dynamics of that period. But providing such an account should not be confused with writing the "history" of the United States since the close of World War II. Our purposes are quite specific. We are interested in understanding the present crisis of the American system. Since that crisis has its roots within the recent past, we wish to explore that past. But the exploration is itself framed and guided throughout by the interest in understanding the present crisis. Our historical exposition therefore is and can only be provisional, a sketch and not a final portrait.

4. PAST

In many of their essential features, both the domestic and international compromises which shaped American life in the postwar period were an institutional response to the economic crisis of the 1920s and 1930s.[1] The details of that crisis cannot be explored here, but it was broadly characterized by severe problems of "underconsumption," or income depression so extreme that goods could no longer be purchased at a rate securing the profitability of their production. Coordinated response to the problem was made more difficult by a chaotic distribution of international financial obligations. This compounded already existing problems of uneven economic development among the major powers, which in turn led many countries to shield their home markets from foreign competition through massive programs of protectionism. The extreme deprivations of the period sharply intensified struggles between workers and already bitterly divided capitalists. Themselves disruptive of economic growth, these struggles reached levels which toppled more than one capitalist democracy. Fascism, imperialism, international disorder, trade wars, world depression, and finally world war were among the many notorious results. Our account focuses on the period after this bloodbath, although that period was obviously shaped by the immediately preceding events, and in the case of the United States, the New Deal figured especially prominently in constructing the arrangements of postwar domestic power.

We observed earlier that the international and domestic compromises of capitalist democracy are closely interrelated.

This was certainly the case during the postwar years, and especially so from the standpoint of the United States. America dominated the world economy in the postwar period and played the classic role of hegemonic state. It was a primary beneficiary of the new international arrangements as well as their chief enforcer. The special international position of the United States had distinct consequences for the organization of power within its domestic system, consequences which may now be only provisionally noted as comprising the peculiar costs and benefits of playing policeman and banker of the world. Because of the special role played by the United States during the period, we will treat the international and domestic accords from the American point of view as two aspects of a single structure, a structure designed to facilitate the process of capital accumulation both domestically and, within the confines of U.S. dominance, on a global scale.

In the international arena, global economic order was sought through a system of incentives to the freer movement of both goods and capital across national boundaries and the progressive erosion of restrictive currency and trading blocs. These international aspects of the postwar accord were given their main institutional features in the Bretton Woods monetary system negotiated toward the close of World War II and consolidated and refined during the late 1940s and the 1950s. Under the terms of Bretton Woods, the dollar, itself directly convertible into gold, became the world's "reserve currency" for use in the conduct and financing of international trade. Among other things, this meant that foreign governments and international institutions would be willing to hold dollars in their gold and foreign exchange reserves for use in international trading. Among different national currencies' a system of fixed exchange rates tied to the dollar was established. The rate of exchange between different currencies was thus stabilized and measured in terms of exchange against dollars. Other institutional arrangements complemented the monetary agreements of Bretton Woods. The International Monetary Fund (IMF) and International Bank for Reconstruction and Development (World

Bank) were chartered and funded as instruments of financial brokering and development assistance for countries adjusting to trade imbalances or seeking funds for additional growth. By reason of their subscription and voting rules, both institutions were dominated by the United States. Finally, the General Agreement on Tariffs and Trade (GATT), which arose from international discussions shortly after the war, provided a negotiating framework for the resolution of trade disputes, and eventually for the substantial lowering of international trade barriers. Like the rest of the Bretton Woods system, the GATT explicitly committed the leading industrial powers to a policy of "multilateralism," or nondiscriminatory trading on a global scale.[2]

The basis of the Bretton Woods system was the overwhelming economic and military power of the United States. In addition to escaping the wartime damage that left Europe and Japan literally in ruins, U.S. economic power was founded on agricultural self-sufficiency, massive export strength, great domestic energy reserves, domination of the crucial international oil business, supremacy in most of the key industries that would shape the postwar world (aircraft, automobiles, computers, electronics, and others), and the enormous growth of its investment and commercial banking sectors that permitted it to replace England as the world's banker. The huge U.S. domestic market permitted the absorption of goods from other countries, while the technological and cost superiority of U.S. goods generated tremendous demand from other countries for American products. This great economic power was the final guarantee both of the dollar's value and of the global U.S. military superiority essential to keeping the postwar institutional arrangements intact. In short, it provided the basis for American hegemony in a free-trade-oriented international order that secured stable conditions for world capitalist growth.

On the domestic level, three major aspects of the accord should be noted. All of them were initiated in one form or another during the time of the New Deal, and then further defined and consolidated during World War II and the immediate postwar period.

The first aspect of the domestic accord was the regulation of labor. Under the Wagner (1935) and Taft-Hartley (1947) acts, the right of workers to form trade unions was explicitly recognized by the state, but subjected to important restrictions.[3] These restrictions were several. While trade unions could, for example, negotiate with employers over the "terms and conditions" of employment, "terms and conditions" was generally interpreted to include only issues immediately related to compensation levels and job descriptions. Federal law also restricted the scope of "union security" clauses, or contract provisions conditioning employment on union membership, and in the "right to work" or "open shop" Section 14B of the Taft-Hartley Act, Congress gave state legislatures the right to abolish such union security arrangements entirely. Coordination between unions in different industrial sectors was limited through sharp restrictions on "secondary" activities, or attempts to pressure the parties to an industrial dispute by pressuring those uninvolved "neutrals" with whom they happen to do business. Those employers with whom unions had direct disputes, or "primary" employers, were thus largely sheltered from indirect or "secondary" attack in the form of strikes, boycotts, or picketing actions against, for example, their principal parts suppliers or customers. Shop-floor militancy was reduced through the removal of dispute resolution to arbitration proceedings between union bargaining representatives and employers. Finally, and most generally, individual workers were accorded procedural rights to "concerted activity," but were limited in their substantive entitlements to the content of particular bargained-for contracts. Thus the federal government recognized the right of workers to join and form unions, but recognized no general right to "just" compensation (beyond the marginal provisions of the minimum wage law). And while language restricting discharge could be built into particular union contracts, workers enjoyed no general protections against willful firing by employers.

First prompted by the radical mass actions of workers in the 1930s, national labor law came to codify the workings of a much less militant movement. It established a fragmented and almost purely economically oriented pattern of interest representation which built upon and further encouraged the segmentation of workers by race and gender into different wage structures. And it guided a system of industrial relations which was crucially dependent upon the administrative apparatus of the government for its legal status and enforcement. Final decisions over the proper scope of bargaining units, the tactics used in organizing campaigns, the permissible subjects of bargaining, the duties of unions to represent their members, the requirements of arbitration proceedings, and the existence of "concerted activity" itself were all made by the state.

The system of labor regulation thus effectively expressed a deal struck between employers and unions through the state. Unions were accorded formal rights to bargain over wages and the conditions of organizational strength necessary to enforce those rights in limited contexts. Employers in turn benefited from the integration of workers into a system of bureaucratic control that was systematically biased against class-based struggles and demands and that encouraged the reduction of organizational activities to the pursuit of short-term economic interests. The prototype of the bargaining agreements that emerged out of this system were sectorally based bargaining pacts, such as the historic "Treaty of Detroit" negotiated between the United Auto Workers and General Motors in 1950, which tied wage increases to productivity increases. The essential terms and conditions of such agreements were often widely emulated in a process that became known as "pattern bargaining."

Within this structure of organized striving for short-term material gain, labor unions soon ceased to comprise a powerful and independent political movement. Systematic purges of more radical leadership and elaborate reward structures for "labor statesmen" accelerated the process of political decline, but its broader material basis was provided by the union wage gains in major industries that flourished after the war. The postwar compromise with labor imposed an outer limit on the ability of employers to shift costs into at least one portion of the work-force. But in no way did it pose any residual challenge to the rule of capitalist democracy. By deradicalizing and integrating the major organizations of workers into the ruling consensus of American life, the first component of the domestic accord thus contributed to the political and economic stability of the postwar system.

The second aspect of the domestic accord was the announced willingness of the state to secure the conditions of economic growth without wide variations in employment, prices, or output, conditions that had been so pointedly absent during the Great Depression. The "Keynesian synthesis" saw the key to such macroeconomic stability in the maintenance of aggregate demand, and efforts to ensure this demand took several forms.

One prong of the demand-based strategy consisted in build-ing mechanisms into the industrial relations system to resist downward wage pressures. Here the already mentioned pattern bargaining in large industries was one contributor to wage stability, and thus to demand maintenance. Additional stability was sought through the Davis-Bacon (1931) and Walsh-Healey (1936) acts, which required that standardized "prevailing" wages be paid on federal public-works projects and supply contracts. These measures were soon widely replicated at the state level for state government spending. And for the first time, general wage floors were adopted in the Fair Labor Standards Act (1938) that established national guidelines for minimum wages and maximum hours. The Employment Act of 1946 reflected the new consensus by explicitly committing the state to maintain-ing high levels of employment by intervening with additional government spending during periods of economic downturn.

In addition to such direct commitments to wage levels and employment, however, the state pursued large-scale programs of public spending. This kept money pumping into the econ-omy and thus helped to maintain demand levels regardless of specific bargaining structures or stages in the economic cycle.

In part such maintenance of demand through public spending went to infrastructural investment in energy development, a massive interstate highway system, and the like. Vastly more important, however, was the "military Keynesianism" explicitly adopted as a policy in the early 1950s. A 1950 document from the National Security Council (NSC-68) noted that "there are grounds for predicting that the United States and other free nations will within a few years at most experience a decline in economic activity of serious proportions unless more positive governmental programs are developed than are now available." But NSC-68 went on to argue that progress in the direction of attaining a high level of economic activity "would permit, and might itself be aided by, a build-up of the economic and military strength of the United States and the free world," and concluded that "if a dynamic expansion of the economy were achieved, the necessary build-up could be accomplished without a decrease in the national standard of living because the required resources could be obtained by siphoning off a part of the annual incre- ment in the gross national product." The link between the military force needed to maintain the international role of the United States and the economic preconditions of the domestic accord was thus explicitly recognized through a call for a "substantial increase in expenditures for military purposes."[4]

The ensuing militarization of the American economy drasti- cally increased peacetime federal spending on "defense" as a percentage of GNP. From 1.1 percent in 1929 and 1.3 percent in 1939, military spending rose to an average 10.7 percent during the period 1951–59. Between 1950 and 1951, mili- tary spending jumped from $14 billion to $33.5 billion, and averaged close to $44 billion annually through the rest of the decade, a more than threefold increase over 1950 levels. Even during periods of economic growth, this buildup required a shift in priorities within the federal budget. Dwarfing other programs, during the 1951 to 1959 period military spending averaged more than 51 percent of total federal spending, and more than 86 percent of federal purchases of goods and services.[5]

The third major component of the domestic accord was the

state's emergence as a direct source of welfare and assistance. The Social Security Act (1935) was but the first in a succession of public programs which helped to ensure demand while shielding individuals from dependence on labor markets and private charity. Even before their enormous swelling during the 1960s, the Great Society years of upheaval, programs of old age and unemployment insurance, welfare assistance, health benefits, and other measures of the "social wage" reflected and heightened the willingness to use public instruments to prevent private disaster. This use extended to capitalists as well as workers. Massive programs of economic regulation, generally beneficial to select business groups, secured order in such previously unstable markets as communications, stock broker-age, and commercial air travel. Government purchasing was directed toward infant industrial sectors such as computers and microelectronics. Use of the tax system to encourage select investment became qualitatively more sophisticated and exten-sive, as in the use of oil-depletion allowances, or in the devel-opment of a vast range of "sheltered" activities ranging from the purchase of pork-belly futures, box-car leases, and land-development rights to investment in uranium mines and suburban real estate. Government guarantees on different sorts of commercial activity were extended, as in the Federal Deposit Insurance Corporation guarantee on bank deposits. Direct subsidies were widely institutionalized in programs ranging from small business assistance loans to farm price supports.[6]

While they directly contributed to growth themselves, both the international and domestic accords were fine-tuned during a postwar period notably auspicious for economic development. In the United States, more than a decade of depression and years of war rationing and wage and price controls had gener-ated enormous potential demand for housing and such consumer durables as automobiles and household appliances. Wage gains under wartime conditions of relative scarcity translated into enormous purchasing power from personal savings which had swollen to $37 billion by 1944.[7] In Europe and Japan, the devastation wrought by the war brought demands for the rebuilding of entire societies, from basic infrastructure on up. Through the $12 billion Marshall Plan for Western European reconstruction and other programs of aid, the United States was able to benefit from this demand from abroad while building a fortress against a variety of forces, including the Soviet Union, opposed to capitalist expansion. Its own huge internal market served as an engine pulling Europe and Japan to recovery. Pent-up domestic demand was accompanied by extremely favorable liquidity positions for both individuals and businesses. Private debt soon grew. Between 1950 and 1970 alone, private debt spiraled from $164.8 billion to $975.3 billion, a more than sixfold increase that dwarfed the growth of public debt and signaled the acceptance of corporate expansion through borrowing and private consumption through life on the installment plan.[8] High levels of peacetime military spending brought important civilian spinoffs that generated yet additional markets, notably in aircraft and electronics. Finally, cheap raw materials and energy were extracted from the Third World to service the enormous demands of a reviving world economy.

The emergence of postwar order under such favorable conditions generated impressive results in growth, employment, and macroeconomic stabilization. Indeed, the postwar generation comprised the greatest period of steady capitalist expansion in the history of the world. In the United States, the period between 1947 and 1968 saw a 107 percent increase in the real net value of structures and equipment in manufacturing, a more than doubling of output per worker, and a 70 percent increase in real personal income per capita.[9] There were substantial reductions in average unemployment rates, compared to pre–World War I and the interwar periods. Between 1890 and 1914, for example, unemployment averaged 10.4 percent, and from 1920–39 it averaged 14.9 percent.[10] During the 1950s it averaged only 4.5 percent, and during the 1960s only 4.8 percent.[11] Although there were still repeated cyclical downturns in the economy (in 1948–49, 1953–54, 1957–58, and 1960–61), the variations and fluctuations of growth and employment were much smaller than during previous periods.[12] The many components of macroeconomic stabilization were having salubrious effects on the workings of the domestic economy.

But the expansion was global as well. The real value of U.S. direct foreign investment doubled during the 1950s, and doubled again during the 1960s, reflecting the mobility of capital in search of profits in an increasingly open international system. Western Europe and Japan steadily rebuilt their economies. The Third World was at least partially integrated into global financial and product markets. During the 1938–67 period, international trade volume grew at an annual cumulative rate of 4.8 percent, an historically astonishing increase 12 times the rate of increase from 1913 through 1937.[13] It was not a peaceful world. Third World rebellions, repeated U.S. interventions, and a variety of showdowns between the superpowers indicated as much. But neither was it a period of major military rivalry between the United States and other capitalist powers. The "American Century" had begun, and the industrialized world rode to prosperity on the back of the apparently limitless boom.

By the mid-1970s, key parts of this elaborate structure had smashed to pieces. The United States was mired in deep recession. Critical industrial sectors were in nearly hopeless decline. Bretton Woods had been abandoned as a monetary system. World trade volume had dropped for the first time since the 1930s. Real spendable earnings were in decline. Growth in the industrialized West had leveled off. Protectionist pressures were mounting globally. Profound liquidity problems constrained the international economy. And large portions of the Third World stood poised on the brink of economic disaster. The international accord was fragmenting, putting additional pressures on domestic arrangements of consent. The boom was decisively over.

Several things had happened. While they do not tell the broader story, changes in the pattern of consumer demand and the increasing costs of energy and raw materials may be given initial notice.

Within broad income-distribution constraints, the market for many of the consumer durables that sustained the long boom was becoming saturated. In 1960, only 7 percent of American homes owned dishwashers. By 1975, roughly 40 percent had the appliance, and the market showed no further signs of growth. In 1960, virtually no one owned a color television. By the mid-1970s, 74 percent of homes had one or more.[14]

One example of such saturation is particularly important. A critical force behind the boom was provided by the automobile industry. Throughout the postwar years, approximately one in seven American workers was employed in the industry or one of its direct suppliers or dependents. Huge levels of employment were keyed to huge and growing levels of demand. Immediately after World War II, only one in five Americans owned a car. But the 26 million automobiles in service then had grown to 102 million by 1973, representing nearly one car for every two Americans.[15] The saturation showed in retail sales figures. The average annual sales of all autos in the United States during the 1961–65 period, including both domestically manufactured cars and imports, was fully 30.5 percent higher than during the years of 1956–60. Sales during 1976–80, by contrast, were only 4 percent greater than during the previous five years of 1971–75.[16] By decade's end the auto industry faced the grim prospect of only 1–2 percent annual increases in the domestic market. Chrysler was a basket case for federal bailouts, and hundreds of thousands of auto workers were unemployed. But what was true of automobiles was true of many industries in the old manufacturing core. An entire industrial structure keyed to mass consumption and tied to the maintenance of domestic aggregate demand was coming to an end.

Raw materials price increases also contributed to the new problems with economic growth by sharply shifting factor prices and scrambling traditional patterns of consumption. Like the saturation of consumer industries, however, drastic price increases in raw materials were far from being "exogenous" shocks to the economic system of the developed world. Upward pressures on resource prices significantly reflected the long

period of steady growth itself. Differential rates of inflation in
the United States for raw materials and finished products
between 1972 and 1974 illustrate these pressures. Wholesale
prices for raw materials inflated at an annual rate of more than
28 percent from 1972 to 1974, while the comparable rate for
finished products was only 12 percent. In the raw materials
category, prices for food and feedstuffs and for nonfood-nonfuel
raw materials inflated at a faster rate than fuel prices until the
recession of 1974–75.[17] Between 1970 and 1973, even before
the major oil price increases that would later mark the decade,
the composite index of raw materials prices increased some
300 percent.[18]

More centrally, however, the boom ended because the accords
that had governed the postwar years were no longer adequate
to the changing relative position of dominant international
economic actors. "Gaps" had developed, and the framework
established to unleash global accumulation was now constrain-
ing it. At the same time, the institutions and powers to which
the accords gave rise effectively blocked the process of their
restructuring. In short, there were no clear rules on how to
change the rules, and any change would necessarily harm
powerful groups of actors.

This general problem of institutional decay and deferred
institutional response unfolded in many stages: (1) the relative
position of the U.S. economy drastically declined, opening a
huge gap between the privileged international position ceded
the United States by Bretton Woods and the economic foundations of that position; (2) within this new position a variety
of competing claims on the U.S. economy produced pervasive
pressures for inflation; (3) the inflation harmed any number of
domestic interests and produced pressures for radical cure
through unemployment; (4) but the unemployment cure no
longer worked the "wonders" it once did, and itself contributed
to further international decline; (5) the resulting impasse of
simultaneous economic stagnation and inflation, called "stagflation," gripped the U.S. economy and underscored the need
for domestic restructuring; (6) but that restructuring was made

vastly more difficult by international instability, itself a function of growing rivalry between the United States and other major capitalist powers, and the nature of the domestic accord itself. These different problems did not unfold in perfect chronological sequence, but they provide an analytic key to understanding the collapse inward of the set of relations we have called the postwar accord. We will consider them in turn.[19]

The relative decline of the U.S. economy can be measured in a number of ways. In the late 1940s, the United States produced 60 percent of the total manufactures in the industrialized West, and 40 percent of the total goods and services. By the late 1970s, both shares had been chopped in half. U.S. export dominance was also eroding. Of Western industrialized countries' manufactured exports, the United States claimed nearly a 30 percent share in 1953. By 1976, the U.S. share had dwindled to a mere 13 percent.[20] The change in the relative position of the United States reflected the growing strength of the economies devastated by the war, particularly West Germany and Japan. By virtually every conventional measure, those economies vastly outperformed the United States during the postwar era. Between 1953 and 1960, the rate of growth of gross domestic product in the United States was 2.4 percent, in Japan 9.4 percent, in Germany 7.0 percent. Between 1950 and 1976, industrial productivity in the United States grew at an annual rate of 2.8 percent, in Japan 8.3 percent, in Germany 5.4 percent. Between 1950 and 1970, the annual growth rate of total fixed capital stock (excluding housing) was 3.8 percent in the United States, 8.8 percent in Japan, and 6.2 percent in Germany.[21]

During the 1956 through 1976 period, the American share of world exports in manufactures dropped from 25.5 percent to 17.3 percent. Germany grew from 16.5 percent to 20.6 percent. Japan grew from 5.7 percent to 14.6 percent.[22] The decline in the U.S. trade position was obvious. In the immediate postwar years that position had been unrivaled. In 1949, for example, the United States showed positive trade balances for all major commodities. But this picture soon changed as other economies rebuilt from the war, and the number of basic classifications of goods showing negative trade balances steadily increased through the 1950s and 1960s. Textiles and manufactured consumer durables balances turned negative in 1955, consumer goods in 1959, electric household appliances and radios in 1962, iron and steel in 1963, and automotive products in 1968.[23] In 1971 the first absolute trade deficit in recent U.S. history appeared. When the overall trade balance of the United States turned sharply negative in 1971, Japan and West Germany commanded an aggregate trade surplus of $12 billion.

The great decline in the relative competitiveness of the U.S. economy during the heyday of Bretton Woods can be traced through the dynamics of the Bretton Woods system itself. Certain distinct advantages to the United States came as a result of the dollar's status as the world's reserve currency. Those advantages had to do with the tremendous demand for dollars from other countries who needed them to finance and conduct their own international trade. Dollars flowing abroad in the form of direct investment, or import acquisition, or foreign aid, or military assistance, accumulated in the reserves of foreign central banks, which used them to buy short-term securities from the U.S. government or redeposited them in U.S. financial markets as short-term deposits. The ability to generate such short-term loans regularly from other countries in turn refinanced additional programs of American spending abroad. The United States was in effect the world's banker. Capital accounts were almost continuously in the red throughout the 1950s and 1960s; the United States was nearly always sending more money abroad in the form of investment and other capital flows than it was taking in. But because of the tremendous demand for dollars, the United States could afford to do this without obvious and immediate damage to its currency. Effectively, it was rewarded for not balancing its books. The French called this the "exorbitant privilege" of international financial leadership.

But with this privilege came many difficulties. Chief among them was the so-called "confidence problem."[24] In making the dollar the world's reserve currency, Bretton Woods effectively required that the United States flood the world with dollars in order to ensure world liquidity and ease the conduct of trade. If the United States did not do this, if a "dollar gap" appeared, then the system of advancing multilateralism might regress to protectionism. Among the many consequences of such a development would be the closure of global markets to American goods themselves. But flooding the world with dollars in turn effectively meant that the United States had to run balance of payments deficits, or deficits on the overall account of its trade and capital flows with the rest of the world. And such imbalances between what an economy takes in and what it puts out cannot continue forever. The confidence problem took its name from the fact that the dollar's role as reserve currency under Bretton Woods required balance of payments deficits by the United States, but those deficits would inevitably undermine confidence in the reserve currency itself. Rather than holding their accumulated dollars against future trading, foreign central banks might choose to exercise their right under the Bretton Woods agreement to convert their dollars to gold. In the postwar years, as more dollars flowed into the world system and the relative demand for American goods slackened, many central banks in fact exercised this conversion option, and as U.S. gold stocks ran down, the confidence problem gained added force.[25]

To mitigate the balance of payments problem, the United States had to maintain trade surpluses to balance as far as possible the capital deficits it continually ran. But there were additional problems here. Bretton Woods accorded the dollar a strong position relative to other currencies, and the tremendous international demand for dollars kept upward pressure on their cost. But a dollar that is so strong relative to other currencies means that imports will be relatively cheaper than goods produced at home, supplementing any possible independent cost advantages of imported goods. It means that the goods of other countries will be cheaper than those of the United States. Thus, in 1950 the dollar cost of Japanese goods was half the cost of American goods, and the dollar cost of German goods was 72 percent of American goods.[26] The situation changed over time, but not as considerably as domestic producers hoped. In 1970, Japanese goods were still one-third cheaper than American goods, and German goods were still 20 percent cheaper.[27] These cost differentials hurt American domestic manufacturers at both ends. It was more difficult to sell their goods abroad, and it was easier for foreign producers to penetrate the U.S. domestic market.

To the extent that American demand for goods increased, it could be expected that pressures to import would increase, thus undermining the trade balance. At least when it was not at war, the United States accordingly adopted relatively restrictive demand policies which were aimed in part at holding income, and therefore imports, below their potential. Full employment was often announced as an official goal during such periods, but it was never seriously pursued.[28] Between 1954 and 1964, from the end of the Korean War to the beginning of the major American escalation in Vietnam, U.S. unemployment averaged 5.4 percent.[29] Relatively high interest rates were maintained. While helping to prop up the dollar's value, these measures further hurt the competitive position of domestic manufacturers and constrained their borrowing, investment, and expansion. At the same time, because of the dollar's strong and unique position in world currency markets, investment abroad was made more attractive. The exercise of the "exorbitant privilege" continued.

Both aspects of Bretton Woods, the extremely strong position it awarded the dollar relative to other currencies and the various measures taken to ensure the stability of that position, thus placed downward pressure on domestic investment and accumulation. But everything else being equal, this in turn tended to weaken the U.S. domestic economy, generating further confidence problems. It was a vicious circle.

But while the free-trade-oriented international accord was causing suffering among domestic producers, it was helping many manufacturing and financial interests to flourish. U.S. multinationals that produced and sold extensively abroad benefited directly from the system and the special position of the

United States within it. A strong dollar encourages multinational expansion abroad by reducing fixed capital and other
costs. A U.S. multinational with reserves of dollars could buy
or build abroad relatively cheaply. While such costs were kept
comparatively low, the multinational had the additional advantage of competing from within often protected foreign markets.
During the postwar years direct foreign investment not only
increased in absolute terms, but also in its relative importance
to the operation of the U.S. economy as a whole. Between 1950
and 1966, for example, the assets of U.S. foreign affiliates as a
percentage of total assets of U.S. nonfinancial corporations
nearly doubled, rising from 6.2 to 12.3 percent.[30]

The fourfold increase in U.S. direct foreign investment abroad
from 1950 to 1970 was primarily directed to other highly
industrialized countries. While wages may have been lower in
less industrialized states, a variety of other conditions, including the presence of appropriately skilled labor, transportation
infrastructure, and political stability made the overall cost
structure more favorable in the industrialized states. Reflecting
such considerations, between 1957 and 1966 the assets of U.S.
affiliates in Western Europe increased from 21.8 percent of
total assets of U.S. foreign affiliates to 37.4 percent. Over the
same period, the assets of U.S. affiliates in Latin America
dropped from 27.9 percent of total assets of U.S. foreign affiliates to 16.3 percent.[31]

International banks also benefited from the growing integration of the world system and the extensive financial brokering
it entailed. Overseas assets of leading international American
banks virtually exploded during the 1960s, rising from $3.5
billion to $52.6 billion.[32]

Even though the workings of the Bretton Woods system placed
substantial pressure on some American interests by the late
1960s, other American interests thus continued to benefit from
the system. And even though the terms of international financial order underscored divisions within the American business
community, that order provided no clear way to resolve those
divisions. The point may be clarified by considering a few of

the many problems associated with readjustment within the confines of Bretton Woods.

By the end of the 1960s, covering the capital account deficits of the United States that were generated by the steady flow of dollars abroad would have required a truly enormous surplus in the American current account (the balance of international inflows and outflows of goods, services, and grants) on the order of $10 to $15 billion a year. In order to generate such a surplus, American goods and services would need to have been made substantially more attractive to foreign buyers through price reductions achieved through dollar devaluation. Such substantial devaluations would have eroded the cost advantage of multinational expansion, destabilized international financial markets, and directly undermined the enormous holdings of the big commercial banks. But quite apart from these immediate political obstacles, substantial devaluations were effectively blocked by the dollar's tie to gold. If the devaluation were to be achieved by simply raising the gold price, then those European countries, in particular France, that had accumulated enormous stores of gold throughout the 1960s would inevitably have pressured for a return to a greater monetary role for gold in the international system. The likely continuation of U.S. balance of payments difficulties even after such devaluation would have made such pressures all the stronger.

Compounding these difficulties was the central role the United States still played in pulling other economies along the path of growth by absorbing their goods in its gigantic domestic market. While devaluation would have helped the position of domestic manufacturers, all other things being equal, sharp increases in U.S. exports and decreases in U.S. imports would have wreaked havoc on the balance of payments of other countries. Particularly in the case of those countries that relied heavily on export earnings, such pressures would have forced substantial domestic adjustment. Such countries could devalue their own currencies in response; but then the price of needed imports would rise, with inflationary consequences for their own systems. Or they could try to reduce imports either by reducing domestic demand through deflating their economies or through protectionism. But if world income contracted or if protectionist barriers increased, then the purpose of American devaluation might be defeated by the resulting shrinkage of international markets. The dollar might be weaker, but the relative position of the U.S. economy might not be any stronger. In such a scenario, downward pressures on the dollar could be expected to increase. These pressures could become overpowering through engineered recessions in other countries, which would further shrink demand and likely strengthen the relative position of other currencies.

If such contraction were to occur, in theory a way out might be offered by vast increases in world liquidity to spur the growth of weaker economies and restore the flow of trade. But such financing could not come from the United States, since by the late 1960s the overflow of dollars was already a problem. And it could not come from the other strong economies like West Germany and Japan, because however much their position had strengthened in the time since World War II, they were not yet capable of fully replacing the United States as dominant international actor. To be noninflationary, increased liquidity would have to come from some reordering of the world financial system itself, perhaps through a cooperative program to increase national reserves. But on any such reordering, the dollar's privileged position would be significantly constrained, or even ended. And although American power was in relative decline, it was still capable of blocking such a move, and could be expected to do so.

What all these scenarios indicate are the serious problems in international readjustment that followed on the relative decline in U.S. economic power. While by the late 1960s the positions of the major parties to the international financial system had shifted, and while "gaps" had appeared, it was not clear how the rules of that system could be changed in a way that reflected the new positions and power of the different parties. Although U.S. power was in relative decline, it was still sufficient to block restructuring. While other national economies were ascendant, none was yet powerful enough to replace the United States as hegemonic state. While the international accord no longer facilitated accumulation the way it once did, no other structure of international coordination was manifestly available and capable of winning the support necessary to implement it.

Within this context of growing international disorder and relative U.S. economic decline, a variety of claims on the American economy generated additional pressures. As in the case of the difficulties associated with Bretton Woods, these claims commonly reflected the normal workings of different aspects of the postwar accord, even as their cumulative effect was to undermine the stability of that arrangement.

Military claims were of particular importance. For years the United States had committed a huge portion of its federal budget to military spending, an expenditure that performed two important functions. The first of these, macroeconomic stabilization, involved detaching a significant component of domestic output from the business cycle without generating competition between the state and private capital. This was the strategy of "military Keynesianism" already noted. The second and more fundamental function of military spending, however, was to enable the United States to enforce the new international arrangements of the postwar period. Military power was a central guarantee of the stability of those arrangements, and of the dominant role of the United States within them.

Military spending developed in two important stages after World War II.[33] The first stage followed on NSC-68's call for massive increases in peacetime defense expenditure levels. The NSC-68 program was enacted after the Korean War, when peacetime spending jumped to a normal 9–10 percent of GNP per annum. Some 50 percent of military expenditures during the 1950s went to nuclear forces. This nuclear emphasis found its official rationale in the doctrine of "massive retaliation," which announced that nuclear capabilities would be used to "deter" any threat to U.S. interests.

The second major stage in postwar military spending came with the Kennedy administration's insistence on the need for "flexible response" in military affairs. In addition to enormously amplifying U.S. nuclear forces through the ICBM program and others, the Kennedy administration called for stronger conventional military capabilities. Enhanced conventional force levels were thought necessary to the conduct of counter-insurgency operations and ground wars during a period of expanding U.S. direct investment in a politically unstable Third World.[34]

Reflecting these many ambitions, by the middle 1960s American military power and commitments had grown to truly enormous proportions. Between 1951 and 1965 the United States spent $675 billion (current dollars) on defense.[35] By 1965 it had military obligations confirmed by treaty with fully 43 countries, and forces and equipment at 375 major military bases and 3,000 minor installations spread around the world.[36] And it was developing generation after generation of advanced weapons systems.

The United States did not merely accumulate this military power. It used it repeatedly. Between 1951 and 1965 military forces were deployed short of full-scale war on the average of once every 40 days. The 138 incidents varied from sending a carrier task force and a battalion-sized marine amphibious force off the shores of Venezuela in 1958 after then Vice-President Richard Nixon was given a stormy welcome in Caracas, to invading the Dominican Republic in 1965, to sending nuclear-equipped bombers to Nicaragua in 1954 as part of the successful U.S. campaign to overthrow the Arbenz regime in neighboring Guatemala. One hundred twenty of the uses of force occurred between 1956 and 1965, with the highest concentration between 1963 and 1964. During that period of "New Frontier" liberalism, U.S. military power was deployed on the average of once every 19 days.[37]

The American invasion of Vietnam added substantially to the economic costs of these military activities. On top of already high levels of spending, between 1966 and 1970 an additional $106 billion was poured into the defense budget to help finance the war.[38] Even under conditions of careful wartime fiscal control, such an acceleration of military spending would have placed a strain on government finances. Under conditions of sagging international competitiveness, a variety of competing domestic claims on the economy, and a refusal to cover the costs of an increasingly unpopular war by raising taxes, its inflationary impact was manifest. The buildup was paid for by printing money.

In addition to the immediate inflationary effects of Vietnam spending, huge and long-standing commitments to high levels of military spending had other adverse effects on the domestic economy. At its core, military spending is wasteful in the elementary sense that the goods produced—bombs, ships, airplanes, tanks—have no use other than destruction. They cannot be eaten or worn. They do not produce other goods. And while their design and production sometimes generate substantial civilian spinoff applications, they do not directly contribute to the physical infrastructure of the American economy the way other public spending on such projects as dams, deep water ports, bridges, and highways does.

More immediately, while the governments of West Germany and Japan were subsidizing their best engineers and highly skilled workers in rebuilding steel plants, gearing up cost-effective automobile production, or exploring the higher technology frontiers of telecommunications, the United States was spending a good deal of its money (regularly more than 50 percent of government research and development funds) subsidizing the design of heat-guided missile systems, antipersonnel weapons, chemical defoliants, rapid-fire machine guns, and the other unproductive paraphernalia of war.[39] As U.S. competitiveness gradually declined, and especially as opposition to the Vietnam War grew, the appropriateness of such research projects and the continued diversion of major national resources to wasteful production was subject to growing criticism on the grounds of their "inefficiency" for the domestic economy as a whole.

Sharply compounding these problems were the independent demands and waste of the military producers themselves. Endlessly subsidized as a critical sector, weapons manufacturers grew in size, but came to depend upon state support. They exerted autonomous pressures for further subsidies and further militarization, even when the resulting expenditures were irrational from the standpoint of maintaining U.S. international economic power.[40] The structure of the subsidized military sector also generated production inefficiencies. The cyclical character of military contracts resulted in long periods of low capacity utilization. High levels of industrial concentration, especially at the subcontractor level, produced important price distortions. The overwhelmingly noncompetitive assignment of contracts exacerbated these tendencies to inefficiency. Cost overruns were only the most familiar sign of this waste.[41] In other respects, the subsidized armaments industry shared certain characteristics with declining industrial sectors. Product innovation dominated process innovation, in part reflecting the orientation of military demand to new weapons systems. This orientation was reinforced by the characteristically technological rather than numerical advantages the United States enjoyed relative to the Soviet Union and other major military rivals, but it implied enormous design and development changes. Thus the increasingly "baroque" American arsenal was produced at ever higher unit costs.[42]

The military link between the domestic and international accords thus placed important pressures on the rest of the political and economic system. But these burdens of the strongest state, while contributing to its decline, were required by the overwhelming desire for a U.S. military presence abroad. They were not the "accidents" or "mistakes" of public policy, although such mistakes were surely made, but the result of that policy's quite deliberate subordination to imperial aims and demands. The policy followed directly from the role of the United States in the international accord, even as it made that role more difficult to play.

Beyond the enormous claims of military spending, many features of the domestic postwar accord, including income floors, wage increases, and programs of state assistance, added to the cumulative strains. Spurred on by the great and often violent civil rights struggles of the period, social programs expanded during the 1960s and were fitted into a broader conception of a "Great Society." While assistance programs for the poor have received the most attention, the bulk of the monies went to solidly middle-class programs in education, social security, medical insurance for the aged, and other such generic entitlement programs not keyed to economic class. Annual spending (in current dollars) on education by all levels of government jumped from $19.4 billion in 1960 to $55.8 billion in 1970. Over the same period, social security and other insurance rose from $10.8 to $35.8 billion, and health and hospital spending increased from $5.2 to $13.6 billion.[43] Between 1961 and 1970, federal outlays for health, education, and income security rose from just over $21 billion to more than $64 billion, an increase of 135 percent in constant dollars. But of the $64 billion spent in 1970, major social insurance programs not keyed to economic class, in particular social security, other retirement programs, and Medicare, accounted for more than $41 billion. Public assistance programs (including Aid to Families With Dependent Children and food stamps) together with Medicaid accounted for less than $8 billion.[44] Unlike military spending, none of these programs represented a wasteful squandering of resources. But like defense expenditures, the social assistance programs that burgeoned during the 1960s underscored the many competing claims made on both political institutions and the economy. The easiest way to meet these claims was, again, through printing money.

Wage claims were also on the rise. Between the recessions of 1960–61 and 1969–70 came a record-breaking boom, lasting from February 1961 to November 1969, that brought with it extremely tight labor markets. Over the period, unemployment fell from 6.7 percent in 1961 to 3.8 percent in 1966, and remained below 4 percent between 1966 and 1969.[45] The mean duration of unemployment fell to a postwar low of 7.9 weeks in 1969.[46] The results were a sharp reminder of the problems posed by high levels of employment in a capitalist economy. The period saw increasing shopfloor militancy, greater inci-

dence of strikes—including both wildcats and strikes over
nonwage issues—and increases in unit labor costs, or the
compensation paid per dollar value of output. After rising at an
average annual rate of 0.4 percent during the 1960–65 period,
unit labor costs rose 3.8 percent in 1966, and averaged 4.8
percent increases during the 1966–70 period.[47] Disrupting the
pattern bargaining premises of the postwar accord, wage gains
were significantly exceeding productivity gains.

More generally, the development of the Great Society programs
and wage gains in an atmosphere of economic growth both
reflected and further enhanced increasing expectations of the
"quality of life" and, with them, of the role of government within
the domestic accord. Americans no longer thought that unemployment should be accompanied by starvation, for example, or
that only the children of the rich should be entitled to quality
higher education. The civil rights movement (and, much later,
the women's movement) shattered old social roles and sharply
altered the expectations of equality of millions. Repeated civil
rights demonstrations and finally outbreaks of urban rebellion
underscored the urgency of these claims. Between 1965 and
1968 there were 300 "riots and disturbances," during which
50,000 arrests and 8,000 casualties were registered. In 1967
there were 150 urban revolts, of which 24 were "major or serious," including the massive upheavals in Newark and Detroit.
In the Detroit uprising alone, more than 43 people were killed
and more than a thousand wounded.[48] Such pressures were
reflected in the steady stream of civil rights legislation that
marked the 1960s, including the 1963 Equal Pay Act and the
Civil Rights Acts of 1960, 1964, 1965, and 1968.

The exposure of vast environmental damage spawned
increasing challenge to the destruction of natural resources by
the private sector. Here too popular concerns placed their mark
on federal legislation during the 1960s and early 1970s, with
the passage of such environmental legislation as the Federal
Water Pollution Control Act (1961), the Clean Air Act (1963),
the Motor Vehicle Air Pollution Control Act (1965), the Water
Quality Act (1965), the Clean Waters Restoration Act (1966),

the National Emissions Standards Act (1967), and the National
Environmental Policy Act (1970), along with innumerable major
amendments.[49]

The routine defrauding of consumers, and the less routine
but increasingly common exposure of such fraudulence, triggered "consumerist" challenges during the period and contributed to the passage of such federal legislation as the Federal
Hazardous Substances Labeling Act (1960), the major drug
amendments of 1962, the Federal Cigarette Labeling and
Advertising Act (1965), the National Traffic and Motor Vehicle
Safety Act (1966), the Fair Packaging and Labeling Act (1966),
the Consumer Credit Protection Act (1968), the Deceptive Sales
Act (1968), the Consumer Product Safety Act (1972), and the
Consumer Product Warranties Act (1974).[50] Health concerns
were reflected in the passage of the Medicare and Medicaid
programs (1965) and the Comprehensive Health Planning Act
(1967). These concerns extended, significantly, to the workplace itself, with the passage of the Mine Safety and Health
Act (1969) and the Occupational Safety and Health Act (1970).[51]

Much of the legislation of the period imposed continuing
burdens of executive administration on the federal government
in an explosion of regulatory agencies. The contrast with earlier
periods was clear. Between 1930 and 1945, during the heyday
of the New Deal and the first major increase in federal supervision of the economy, some 16 federal regulatory agencies
were created. Between 1946 and 1963, another 10 regulatory
agencies were added. Between 1964 and 1973, fully 29 new
agencies emerged, including such major ones as the Equal
Employment Opportunity Commission (1964), the Office for
Civil Rights (1964), the Office for Consumer Affairs and Regulatory Functions (1968), the Office for Fair Housing and Equal
Opportunity (1968), the Environmental Protection Agency
(1970), the Consumer Products Safety Commission (1972),
and the Occupational Safety and Health Administration (1973).[52]

Imperial maintenance of authoritarian regimes whose actions
did not directly benefit ordinary Americans even prompted
widespread discussion of foreign policy. As in the case of protests

against the Vietnam War, in which millions participated, that discussion sometimes took place in the streets. Here too the success of economic growth generated political contradictions. Less fearful about their future, at least some Americans became less docile, and engaged in the risks of unapproved political action.

The successful workings of the domestic and international accords thus generated contradictory pressures which tended to fracture those accords themselves. The cumulative strain took its toll on the bottom line of postwar prosperity, the profitability of accumulation itself. Profit rates declined in 1966 and dropped sharply in 1967. After averaging approximately 16 percent during the 1947–65 period, the net before tax rate of return of the nonfinancial corporate sector would drop to an average rate of 12 percent during the next decade.[53] The annual rate of increase in real nonresidential fixed domestic capital formation followed suit. Having averaged 9.6 percent during the 1961–65 period, it would drop to 2.5 percent during 1966–79.[54] During the 1966–79 period, productivity increases fell to an average 1.4 percent annual rate.[55] During the 1949–66 period, when real nonresidential fixed domestic capital formation had grown at an average rate of 5 percent, productivity increases had averaged 3.2 percent per year.[56]

Thus, as the United States entered the 1970s, many of the problems that were to plague that decade were already evident: sharpening international competition; relative industrial decline; splits within the business community over the appropriate response to these phenomena; declining profits, investment, and productivity at home; increasing claims made upon the state; increasing claims by the state upon the economy. All these problems converged in the new economic phenomenon of stagflation that would define U.S. economic performance during the next several years.

"Stagflation" refers to the simultaneous persistence of stagnation and inflation. While periods of economic growth always bring pressures for inflation, stagflation describes a situation in which inflation tends to persist even when the economy is stagnant, and in which the economy tends to stagnate until measures are taken which are even further inflationary. The relative decline of U.S. industrial power spelled the beginning of stagnationist tendencies at home, the first aspect of the stagflation problem. With them came sharpened pressures for inflation within the system.

Formally understood, inflation reflects the nominal satisfaction of conflicting demands on an economy that are not being satisfied by the current level of production and distribution of benefits. Unless it leads to further offsetting increases in production, such a "solution" to conflict will be only temporary, and if it is, can lead to further inflationary pressures. As already noted, the demands made upon the American economy in the late 1960s were several, ranging from the costs of military empire to the costs of education and welfare. But these many demands may be approached by considering that critical demand which drives the domestic system, the demand by manufacturers for profits.

Facing declining profits in the late 1960s, one "natural" response of manufacturers was merely to increase their prices. This was less costly than reducing current consumption to secure funds for investment for future profits, and easier to accomplish than facing down the growing nominal wage claims of workers. But such price increases are inflationary. For goods to be bought at higher prices, more money must be made available. Increases in the money supply which do not correspond to increased production are inflationary in the basic sense that there is simply more money chasing the same bundle of goods.

In the United States, the strategy of inflating away workers' wages was generally successful. In contrast to Western Europe, where the share of wages in manufacturing income actually increased substantially during the late 1960s and early 1970s, American wage increases generally did not keep up with prices during that period.[57] The apparent inability of American workers to keep up with inflation may seem surprising against the background of worker militancy that was evident during the long 1960s boom. But that militancy produced no organizational or institutional shift to consolidate wage gains or more permanently boost the power of labor. While strikes increased during the 1960s, the level of unionization of the labor force continued its postwar decline. No change in labor legislation was enacted that would have lowered the costs of organization or contributed to overcoming the labor movement's fragmentation across industry lines. Nor was there a strengthening of labor's position within the Democratic Party. Democratically controlled Congresses consistently failed to amend Section 14B of the Taft-Hartley Act, the "open shop" provision that encouraged the regular movement of capital to antiunion havens in the South. And Democratically controlled trade policy under both the Kennedy and Johnson administrations showed apparent indifference to labor's concern about the loss of jobs in manufacturing associated with increased imports. While such core union industries as textiles and shoes lost hundreds of thousands of members to the inroads of foreign competition, the "Kennedy Round" of GATT negotiations resulted in roughly 30 percent cuts in tariffs and other barriers to the flow of trade.[58]

When the long 1960s boom ended, signs of labor's weakness quickly appeared. Real disposable income for a worker with three dependents, which had only remained constant from 1965 through 1968, dropped sharply in 1969. A decade later it would even be below 1969 levels.[59] Real average gross weekly earnings, which increased only 2 percent between 1965 and 1968, fell in 1970 below their 1968 level, and by 1979 would fall to their 1965 level.[60] Unionization rates showed a continued drop in the 1970s, and strike levels steadily declined after a brief upturn in the early 1970s.[61] Social programs of course continued to provide some measure of income security for workers, but this "social wage" continued to be financed through regressive tax measures.[62]

But while inflation may thus comfort manufacturers seeking to protect their profit share from an already debilitated labor movement, it severely threatens financial interests by reducing the value of accumulated reserves and of loan repayments. If the buying power of money declines, the power of creditors and those who hold money also declines, while the burden on debtors is lessened. Paying back a loan with 10 percent interest during a period of 10 percent inflation is equivalent to being able to borrow for free. The increased prices that accompany inflation can also hurt international competitiveness. If a car costs $4,000 one year and the same car costs $5,000 two years later, everything else being equal (including the rate at which foreign currencies can be converted to dollars), that car will be more difficult to sell abroad. If the value of the dollar relative to other currencies were to drop to an extent equal to the rise in nominal price, then this effect could be corrected. But such depreciation of the dollar's value, which was in any case effectively prohibited under Bretton Woods, would hurt the interests of multinational manufacturers and international finance. Their dollar reserves would be worth less, and their buying power in foreign markets would be proportionately reduced. Depreciation also commonly leads to inflation, since domestic actors (workers and manufacturers both) will struggle to increase their own wages or prices to recover the buying power they have lost through the higher costs of imports. Such inflation hurts financial interests further. While there are a variety of ways in which financial interests can try to adjust to inflation, the value of previously negotiated credit repayments will be threatened, and uncertainty over future variations in inflation makes current adjustments difficult. Finally, a sustained cycle of inflation, depreciation, more inflation, and more depreciation holds the eventual threat that speculation against the home currency may be triggered in international markets in expectation of further deterioration in that currency's relative position. The mere existence of such speculation commonly applies further downward pressures and can have a cumulative effect.

Inflationary pressures thus exacerbate tensions between manufacturing and financial interests. They underscore again this important line of division within the business community, while adding to the difficulties of responding to the division in concerted fashion. As in virtually all such situations, no ulti-

mate incompatibility among different business interests need
be assumed to understand their continued conflict. Manufacturers have an obvious stake in the health of banks, for example, because banks are important sources of credit. Financial
interests have an obvious stake in the welfare of manufacturers, since the welfare of manufacturers is the precondition of
their repaying their loans. But when business interests come
into conflict, neither is there any reason to assume that social
mechanisms are already in place for the resolution of such
conflicts. Again, it is possible that socially irrational results will
derive from individually rational decisions. The business
community may founder, but not because its members are
either stupid or crazy. Inflation may continue.

If inflation does continue, fed by its many claimants, the
financial community, which tends to suffer disproportionately
from the phenomenon, will eventually attempt to halt it by
tightening money or credit, and thus inducing recession.
Recession ordinarily breaks the inflation spiral by throwing
workers off their jobs, thereby increasing the pool of unemployed workers, or what is commonly called the "reserve army"
of the unemployed. An increase in the size of this army tends
to weaken the bargaining position of those workers who are
still employed, and thus places downward pressure on their
wages. As jobs become more scarce and unemployed labor
more plentiful, the "cost" of labor, or the wages necessary to
pay someone to work, can be expected to decline. In theory,
reduced labor costs and generally reduced aggregate demand
from slowed production and shrinking employment should lead
to a decrease in prices. But in addition to the damage it does to
workers, recession hurts manufacturing interests by reducing
sales and thus, everything else being equal, reducing profits.
In addition, if factories are running at less than their full capacity and the demand for goods is low, there are few reasons to
invest in new production. But in an increasingly competitive
global economy, missed investment opportunities commonly
translate into a weakening of relative position. Each downturn
in an economy thus makes a future upturn more difficult under

competitive conditions. Sustained recession of course also generates increased bankruptcies and a decline in debt service. Manufacturers are less able to pay off their loans, and this poses barriers to the realization of the interests of the financial community as well. Recessions should thus "ideally" be short, sharp expressions of the reserve army effect. By increasing unemployment, they should quickly reduce costs and demand-side pressures for price increases. Above all, they should not go on too long.

For a variety of reasons having to do with the postwar accord, however, by the 1970s recessions had to go on longer and longer to produce the downward movement in wages desired by both manufacturing and financial interests and necessary to satisfy their common concern for profits and price stability. While the power of labor to extract affirmative concessions from employers had not increased, the resilience of the wage floors constructed by the domestic accord proved considerable. The existence of unemployment insurance, social security payments, pattern bargaining pacts, and the other floors constructed under wages all meant that wages and prices were harder to drive downward than they were to push up. This asymmetry in resistance to movements in one direction as against another, or "ratchet effect," underscored the presence of inflationary pressures while reinforcing inflation as a policy choice in dealing with declining profits. It derived importantly from a commitment to the maintenance of aggregate demand, that is, to ensuring that there would at no point be huge income losses suffered by workers within the system. But for manufacturers facing profitability problems, and either unwilling or unable to make the investment for the restructuring necessary to face global competition, it was an increasingly costly commitment and a constant spur to seek the inflationary route to profit protection.

Some of this resilience of basic wage floors is indicated by the diminishing significance of the reserve army effect in the postwar years. Contrast the recession of 1920–21 with that of 1973–75. During the former, wage inflation fell by 37.4 percent and price inflation fell by 56.8 percent. During the latter, wage inflation actually increased by 2.9 percent and price inflation increased 8 percent.[63] While this particular case was an extreme one, the dampening of the reserve army effect increased steadily throughout the postwar period. Taking the downturn between the peak quarter in the business cycle and two quarters after the trough, the 1948–49 recession saw a 4 percent increase in unemployment and a 2.1 percent decline in real wages. During the 1953–54 recession, unemployment increased 4.2 percent and real wages declined 1.9 percent. During the 1957–58 recession, unemployment increased 4.7 percent and real wages actually increased 0.2 percent. During the 1960–61 recession, unemployment increased 2.2 percent and real wages increased 0.1 percent. During the 1969–70 recession, unemployment increased 3.4 percent and real wages increased 2.2 percent.[64] The 1973–75 result was especially strong, but not out of line with the general trend. To reduce wages, recessions would have to go on longer.

Especially in the context of increasing international competition, the required length of recessions meant that their costs to manufacturers would be ever more pronounced. Soon cries would go up for government policies to stimulate the economy out of recession. But such policies of economic stimulus would likely bring inflation in their train, and unless that inflation kept prices well ahead of wages and led to sustained productivity growth relative to other industrial powers, it would be self-enforcing. Financial interests would again be harmed, and the relative position of the economy would not be substantially improved. Inflation could be mitigated through fiscal policy, by cutting spending or raising taxes, but the first was difficult at a time of huge claims upon the state for both military and social spending, and the latter was powerfully resisted by business interests unwilling to sustain an increased tax burden during a time of declining profits. Once again, the successful workings of the domestic accord had generated problems, but provided no clear solution.

Against this general backdrop, the stagflationist pressures

that buffeted the U.S. economy were highlighted during the 1970s by the two great international economic events that marked the decade. In August 1971 the United States suspended the dollar's convertibility into gold, yanking out the linchpin of the Bretton Woods system and initiating a series of fluctuations and devaluations that finally led to the outright collapse of the system with the abandonment of fixed exchange rates in 1973. Later in 1973 and early in 1974, the nations of the Organization of Petroleum Exporting Countries (OPEC) announced a series of price hikes that more than tripled the price of oil.

Detaching the dollar from gold, and eventually abandoning fixed exchange rates altogether, effectively eliminated the balance of payments constraint imposed on the United States by Bretton Woods. Dollars could continue to pour out, but with no clear check on their value. More aggressive strategies of economic expansion through looser monetary policy were thus permitted. While inflationary for the United States (and for the rest of the world system), when such looser expansionary policies were pursued, as they were during the early and late 1970s, they produced some of the highest growth rates in postwar U.S. history. During the 1976–78 period, for example, while many other countries were still barely climbing out of the massive mid-decade recession, annual growth in U.S. real GNP averaged more than 5 percent annually.[65]

Now that the dollar was no longer convertible to gold at fixed rates, dollar depreciation as an instrument of international trade rivalry, as a way of making U.S. goods cheaper on foreign markets, became a more attractive option. Depreciation was actively pursued in 1971, 1973, and 1977–78 in a repeated quest for renewed international competitiveness. Between 1969 and 1979, the dollar fell roughly 50 percent against both the West German mark and the Japanese yen, the currencies of America's major industrial rivals.[66] By the late 1970s, average unit labor costs in the United States had dropped below those of much of the industrialized world, and the dollar cost differentials between U.S. and West German, Japanese, and French goods had shifted to a significant American advantage. The eroding strength of the dollar pulled foreign investment into the United States for the same reasons that the great strength of the dollar relative to other currencies under Bretton Woods had driven U.S. investment abroad. Between 1972 and 1980, direct foreign investment in the United States increased 340 percent, while U.S. direct investment abroad increased only 137 percent.[67] The prospect of a full-scale disinvestment in the American economy was thus at least temporarily avoided.

Impulses toward dollar depreciation were given additional impetus during the 1970s by the explosion of raw materials prices. Reflecting the long boom of the 1960s, these prices increased sharply between 1970 and 1973. The OPEC price hikes that soon followed on this movement only increased the impetus. Raw materials and OPEC oil were almost exclusively indexed in dollars. One way of reducing their price was therefore to reduce the price of dollars themselves. This "funny money" approach to dealing with the increasing costs of raw materials was very popular with U.S. importers, and while OPEC eventually responded to such tactics with mammoth price increases, as in the double-digit hike of 1979, inflation was working at home to keep manufacturers' prices well ahead of wage increases. That year alone, real wages in the United States declined by $45 billion, more than enough to foot the increased oil bill.[68]

As already noted, currency depreciation is normally inflationary for the country that depreciates. With a decline in the relative value of a currency, the cost of imports increases. Import consumption may thereby be reduced, and it very often is, but where the imports are primary goods necessary to domestic production, their higher cost remains and seeps through the domestic system in the form of higher prices for finished products. While not immune to this problem, the United States nonetheless has an advantage in depreciation strategies because it is less dependent on imports for domestic production than most economies. Indeed, since raw materials prices are indexed in dollars and respond relatively quickly to changes in the dollar's value, U.S. devaluations effectively *export* inflationary pressures to other countries, yet another phenomenon that marks the centrality of the United States in the global system.

Depending on their own economic strength, different countries respond to such pressures in different ways. West Germany and Japan, both very strong economies, responded to the oil price hikes and the expansionary American policies of the late 1970s by deflating their economies. This reduced income and with it, the demand for imports. In addition, West Germany and Japan both engaged in aggressive export drives to generate the reserves needed to pay their bloated oil bills. Between 1975 and 1978, for example, West German exports increased more than 58 percent, Japanese exports more than 76 percent.[69]

The responses of other major countries to the OPEC price hikes and American trade strategy generally is in part explained by the differentiated impact the price rise had on different industrial economies. When OPEC first increased prices in 1973, the United States supplied more than 80 percent of its energy from domestic sources. Japan supplied only 10 percent of its energy needs from domestic sources, and imported more than 99 percent of its oil. West Germany relied on imports for 56 percent of its energy consumption, and Western Europe as a whole relied on imports for more than 60 percent of its energy needs.[70]

In addition to the OPEC price increase, West Germany and Japan were forced to contend with the relative reduction in the cost of American goods on foreign markets that followed from dollar depreciation. They used the constraints of the late 1970s as an occasion to restructure their economies toward higher-technology industrial sectors. Through the granting of long-term credit and direct investment abroad, West Germany and Japan, like the United States of a generation before, also subordinated other economies to their own export dominance. As Chancellor Helmut Schmidt remarked of a West German loan to Italy during the period, "We have given Italy enough to keep its head above water. . . . It is necessary that a precise division of labor be brought about in Europe."

In contrast to a generation before, however, this restructuring of global competition did not come during a period of world-wide boom and overwhelming U.S. dominance. It came instead during a period of deepening economic turmoil in which the United States, now a less dominant economic actor, could no longer pull the rest of the international economy to stable recovery. Here the dilemmas of international competition and the crumbling assumptions of the postwar accord were again squarely posed. By shrinking their own domestic markets, the restrictive policies of West Germany and Japan constrained movement out of the recession that gripped much of the world. But the ever-sharpening rivalry among the great industrial powers prevented their cooperation in some rearrangement of the international financial and trading order sufficient to bring about recovery.

During this period of mounting conflict among the leading industrial economies, other countries paid the price. Sharp growth in the Third World and southern Europe gradually slowed. Faced with enormous oil costs of their own, but unable to generate reserves through export, the weaker economies went heavily into debt. Between 1973 and 1980, the long-term external debt of nonoil developing countries almost quadrupled, from $97.3 billion to $370.1 billion.[71] Over the same period, debt service in those countries rose from 14 to 18.2 percent of exports of goods and services.[72] This debt was supplied increasingly through private channels. Among middle-income oil importing countries, the share of total debt from private capital sources rose from 56 percent in 1971 to 70 percent in 1980.[73] Where not supplied through private banks, it came largely through institutions like the IMF or World Bank, still dominated by the United States, or through a variety of bilateral and regional lending authorities, with the United States again being a primary source of funds and controller of the terms of credit.

The U.S. dollar devaluations, while delivered from a position of strategic advantage, thus brought ambiguous results. By forcing revaluation on its major rivals in West Germany and Japan, the United States also induced deflationary strategies there, which helped ensure world recession, which in turn reduced demand for American exports. By upping the costs of international competition, the United States had invited international economic instability and decline. Within this context, the relative position of the United States vis-a-vis its major rivals did not significantly improve. Devaluations prevented further precipitous slides in export shares, but were insufficient to restore anything approaching former U.S. dominance of international trade. At the same time, the expansionary policies the United States pursued domestically in the late 1970s brought high import levels. While West Germany and Japan ran trade surpluses during 1977–78, the United States suffered a trade deficit of $64.7 billion.[74] The trade problem was not solved.

American productivity growth continued to slide. Between 1975 and 1979, in part reflecting the deteriorating living standards that forced many families to move to double-wage-earner status, in part reflecting the maturation of the American baby boom, total nonagricultural employment in the United States increased a startling 15.8 percent.[75] The rate of growth of capital/labor ratios, key to increasing worker output, fell during the period. There was more investment, but it was dwarfed by the increase in the hours of work logged by a vastly expanded labor force. The rate of annual growth in hours worked during 1977–79 reached 4.4 percent, fully 11 times the 0.4 percent average annual rate that marked the golden days of 1948–65.[76] During the periods 1959–69 and 1974–79, almost identical percentages of American GNP were invested, but during the former period the rate of growth of the ratio of capital stock to hours worked was 3.3 percent, while during the latter period it was only 0.2 percent.[77]

But dollar devaluations and loose monetary expansionism did have one unambiguous effect. They generated tremendous pressure on financial interests that were already operating within an increasingly competitive international environment. Banking boomed during the turbulent 1970s. One indicator of its growth was the increased size of the Eurocurrency market,

which ballooned from $150 billion in 1970 to $1.44 trillion by
the end of the decade, representing a 29 percent annual growth
rate, almost five times the annual growth rate of international
trade and an even larger multiple of the rate of growth of sagging
industrial production.[78] Such booming conditions brought many
competitors and lower profit margins for the banks. The average markup on loans over the cost of funds declined during
the 1970s. In the 1975–79 period alone, it declined 50 percent.[79]

For the huge American international banks that had long
dominated world financial transactions, the continuing relative
decline of the U.S. economy and the growing instability of the
dollar itself powerfully accelerated the effects of banking
competition. Between 1969 and 1979, the share of the top 50
American banks in the loans made by the world's top 100 banks
dropped from 40 to 21 percent. Between November 1972 and
May 1977, assets of foreign banks increased at more than four
times the rate of American banks. Between 1974 and 1979,
American banking's share of world international banking loans
and other claims dropped from 45.7 to 30.3 percent. A 16
percent decline in share was registered during the 1977–78
period alone, when the dollar was rapidly depreciating. Uncertainty over the continued strength of the dollar was particularly
evident in the case of the OPEC countries, whose huge dollar
surpluses during the period had at first immensely advantaged
the position of American bankers. The share of OPEC deposits
going to American banks dropped from 42 percent in 1975 to
36 percent in 1978. During the heavy devaluation period between
late 1977 and early 1979, the American share of lending to
OPEC declined by more than one-third.[80]

Within the constrained global economy of the late 1970s,
such decline in banking market shares paled next to the consequences for American financial institutions that would follow
on sustained speculation against the dollar. The confidence
problem of Bretton Woods could reappear with tremendous force,
as huge dollar sales drove down the value of the currency,
inspiring further sales and additional downward pressures in a
vicious diving spiral.

But there were important cross-cutting pressures acting against a policy of financial restraint. American banks had participated heavily in financing the exploding debt of the non-OPEC Third World. Much of this financing was done through "recycling" OPEC bank deposits as private loans. Here too the share of the action held by American banks had declined. The U.S. banking share of the debt of non-oil-exporting developing countries dropped from 54 percent at the end of 1975 to 38 percent by the middle of 1979. But the vast exposure and concomitant risks for American financial institutions had not decreased. In their loans to non-oil-exporting countries, the nine leading American banks had by 1979 loaned out more than 180 percent of their capital.[81] By 1979 the cumulative lending of American banks to the Third World had reached $55 billion in outstanding loans. The making of these loans tended to be a self-enforcing process. Increased Third World exports would be necessary to repay already outstanding loans. Achieving them in turn required further infusions of capital. The highly competitive international banking environment of the late 1970s added to these pressures. Banks had to compete aggressively against one another in the terms of credit offered to Third World countries. They had to be willing to assume greater amounts of risk in order to play the game at all.

But the extension of Third World debt also had consequences for the U.S. domestic system and the attitude of financial interests toward inflationary domestic expansion. For Third World loans to be repaid, the United States would have to be prepared to accept the exports of debtor countries that were necessary to generate foreign exchange, and such acceptance was unlikely under conditions of slower growth in the United States. If workers were thrown out of their jobs or manufacturers out of their businesses during a period of high levels of Third World imports, the already considerable protectionist pressures building within the U.S. domestic system might be expected to increase sharply. Such a protectionist reaction might have far more drastic long-term consequences for the well-being of international finance than those posed by inflation. At the same time, years of inflation had sharply increased the advantages of debt financing for U.S. corporations, and by the close of the decade their liquidity positions were severely strained. Between 1976 and the end of the decade alone, the ratio of liquid assets to current liabilities for nonfinancial corporations dropped from 38 to 18 percent, the lowest point in American history.[82] Cutting back on the expansion would pose severe problems of repayment. Thus many of the pressures that led banks to continue extending credit to the Third World also created inducements to letting the domestic expansion continue.

But at the close of the 1970s, the cumulative international pressures against the dollar became too great. Bouts of speculation broke out. In a flurry of activity, everyone rushed to cut losses. After years of letting the dollar slide on international markets, the Carter administration moved to support it in November 1978. A month later Iran, a major oil exporter, exploded in a revolution that cut off imports, and OPEC announced another major price hike. The dollar continued to fall through the spring of 1979. In the summer, Jimmy Carter rearranged his cabinet and announced that a "malaise" now gripped ordinary Americans. The dollar continued to fall. In October the Federal Reserve, representing the banking community, finally stepped in with restrictive monetary policies. The Fed hiked the discount rate charged to its member banks to what was then a record 12 percent, and sharply increased reserve requirements. Another oil price increase came in January 1980. Straining under the tightening policies of the banking community, the economy declined, but the Consumer Price Index jumped to a 17.5 percent annual rate of increase. Further tightening and credit controls came in March. Despite continued pumping from increasing government spending, the April–June second quarter of 1980 saw a record-level 10 percent annual rate of decline in real GNP. While there were many more maneuvers during the 1980 election year, the stagflation circle had again been closed. The economy was in deep recession.

Thus, during the turbulent 1970s, both the domestic and

international accords that had long shaped American life finally collapsed inward. All the accumulating signs of disorder—growing competition between the United States and other advanced industrial states, the tremendous burdens such competition placed on weaker economies, increased instability in world trade patterns and behavior, deepening conflict at home between successful international traders and protectionist domestic producers, sharpening disputes between financial and manufacturing interests, exploding oil prices, and the general decline of profit rates in the industrial core of the developed world—pointed to a period of crisis and necessary restructuring that extended beyond America to all of the global economy. By decade's end, almost every conceivable pressure that had appeared in the 1960s had been powerfully restated, and continued to push upon established institutional arrangements with ever-mounting force.

In contemplating the restructuring of international and domestic institutions that the crisis required, American corporate elites were bitterly divided over crucial questions of trade and the role of the dollar. But on two key items there was almost universal assent in business circles. It was clear to all that despite disagreements about the pace and direction of defense spending, during a period of mounting instability increased military power was essential to the defense of private interests. It was also clear that any restructuring at the domestic level should ideally begin by forcing massive income losses on American workers, thus reducing the temptations to inflation that divided manufacturing and financial interests while eroding the profits of both.

During the presidential campaign of 1980, the first proposition was presented to the public as a set of arguments about the dimensions of "the Russian threat." The second was offered as a variety of plans to "get the government off the backs of the people" and thereby unleash the creative energies of individuals and private enterprise. Most professional observers ranked it a dull campaign, and nearly half the voting age population stayed at home on election day. But for those who found their way to the polls, the choice of candidate was clear. After four years of decline and months of outright misery, they thought it was time for a change. Promised tax cuts, high employment, and renewed national self-respect, millions of working Americans rushed to the bright light of Reaganism that signaled an exit from their tunnel of confusion and fear.

It was only an oncoming train.

5. PRESENT

As they enter the middle 1980s, both American society and the international system remain in turmoil. Despite the endless political initiatives and mobilizations of the past few years, the broken accords have not yet been replaced. Political disorder proliferates. The crisis continues.

Dangers of course always accompany such periods, and any number of disasters now loom as distinct possibilities.

Military disasters are among them. Escalating conflicts are possible in such improbable places as the Falkland Islands, or in such obvious ones as the Middle East. Conventional wars between allies of the United States and the U.S.S.R. could lead to global confrontations between American and Soviet forces. Consider a scenario of total destruction that begins with fighting between Israeli and Syrian troops in Lebanon, and escalates to a nuclear exchange between the superpowers. In a few bright seconds, the world would end.

Less apocalyptically, imagine a financial disaster. The conditions are all in place. The external debt of the developing countries has risen to more than $600 billion, much of it supplied by private Western banks. Huge Third World foreign exchange earnings are necessary to pay off such sums. But those earnings are constrained by the decline in raw materials prices that has accompanied world recession, and by the general slackening of demand for Third World goods within the depressed markets of the industrialized states. Debt service payments now comprise a larger and larger share of Third World exports. Some thirty-odd countries are already in arrears on debt payments, and global financial entanglements are becoming ever more extreme. While the rollovers of debt in Mexico and Brazil indicate that the restructuring of obligations can be accomplished in a way that satisfies major creditors, there is no guarantee that this will always be the case. In the meantime, major banks are more reluctant to cover already shaky debts with new infusions of capital, and international authorities such as the IMF may be unable to raise sufficient additional funds to guarantee unsteady loans. If something gave way suddenly, the absence of clear international regulations on lending and credit would preclude any easy division of claims or allocation of losses. Chain defaults are thus a possibility. Starting with some relatively small country, they could escalate and expand to include larger and larger ones, precipitating speculation against particular currencies, inducing spreading bankruptcies, and finally dragging all the major global economic actors down into the turmoil of international financial collapse.

But periods of crisis are not only dangerous. As noted earlier, they are also highly uncertain, and this uncertainty pervades U.S. politics at present. Any number of programs of action are now promoted by elites, and any number of conflicting proposals on economic renewal, military spending, tax reform, budgetary restraint, monetary policy, and international competitiveness are currently advanced by competing groups. Especially among major private actors, the conditions of mobilization and organization are now highly fluid, and even barring catastrophes of the sort just described, the success of any of these initiatives may be decided by any number of unforeseeable events. But despite all the confusions of conventional politics in the United States, there are a few broad strategies that dominate present maneuverings and debate. Within the peculiar conditions of political fragmentation, labor weakness, and declining international power that mark the American system, each of these lines of action can plausibly satisfy the general conditions required for the maintenance of capitalist democracy. Each can secure the consent of an important group of profit-seeking capitalists. Each can forestall radical challenge by workers from below. Each can provide for state legitimacy through a process of orderly elections.

In this chapter we sketch three such lines of action. The sketch is brief, and is intended neither as a complete inventory of actual political programs nor as a set of predictions about the future course of politics in the United States. Our purposes are more limited and specific. We are interested in extending the previous analysis of the structure of capitalist democracy to the problems of the present, in seeing how the current course of politics can be illuminated by considering the constraints imposed by that structure, and in seeing above all how that structure might accommodate a variety of distinct lines of action. Again, our interest in understanding capitalist democracy is informed by a desire to transform it. In outlining different strategies of response, we are not only attempting to trace the broad dimensions of contemporary politics. We also wish to emphasize that despite conditions of crisis, conventional politics can in fact continue. However grim "objective" conditions now are, they do not require the radical transformation of capitalist democracy, and those who wish to move beyond capitalist democracy therefore cannot presume that such a movement will inevitably arise from the worsening of those conditions.

The first line of response we consider consists merely in continuing with politics as usual, albeit under unusual conditions. We argued earlier that when a capitalist democracy enters a period of crisis, there is no guarantee that mechanisms of readjustment will be available for a coordinated response to that crisis. Individual actors or groups of actors may continue to pursue their interests rationally, but within a structure that no longer aggregates their decisions to socially acceptable outcomes. The state may be unable to impose the costs of necessary restructuring on powerful private actors, and the continuation of politics within existing institutions may be more attractive as a course of action than assuming the burdens of establishing new ones. As a result, there is very often in state policy a tendency toward "muddling," or the repeated application of piecemeal, partial, and often contradictory solutions to what is a broader social problem.

The decentralization and relative weakness of the American state contributes to this tendency toward muddling, as does the relatively undisciplined and unprogrammatic character of American electoral politics. The United States has what James Madison once described as a "feudal constitution," a framework of basic law and institutional structures deliberately designed to block the emergence of a strong centralized national government. This constitutional tradition is ratified by the existence of 50 different independent state governments that compete with federal authority, and with one another, and whose workings produce innumerable blockages and coordination problems within American politics. Within this highly federated framework of public power, concerted response is especially difficult to achieve. But the nonideological and demobilized character of the American electoral system also effectively encourages muddling by making it less likely that failure to achieve concerted action will prompt concerted challenge in public arenas. At the same time, the absence of substantial worker opposition from below provides such a strategy with a material base. The hope is for the resolution of crisis through attrition, with the costs of that attrition visited most squarely on workers. Given the many problems that plagued the American business community in the 1970s, a 1980s strategy of muddling would naturally feature broad attacks on workers, broad attempts to revive U.S. international dominance through military buildup, and sharp and continuing disagreements about virtually all other details of public policy. Nowhere is this more evident than in the muddling that now goes on in American politics under the name of Reaganism.

By the time of his election in November 1980, Ronald Reagan had garnered nearly wall-to-wall support from the American business community, and the program he has since put forward as president faithfully reflects the lowest common denominator of that increasingly divided group. Reaganism stands for social cutbacks, increased military spending, real income losses for workers, upward redistribution of wealth, and restrictions on democratic process and the articulation of political interests. As its vast military buildup attests, Reaganism is hardly "dismantling" the state. But in weakening Legal Services or such agencies as the EPA, FDA, or OSHA, or changing the rules of federal land use management, or limiting scrutiny of government action through new executive orders on classification, it is changing the practices and procedures of select state institutions and making it more difficult for citizens to defend themselves against the abuses of government and private power. The Reagan program will thus have cumulative and long-lasting effects. The pain it has already brought to millions should not be underestimated. Nor should the pain it will continue to inflict in years to come.

As ambitious as this program is, however, it is also notably incomplete. Nothing that has happened since Ronald Reagan came to office has relieved the pressures on the American economy that prompted his victory. Sharp international competition remains at the core of the present crisis, and responding to America's changing role within the global economy will largely define national politics for the next several years. But no concerted program to address these problems has been forthcoming from the Reagan administration. Thus far, that administration has only succeeded in restating the many competing demands of its business supporters as contradictory policy "choices."

From virtually its first day in office, the only stability in the administration has come from its aggressive military buildup and posturing and its almost unrelenting attacks on working people and the poor. Everywhere else it has shown signs of fluctuation and inner turmoil. The administration has waffled or repeatedly reversed itself in arguments over trade barriers, tax increases, monetary restraint, deficit spending, and the international position of the dollar, while relations with NATO allies, the Soviet Union, China and Taiwan, and the countries of the Middle East remain subjects of sharp White House dispute. Reflecting its many internal divisions, the Reagan "team" has repeatedly reshuffled and rearranged itself. Dozens of top administration officials have departed its ranks, from supply-side advocates at the Treasury to "Atlanticist" figures, including the secretary himself, at the Department of State. Clark has come in for Allen. Shultz is mopping up after Haig. Meese has acceded to Baker. Nofziger occasionally replaces himself. But even now, after all the shifts and fits and starts, aside from the militarism and attacks on workers that comprise Reaganism's common denominator program, there is very little that unites figures as diverse as Caspar Weinberger, George Bush, James Watt, George Shultz, William Brock, William French Smith, Elizabeth Dole, David Stockman, Donald Regan, James Baker, Terrell Bell, Margaret Heckler, Ray Donovan, and Jeane Kirkpatrick.

But while Reaganism provides one example of a muddling strategy, such a strategy need not take the peculiar form of Reaganism. Indeed, an entire system of politics based on muddling is easy to imagine. Democrats can muddle along with Republicans, and as long as there is no serious challenge to the major institutions of national life, electoral competition between the muddlers could continue. If party programs are not clearly stated, muddling could be promoted as "pragmatic" public policy, and in the case of Democratic candidates or administrations, such policy might even be advertised as a "nonideological" alternative to Reaganism.

Social programs, for example, may be cut without deliberately invoking racism. Declines in food-stamp funding do not have to be justified in the style of administration adviser Peter Grace, who declared food stamps "basically a Puerto Rican program." The removal of public control over environmental resources can proceed without announcing, with James Watt, uncertainty over the number of future generations that will precede the Second Coming of the Lord. And where the costs of political action are simply too great to be sustained by either party, as they were in the case of Social Security cutbacks, then blue-ribbon bipartisan commissions can be formed.

Even if they had no relief to offer, muddling politicians could still urge the public to "face the hard facts" and "confront the hard choices" posed by continuing economic disorder. Widespread agreement that the regressive supply-side tax cuts of Reaganism had done much to enlarge structural budget deficits, but little to stimulate investment, might lead to yet additional programs of regressive tax reform. This could even be sold with much ado about equity and simplification, as through the "flat tax" proposals now making the rounds that would constitute another huge upward distribution in after-tax income for the wealthy.

If workers remained passive, the politics of muddling would provide room for much maneuver. Divisions over the pace and pattern of military spending, for example, might be papered over by a general agreement on the need to deepen cuts in social programs. If military spending was still getting out of hand, it could simply be announced that the window of vulnerability had begun to close. Or yet another blue-ribbon bipartisan commission might agree that the window could be shut without a B-1 bomber, or by building more submarine-launched Trident II missiles in place of an unbasable MX, or with killer satellites on the "high frontier." Such a movement of military "reform" would cut the rate of increase, though not spending levels themselves.

In the arena of international economic policy, a combination of aggressive pressure and posturing along with sidebar agreements on select items of trade could hold together general trade flows and dollop out benefits to some of the larger product constituencies without embarking on a concerted restructuring of the national economy. Japan might agree to postpone an all-out invasion of the American car market for a few more years while American automobile manufacturers retooled their plants. Some arrangement might be reached with Western Europeans to tolerate U.S. quotas on their steel products in exchange for restraint by American agricultural producers.

But while it can continue, and probably will continue, in the near term, such muddling may not be able to go on forever. If it were brought to an end, that end would not necessarily come from world war or international collapse. It could be brought on by the growing international competition that is central to the current crisis. At a certain point, the question of the relative position of the United States within the global economy might have to be more directly addressed. Here again, an almost infinite number of variations might be pursued, but there are two basic approaches. Each will appeal to certain major private interests and will provide some benefits and satisfactions to ordinary people. Each thus has a chance to win sufficient support to meet the basic conditions for the reproduction of capitalist democracy.

The first approach would address the decline of U.S. industry through a coordinated national "industrial policy" aimed at restoring American economic competitiveness within a global system of free trade. Such a policy would include the reductions in social spending and sharpened capacity to project military force abroad that comprise the key components of the lowest-common-denominator program. But it would couple these with targeted tax relief for corporations, other specific investment incentives, and some control of the pattern of investment, exerted either through the state or, more likely, through the private financial sector aided by the state. Austerity budgets and a less restrictive monetary policy would provide the program's financial basis.

Appealing to competitive or near-competitive business sectors, the components of this program, suitably packaged, would have at least some popular appeal as well. Because it would start from the presumption that the development of other countries has moved them to the point of comparative advantage in certain areas of basic manufacturing, it would logically be coupled with retraining and education programs for workers. There would be revival of the post-Sputnik-style state support for education. As the United States moved steadily toward higher-technology industries, select services, and batch-styled production of basic goods, the traditional role of large-scale unions could become even more irrelevant to organizing the workforce than it is now. Because restructuring would in any case require relatively loose labor markets and the mobility of workers, within the regime of austerity it might be useful to employ labor policy as an arena for costless moralizing. The destruction of communities could be coupled with a proclamation of renewed commitment to achieving the goals of sexual and racial equality, albeit within depressed labor markets. The need for humane industrial relations within profit-making enterprises could be stressed, not least for its promise of increased worker productivity. The more complete integration of workers into the traditional goal structure of corporate firms could be sought through the formation of "quality circles" to discuss toxic waste on the shop floor or the encouragement of regular production-line powwows on the need for speedup and automation.

The costs of these innovations need not be paid for by an explicit attack on income. There could be a conversion of the tax system to a consumption tax program accompanied by a call to replace the society of consumers with a community of savers. Promises of a better future through current savings and formally equitable austerity measures could be enriched by a program of job generation through infrastructural investment, an investment which is in any case necessary to industrial renewal. Funding for this program might require a decline in the rate of increase in military spending. Accordingly, instead of a 7 or 8 percent annual increase in defense outlays, increases as low as 6, or 6.3, or 5.5, or even 5 percent might be proposed. Such trivial cuts could be given a high moral tone to generate popular support for the overall program. Since the United States already possesses more than enough nuclear tonnage to destroy the world several times, a commitment to a freeze on stockpiling additional nuclear weapons could be announced. Marketed properly, such a "brave move toward peace" might be applauded by millions.

Structural unemployment within such a regime would be very high, but for those who could find jobs, the benefits of competitive free trade would be clear. As the national destiny was redefined as the quest for renewed competitiveness within an international environment of competing firms, low-cost consumer goods and high-tech home gadgetry would permit stylized local consumption. In sum, a more ambitious reordering of the economy to gear up for international competition could be sought with potentially broad support.

All the forces that militate for muddling militate against such an aggressive industrial policy. Even on the assumption that workers acceded to continued welfare losses, any concerted industrial restructuring would force explicit government decisions about who would gain and who would lose among capitalists themselves. The largest and most powerful industrial sectors, employing the largest number of workers in basic manufacturing, are the older and less competitive industries which would lose most under such a plan to shift production upward to higher-technology plateaus. While there would be much discussion about saving workers, not capitalists, it is highly unlikely that those industries that cannot now compete effectively in international markets, and whose domestic markets are being eroded by international competition, would sit idly by as their assets gradually declined into worthlessness. Under such circumstances, "orderly retreat" from declining sectors would be very difficult to achieve.

In addition, funding the transition would be extremely expensive, and coordination costs would be high. The model for advanced industrial development offered by West Germany and Japan features substantial government involvement and support for industrial restructuring. The degree to which the decentralized American political system could achieve or sustain such involvement is notably uncertain.

Finally, any strategy of international competitiveness would require some resolution of the currency problems associated with the collapse of Bretton Woods. One highly touted proposed solution to these problems would consist in moving toward some form of "global Keynesianism," or the redistribution of large amounts of money and credit to the developing world to ensure the stabilization and growth of markets. But the residual strength of the United States encourages highly aggressive international financial strategies and relatively little cooperation with other powers. An entirely new order for the handling of international financial claims and payments should ideally be constructed. But the terms and conditions under which that order might emerge would virtually require a relative reduction in the role of the dollar on a global scale, and that reduction is powerfully resisted by the United States.

Short of such international financial renovation, a huge interim problem looms. Even if the United States were to regear for increased international competition, its ability to dump products on foreign markets may be constrained by weak international demand and the foreign counterparts of those protectionist pressures that have recently marked American politics. In a declining world economy, an aggressive export drive from the United States would face substantial opposition abroad.

In the face of such problems, a nationalist protectionist response to deteriorating international competitiveness might grow more attractive. This final sort of approach, a program of gradually sealing off the American economy, would draw support from those important declining industrial sectors which cannot now compete in international markets, or whose competitiveness is severely threatened. Its popular appeal might consist in ever more strident assertions of national chauvinism, coupled with promises of job security for those workers employed in the older sectors, or those tied directly to national defense.

As in the free-trade response, the state would be forced to play a greater role in order to acquire the markets and material needed for profitable production without opening the home economy to foreign competition. The continued stagnation of the American domestic market, itself reinforced by the low-wage regimes necessary to secure profitability for decaying private industry, would produce increasing pressure for that market's internal expansion. Sealing off California and New York might lead to attempts to seal off North and South America, perhaps along with other parts of the world. Such a strategy could converge with a weakened free-trade response baffled by the uncertainties of global restructuring. Hemispheric preferential trading zones dominated by the major industrial powers would be one prospect. They would be large enough to permit industrial diversification while easing some of the strains of competition. In theory, such a division of the world, with the United States dominating Latin America and the Middle East, France and Germany dominating Africa, and Japan dominating Asia, could provide a period of renewed international stability. But it is highly unlikely that the United States would willingly accede to such limited demarcations as these. It is for example difficult to imagine the United States giving up South Africa to the West Germans or the French, or tolerating complete Japanese domination of the Philippines or South Asia. And it is equally difficult to imagine any of the other great powers giving up the much-contested Middle East.

However structured or achieved, a nationalist protectionist strategy could supplement a shrinking wage package with costless cultural substitutes, sometimes encouraged through minor market incentives. Tuition tax credits could spawn a vast network of private schools teaching creationist biology, Christian fundamentalism, and other familiar antidotes to secular humanism. The removal of workers from the ranks of the unemployed could be facilitated by an emphasis on traditional sex roles and the maintenance of women near hearth and home. Revitalized cottage industries such as animal breeding, shopping services, and sewing could be promoted as domestic supplements to family income. Larger and larger scales of militarization could perform many of the socializing functions now performed by the public-school system, while simultaneously contributing to lowering youth unemployment. Atavistic cultural expression could be given a high-tech glaze as proliferating cable networks beamed a steady supply of consensual "family" entertainment into homes.

The costs of an imperial protectionist strategy would of course be great. Depressed wages and residual public opposition to war would increase the likelihood of internal resistance in the United States, and thus the need for an enhanced police presence and more authoritarian ways of dealing with internal dissent. These internal costs would be modest in comparison to the burdens of maintaining an overtly oppressive military empire superintending the imperial region. But if resistance could be sufficiently fragmented or suppressed, progressively higher levels of exploitation might permit economic growth and restructuring. Public knowledge of what the United States was doing elsewhere in the world could be constrained even more effectively than it was during the postwar generation through a variety of controls. The circulation and revelation of internal government documents could be effectively stanched through ever-broadening definitions of national security and a more restrictive system of information classification. Traditional media reluctance to challenge business and government could be raised from its already stratospheric levels by discrete changes in libel legislation or more direct state supervision. Free speech and associational rights could be further eroded for individuals, while carefully preserved for the "commercial speech" and political activities of major corporate actors. Many things could be done.

As we have suggested, it is more likely that some shifting combination of the free trade and protectionist programs will be attempted, sometimes featuring more determined efforts to secure international competitiveness through restructuring, sometimes bending to particular protectionist pressures. At least in the near term, higher and higher levels of muddling will likely comprise the American response. National politics will most probably continue with a mishmash combination of securing international markets for competitive industries, while asserting U.S. strength to protect declining ones, along with a mishmash of relatively costless ploys to secure worker consent to continued rivalry within the business community.

Whatever scenario is finally adopted by the American system, it will not be pursued in splendid isolation. Some Third World countries will resist oppression. West Germany and Japan will resist attacks upon their markets. The Soviet Union may resort to greater use of military force. And the threats of nuclear war and international financial disaster remain.

But none of this is to say that the current global crisis is somehow irresolvable. This is no final crisis. The dynamics of capitalist development are constrained chiefly by the institutional structures through which they are expressed, and as indicated here, a variety of options are available now and are likely to continue to be available for some time to come.

It might be argued that such global decline and restructuring will prepare the possibility of a transition to a different and more just ordering of social life. But that possibility currently exists, and its "ripeness" does not in any way guarantee its realization. There is no future point to be awaited which will guarantee a more just restructuring of society, or even guarantee the unambiguous alternatives of a just society or barbarism.

Continued economic decline is itself not assured. But even if it were, within all the possible futures just sketched, the distribution of action would still encourage the search for a separate piece. There will always be structures of individual reward. It will always be possible to hope for a better future, at least for oneself. There will always be some jobs, for some of the people, some of the time. Some will be better than others. There will always be commercial options, and pursuing those options can always be dressed up or justified as individually satisfying, or contributing to the public good, or comprising at the very least another expression of hard-nosed "realism." Academics can do risk assessment for major corporations seeking investment opportunities in an ever more unstable world. Engineers can work in the massive military sector. Skilled workers can operate machine tools. Unskilled workers can assemble the computer parts to displace them. Data processors can manipulate programs. Secretaries can switch from IBM Selectrics to Wang word processors.

And though the world will surely change, many things will surely remain the same. There will still be lifestyles. All of them will have internal sources of meaning, however distorted that meaning may now appear. There will still be secular enchantments provided by the magic of the market. There will still be designer jeans, hot dogs, Big Macs, and professional baseball. There will still be fashions in what one wears or eats or reads or thinks. There will still be disaster movies, sports cars, beach houses, and celebrities. There will still be alcohol, barbiturates, cocaine, and sinsemilla. The structuring of demand will still make it economically irrational to cooperate with others in changing the system. The multiplicity of material rewards will still foster consent to the reduction of politics to short-term material gain. And while almost all substantive public control of almost every important public decision will be surrendered or forcibly eliminated under all the likely avenues of response, it will still be possible to vote. Within such a life, there will always be something to lose. There will always be reasons for going along.

Or a decision can be made not to go along. A decision can be made for a different set of rules. There are grounds for such a decision. It is not arbitrary. But it is also not yet another calculation within the endless private strivings of the present economic order. It is a choice.

6. DEMOCRACY

The choice for an alternative set of rules is a choice against capitalist democracy. The many undesirable consequences of the operation of capitalist democracy provide many grounds for such a choice. But if that choice is to be a reasoned one, it cannot be directed only toward the consequences of capitalist democracy. The choice must be directed as well against the basic institutional structure of that social order.

In our previous discussion we emphasized two aspects of that structure. First, while capitalist democracy cedes workers certain rights and liberties, including suffrage, it does not eliminate the subordination of the interests of workers to the interests of capitalists which is characteristic of capitalism in general. Within capitalist democracy, the satisfaction of the interests of capitalists remains a necessary though insufficient condition for the satisfaction of the interests of workers, and the welfare of workers is thus dependent on the welfare of capitalists. Second, this structural subordination of the interests of workers is reproduced through the reduction of political struggle to struggle over short-term material gain. The operation of capitalist democracy rewards and thereby encourages a narrow economic rationality oriented toward the satisfaction of short-term material interests. The satisfaction of such interests in turn provides a basis for consent to the continued operation of the system.

The choice against such an institutional structure can take many forms. It can for example be a choice for fascism or totalitarianism. Such choices are paradoxical, however, since they endorse systems that do not respect the capacity for reasoned choice itself. There is only one system of social relations that does fully respect that capacity. That system is democracy. To choose democracy is to choose a form of social association which manifestly respects such capacities within an order of equal freedom.

In what follows, we spell out a democratic conception of politics, a political philosophy for a social order that is alternative to capitalist democracy.[1] Because that order does not yet exist, parts of the following discussion must be abstract.* And because that discussion is in part abstract, a few preliminary remarks may be useful in clarifying its structure and aims.

First, the general focus and intent of our account of the democratic conception should itself be clarified. Some elements of this conception—civil liberties, distributional measures of equality, full employment, and a humane foreign policy—are already familiar demands within the universe of contemporary politics. Other elements—including public control of investment, workplace democracy, and certain aspects of what we will interpret as requirements of equal opportunity—are not. Whether the elements are familiar or unfamiliar, however, our presentation of them is primarily directed toward showing how they fit together into a coherent view of social order. In emphasizing the interrelation of these different elements, in underscoring their status as aspects of a unified political view, we are not intending thereby to deny the force of particular aspirations, be they for racial and sexual equality, for work under decent conditions, or for peace. Rather, we are attempting to

---

*When we say the democratic order does not yet exist, we do not limit that claim to the United States. As should become clear from the presentation of the democratic conception, we certainly do not for example regard the Soviet Union or any other case of "actually existing socialism" as a democratic order.

show how many such aspirations have an affinity with one another, and can be accommodated and related more forcefully to one another by the broader political vision of democracy. While the discussion is theoretical, its intent is thus practical. In showing how the democratic conception can accommodate and relate more particular claims or aspirations, we are attempting to strengthen the appeal of that conception. And in so doing, we are attempting to give those particular claims themselves additional force and appeal. In short, in arguing for the affinity among particular claims, we are not only attempting to indicate the theoretical coherence of those claims, but their practical and political coherence as well. In showing how the democratic conception can unify the aspirations of different movements of opposition, we thus hope to show how that conception can unify those movements themselves.

Briefly noting the intellectual and political background of the discussion that follows may clarify its purposes in a second way. The democratic conception owes much to the socialist tradition within modern politics. That tradition is squarely associated with the claim, elaborated in our discussion of capitalist democracy, that the taking of profits under capitalism necessarily subordinates one class of individuals to another and thus, even under conditions of formal equality, subverts the conditions for equal freedom. But the democratic conception owes much as well to the liberal tradition within modern social philosophy. Although it does not hold a monopoly on the claim, liberalism is traditionally associated with the strong belief that individual liberties require some recognition not only in principle, but also in the actual institutional arrangements of political order.[2] We share that strong belief, and here again wish to show how it is an aspect of the belief in democracy itself.

Finally it should be noted that the democratic conception is explicitly a conception of a *political* order. It is a conception of a social system in which public debate over the direction of social life would not only be expected, but would in fact be

publicly encouraged. Implicit in this conception is the convic-
tion that the removal of familiar barriers to free deliberation
would not eliminate all grounds for political disagreement. Thus
the task of the democratic conception is not to describe a social
order in which all disputes would be trivial, or indicative of a
failure to realize the principles of the order. The democratic
conception is not a utopian conception, dedicated to the ideal
of perfectly harmonious community, and the burden of the
conception is not to outline a political order in which such an
ideal is realized. The burden rather is to outline a political order
in which disagreements over the direction of that order could
be socially addressed through free deliberation.

In view of these considerations, and the general aims they
set for the discussion of the democratic conception, our
elaboration of the democratic order must satisfy three major
conditions. The principles of that order must be clarified by
describing more fully the idea of democracy, at least in its most
fundamental aspects. Some indication must then be given of a
set of institutional requirements rooted in those principles. And
an account must be offered of the motivations that might plausibly lead people to struggle to create such institutions under
conditions in which they do not yet exist. In describing the
democratic order, we consider these three conditions in turn.

The first condition has already been met implicitly in our
previous discussion, but we can make it more explicit here. A
democratic society is an ongoing order characterized in the
first instance by a certain principle of justification, or principle
of democratic legitimacy (PDL).[3] The PDL requires that individuals be free and equal in determining the conditions of their
own association. In part the PDL articulates a claim about the
nature of sovereignty in a democratic order. That members of
the order together determine the institutions, rules, and conditions of their own association means that they themselves are
sovereign. This sovereignty is *freely* exercised in the sense that
participants in the order have, and are recognized as having,
the capacity to form reasoned judgments about the ends of

social life; that they are constrained in making those judgments only by the conditions necessary to preserve reasoned
public deliberation; and that nothing actually determines the
ends of social life other than the judgments arrived at by
the members of the order. Sovereignty is *equally* exercised in
the sense that the views of each member of the democratic
order are accorded equal weight in public deliberation.

The PDL thus cannot be satisfied merely through a proper
arrangement of formal arenas of politics, if those arenas remain
prey to the intrusions of private power. As indicated in our
discussion of capitalist democracy, the power of formal guarantees of freedom and equality is severely limited if political
activities within those formal arenas are constrained by material
inequalities in resource allocation and control. Satisfaction of
the PDL's requirement of equal freedom thus requires attention to such background constraints on formal freedom. It
requires that the conditions of equal freedom be satisfied in the
arrangement of all social arenas that bear on the conditions of
public deliberation.

For the PDL to serve as a principle of public justification, the
satisfaction of the PDL must, like the satisfaction of any principle of legitimacy (e.g. the process of orderly elections), be
manifest or clearly visible to members of the order in the actual
workings of its institutions. The institutions of the democratic
order must in other words be organized in such a way that they
not only in fact satisfy the requirement of equal freedom and
reasoned deliberation, but do so in such a way that members
of the order recognize this satisfaction as having been achieved.
Such manifest satisfaction of the PDL in turn provides a plausible basis for the *stability* of the democratic order over time,
that is, for the ability of the order to remain democratic. In
seeing that the institutions of the democratic order satisfy the
announced principle of legitimacy of that order, members of
the democratic society have plausible grounds for loyalty to that
society and its arrangements. While the stability of capitalist
democracy rests upon its ability to satisfy the interest in short-

term material gain which it systematically generates, the stability of the democratic order rests upon the respect for individuals as free and equal that is expressed in its basic institutions, and upon the recognition of that respect by its members.[4]

Finally, this general conception of democratic society has consequences for the sorts of claims that members of a democratic order can make on one another. There are many such claims that can be made by free and equal participants in the exercise of sovereignty, but of particular importance is the claim to *autonomy*. Autonomy consists in the exercise of self-governing capacities, such as the capacities of understanding, imagining, reasoning, valuing, and desiring. Free persons have and are recognized as having such capacities, and in a political order centrally dedicated to securing the conditions of free deliberation for its members, those members can legitimately expect of that order that it not only permit but also encourage the exercise of such capacities, that is, that it permit and encourage autonomy. But since the basis of the claim to autonomy is the claim to the status of an equal member of a free association, to claim autonomy for oneself is to recognize the perfectly reciprocal and equally legitimate claims to autonomy by others. Thus the claim to individual autonomy is really a claim about how the social order should be constructed. It effectively consists in the acknowledgment of and accession to a social structure of *mutually* recognized autonomy.

The PDL thus requires an ongoing order of mutually assured and encouraged *autonomy* in which political decisions are *manifestly* based on the judgments of the members as *free* and *equal* persons. It requires that the expression of self-governing capacities operate both within the formal institutions of politics and in the affairs of daily life. And it requires that the democratic order *stably* satisfy the conditions of equal freedom and autonomy that give it definition.

Taken together, these conditions provide the basis for considering the more specific institutional requirements of the democratic order. Elaborating these requirements comprises the second element in our discussion of the democratic conception. That elaboration can proceed only in general outline. Like other political conceptions, the democratic conception states a broad framework of social cooperation. How exactly that framework will be expressed institutionally will vary under different conditions. In outlining the democratic conception our aim is to anticipate neither the details of such varied institutional expression nor the variety of conditions under which democratic institutions might arise. Our aim is only to state the basic requirements of a democratic political order, and in some cases to try to clarify the content of those requirements by outlining what they would imply under current conditions. In describing the institutional requirements of the democratic order, our discussion must therefore remain somewhat abstract and provisional. But it is worth underscoring that such abstract specification of basic institutional principles is a precondition for pursuing the important but subordinate task of providing a more detailed specification of institutions themselves. And however abstract and provisional the discussion here may be, it is worth underscoring as well that the various requirements on institutions within the democratic order do comprise a system, an interrelated set of constraints and conditions which together define a distinct social structure of coordination and power. They thus require one another for interpretation and justification, and this fact is reflected in our presentation here. While we take up various elements separately, as the presentation proceeds there will be need for reference back to the basic framework of principle, and for cross-reference among the different institutional conditions. Finally, the order in which the conditions are presented does not indicate any priority among them. Since they comprise a system, no such priority can be assigned.

With these provisos, the institutional requirements of the democratic order follow immediately:

1. Formal guarantee of the individual freedoms necessary to autonomy and reasoned public deliberation must be secured.

Thus the basic liberties of thought, speech, association, assembly, and participation that might ordinarily be exercised by free individuals must be inviolate. By themselves, formal public liberties are notoriously incapable of addressing the distortions of politics by private advantage. But that plainly provides no argument for their destruction. Within the democratic order, politics would continue. There would still be debate and disagreement over the direction of public policy and the proper ends of social life. For the free deliberative process among equals that lies at the core of the democratic order to proceed, individual expression and participation must be absolutely protected activities. And for the PDL's requirement of manifestness to be satisfied, it is important that the protections afforded such activities be part of the visible framework of social regulation — that is, that they assume the form of law.

It is worth emphasizing that such protection must extend significantly beyond traditional "political" liberties. Free public deliberation follows upon and itself requires the exercise of individual self-governing capacities in arenas that are not commonly recognized as political. That exercise in turn depends on the protection of freedom of expression, speech, belief, and thought within those arenas. Autonomy thus requires not only explicit political liberties and protections, but more personal ones as well. As a means of guaranteeing the exercise of autonomy, the scope of such protections must of course conform to the requirement that autonomy be recognized as mutual. Individual exercise of such self-governing capacities would not be protected at or beyond the point at which it constrains the autonomy of others. But within the democratic order, the fact that some forms of private activity or expression are offensive to the tastes and sensibilities of others within that order does not by itself provide any argument for curbing that activity or expression.[5]

2. While such protections of individual autonomy are a necessary condition for the social exercise of deliberative capacities, they are not sufficient. The democratic conception

requires as well that the organized expression of political debate
be recognized as a goal of a democratic order and be conducted
in a manner attentive to the PDL's more general requirement
of manifest equal freedom. Public assumption of the costs of
competition among multiple political parties would be a natural
way to provide such recognition consistent with the PDL's
background requirements.

That the costs of group political activity should be publicly
assumed follows from the requirement that the institutions of
the democratic order *manifestly* respect the condition of equal
freedom. As our discussion of capitalist democracy indicated,
there are many reasons to believe that in the absence of public
funding, both political activity and the results of that activity
will reflect the distribution of private resources among individuals in the political system. Some guarantee against such
distortion is needed if the democratic order is to be one in
which political outcomes are to reflect the judgments of its
members. But in a democratic order it is not enough that political outcomes *in fact* reflect the political judgments of its
members. It is also crucial, as the condition of manifestness
emphasizes, that this fact be *evident* to the participants in the
order. The organization of the political arena must itself be a
source of confidence in the satisfaction of the requirement of
political equality. Public assumption of the costs of deliberation
is needed to secure this confidence, although it is not sufficient
on its own.

The second aspect of meeting this requirement, that such
public assumption of the costs of deliberation take the specific
form of a subsidy to *competitive political parties*, is also based
on the PDL. As indicated already, the achievement of a democratic order does not imply the end of politics. Disagreement
over the ends of social life continues, and it would be expected
that questions about the proper level of current savings, the
rate of economic growth, and the allocation of public resources
to different ends would still be objects of social concern and
public debate. In helping to shape that concern into coherent

public debate, the role of competitive political parties is crucial, although not for the reasons commonly offered. In one especially important traditional view of party competition, such competition is necessary to the winnowing out of "bad" or "untrue" political views. Here the aims of the political order are defined as the achievement of the "best" policy outcomes, and the value of political party competition is understood in terms of the value of achieving those aims.

But as indicated by the examples of possible disagreement within the democratic order, under democratic conditions the "truth" of different policy views is a notion without clear content. It is not clear, for example, that there is a single "correct" level of current savings or economic growth that should be sought or achieved, or that there is a "correct" pattern of allocation of social resources between education and health. Even if there were "correct" solutions to such problems, it is not clear what sort of political arrangement, if any, could guarantee their achievement. And even if there were some arrangement that could guarantee their achievement, that arrangement might very well be unacceptably oppressive.

While not relying on a view of party competition as necessary for producing "correct" policy outcomes, the democratic conception nevertheless supports such competition as an expression of a democratic order's commitment to the enhancement of deliberative capacities in public arenas. Satisfying the conditions of reasonable deliberation requires that public discussion proceed against a background of alternative coherent views. The presentation of such views comprises one function of political parties. Within the democratic conception, the coherent statement of alternative policy choices is thus not taken as an end in itself, nor as a means to guaranteeing correct choices, but as a precondition for public deliberation. Political parties and their competition are required not to discover the "truth" of correct policy, but for the exercise of autonomy itself.

The third aspect of the requirement regarding political parties, that the democratic order provide for the competition of a multi-plicity of such parties, follows directly from this conception of their role. The subsidy of one party alone would, of course, make a mockery of the commitment of a democratic order to an equal consideration of views, since the views of the single party would in any case determine the outcome of such consideration. But the existence of several parties is important for another reason as well. Just as the total absence of political parties would for most citizens effectively block the consideration of many issues of public concern, so too the existence of only a single party—even one with a highly coherent program and set of views—would impair the process of comparing and evaluating alternative policy choices that is required for reasoned political judgment.[6]

As a public expression of the principle of free deliberation, public funding of party costs would logically be tied to allegiance to that principle. It would violate the principles of the democratic order to divert the monies of that order to groups actively opposed to its very existence. But this in no way precludes the legal existence of such groups, and indeed the legality of their existence at the level of expression and peaceful participation would have to be assured. Thus, the existence for example of a fascist party would be permitted, but would not be subsidized with public funds.

Additional limitations on the collective assumption of the costs of party competition might be built into the democratic order through political judgments on the aggregate number of parties to enjoy such subsidy, the level of subsidy, and the requirements of achieving "public" party status. Such judgments would in turn have to be the products of social deliberation.

Within a democratic order, meeting the condition of free competition would finally require the elimination of any formal barriers to equal participation and representation. The participation requirement is effectively met through the guarantee of formal liberties of expression and participation already noted. Under conditions of representative democracy, the representation requirement might be achieved through the establishment of a system of proportional representation.* While other systems of representation may plausibly claim to meet the requirement as well, proportional representation has the merit of manifestly satisfying the requirement that the views of individual members of the political order be given equal weight. In addition, the exercise of deliberative capacities in social arenas is enhanced by the ability to judge as far as possible the capacity of different parties to act as responsible agents of representation. Since proportional representation ensures that parties with significant support actually have the opportunity to participate in government, it helps to ensure that deliberation over support for those parties is more fully informed.

3. Since the absence of material deprivation is a precondition for free and unconstrained deliberation, a basic level of material satisfaction, which would be more precisely specified through a free process of deliberation, would be required for all members of the political order. This might at first be satisfied through the achievement of full employment, but since the goal is not employment per se but the absence of material deprivation, the democratic order might soon devote itself, within conditions of

---

*A system of proportional representation (PR) is a system in which the votes of participating citizens are directly reflected in the composition of legislative bodies. Such a system can be clarified by its contrast with the "winner take all" balloting and representation procedure of the United States. In the United States, for example, if 50 percent of the participating electorate vote for a Democratic candidate for the House of Representatives, 40 percent vote for a Republican, and the remaining 10 percent divide their votes among a variety of lesser parties, then the Democratic candidate wins the seat. The winner takes all. If the results above were consistent across districts, a Democrat would win in each district, and the composition of the House would be 100 percent Democratic. If the same pattern of voting obtained within a pure PR system, on the other hand, then the composition of the legislative body would be 50 percent Democratic and 40 percent Republican, with 10 percent of the seats divided among the lesser parties. The overall pattern of voting would thus actually be reflected in the composition of the legislature. It is common for states to

full employment, to the reduction of the labor time necessary to secure an acceptable level of material well-being for all. Such reduction would in obvious ways enhance the conditions of individual autonomy and social deliberation by increasing the availability of free time within conditions of basic material satisfaction.[7]

Material inequalities are not inconsistent with such a requirement of basic material satisfaction for all. But as noted repeatedly, material inequalities can subvert a structure of free and equal public deliberation by translating into sharply unequal capacities for political action. This is especially a problem in view of the requirement of full formal political freedom (requirements 1 and 2 above). Since the democratic conception prohibits restrictions on political expression, it must set limits on the material background of that expression. Thus the democratic order would have to discriminate between those inequalities that were consistent with the conditions of the order and those that were not. The discrimination between different material inequalities would have to take the form of permitting those material inequalities that contribute to the

---

impose minimal barriers to representation within PR schemes. The Federal Republic of Germany, for example, has a "5 percent rule," meaning that to have any representation within the Bundestag a party must garner at least 5 percent of the national vote. Even on such modified plans, however, what distinguishes PR systems of representation from "winner take all" systems is the way in which the votes of participating citizens are aggregated to social decisions. Within "winner take all" systems like that featured in the United States, the final distribution of representation (Democrats versus Republicans versus other parties) may not and usually does not reflect the aggregate levels of support for different representing parties. Within a PR system, the procedure for allocating seats comes closer to providing the basis for a distribution of representation that does reflect these aggregate levels of support. By providing representation for political parties that do not win majorities in any single district, a PR system removes a formidable obstacle to the formation of "third parties," and thus helps to ensure representation of minority views.

material well-being of those least well-off.[8] It is worth emphasizing that the operation of such a principle of distributive equity
does not disturb the requirement of providing basic levels of
material satisfaction for all members of the democratic order.
Nor, surely, does it mandate the proliferation of inequalities
within that order. Rather, it comes into play as a restrictive
control on inequalities, a control that is itself attentive to the
requirements of the PDL. This may be clarified by briefly indicating the sorts of conditions under which the principle might
come into play, and then indicating its rationale within the
democratic order.

Take the example of material incentives. If attracting people
to some sorts of work requires special material incentives, the
PDL does not provide an absolute and general bar to their use.
It does, however, require some evident connection between the
existence of such incentives and the material well-being of
those who do not receive them. The point of such incentives in
a democratic order is not per se to reward the skilled or the
talented, but to encourage contributions to the overall level of
material satisfaction. For incentives to be justified, it must be
shown that the material inequalities they generate contribute
to the material well-being of the least well-off. That is, it must
be demonstrated that they would be even less well-off, in absolute terms, under a scheme that did not feature the particular
incentives or material inequalities whose justification is sought.

The rationale for limiting inequalities in this particular way
follows from the democratic conception's requirement of a
manifest structure of equal freedom. Requiring that incentives
contribute to the well-being of the least well-off respects the
equal status of the least well-off within the political order. It
does so by taking improvements in their material position as a
necessary precondition for justifying the existence of any kind
of material inequality.

Such stringent requirements on distributional equity may be
controversial. As such, they provide occasion for anticipating
what may be a recurring objection to the democratic conception outlined here, namely, that instead of enhancing the exer-

cise of democratic judgment, such a conception actually constrains it. Thus the requirement of distributive equity might be thought inconsistent with the general concerns of the democratic conception, since it may appear to "constrain" the exercise of democratic judgment in the area of material equality. Suppose that members of the democratic order wanted to allow greater material inequalities. Does it not violate the idea of a democratic order to constrain such desires by insisting on the satisfaction of the requirement of distributive equity?

In responding to this concern, it might be useful to notice first how such a question could be generalized to any of the institutional requirements presented thus far. Thus it could equally well be argued that it violates the idea of a democratic order to require that there be protection of individual political liberties. After all, could it not be decided "democratically" that some minority group should be excluded from the protections of those liberties? No, it could not.

The PDL does not specify an initial starting point from which any departures are legitimate if they are made from that point according, for example, to a requirement of majority rule. It specifies a *standing requirement* of an ongoing order, and thus requires that democratic conditions be preserved over time. Insofar as the PDL requires political liberties, it requires that those liberties be preserved. If they are not preserved, then the order is no longer democratic, and therefore the denial of such liberties is itself undemocratic, since such denial violates the very principles which make the existing procedures of social choice legitimate. Once the principle of individual liberties is violated, then individuals no longer retain their status as participants in an order of equal freedom.

The same may be said of the requirement of distributional equity. It too is a standing requirement of the ongoing democratic order. It too is not merely a condition to be secured at some starting point of social deliberation. And its violation, like the violation of political liberties, cannot therefore be accorded legitimacy as a "democratic" act. A genuinely democratic order sets requirements on the structure of formal arenas of social deliberation, and on the material background of those formal arenas. Both sorts of requirement must continue to be satisfied if the order is to continue to express in its manifest structure the conditions of equal freedom and autonomy that give it definition.

4. As indicated already, the democratic conception requires the maintenance of conditions of formal political equality, but it requires as well attention to the material background of such formal structuring of political arenas. In part this attention is provided in the stipulation of public funding of party competition and the distributional measures just discussed. But as our previous discussion of capitalist democracy indicated, such measures are not adequate to address the structural constraints on political decision-making that accompany any system in which investment decisions remain in private hands. Investment is effectively the only guarantee of a society's future. If that future is not available as a subject of social deliberation, then social deliberations are fundamentally constrained and incomplete. It was this point that provided a central focus in our discussion of capitalist democracy, and it is this point which must be directly addressed by the democratic order. That order cannot proceed under free and equal conditions if some of its members have a restrictive monopoly on decisions over the disposition of social surplus. The democratic conception therefore requires that formal political freedom, public funding of party competition, and distributional measures of the sort described be accompanied by public control of investment.

Such public control of the investment function must not in turn provide another occasion for removing control over the economy from arenas of democratic deliberation. Investment decisions must be made by a body either subject to control by a democratic legislative body or itself subject to direct democratic accountability. They cannot be the exclusive purview of some unaccountable administrative or police elite. For decisions over social surplus to be "public" means that those decisions are centralized and subject to national political debate, but it means as well that that debate cannot itself be constrained by other structures of decision-making or authority that members of the order do not enter as free and equal. Here again the role of political parties and the existence of grounds for debate within the political order are highlighted. There may well be serious disagreements as to the direction of investment— disagreements over the pattern and rates of growth, over the correct manner of "signaling" from firm to public authority, over the level of present surplus extraction necessary to sustain future growth, over the extent of present obligations to future generations. It is the task of the political arena to present these disagreements and the probable consequences of different policies in as coherent a fashion as possible, and thus facilitate reasoned choice and deliberation by the members of the order.[9]

Public control over investment does not imply a new principle of workers' sovereignty, embodied for example in a system of councils rooted in the workplace. A potential problem with councilist organization is that producers' interests are, as such, particular interests, and representation of interests organized exclusively on this basis may tend to select out those social interests (such as those of communities or those of consumers) not easily organized from the standpoint of the workplace. This problem may be susceptible to resolution within the framework of democratic legitimacy. Organizational experimentation would be needed to determine specific forms of coordination between decisions of particular enterprises and broader political judgments of the system as a whole. The objection to a workplace-based form of council democracy is not one of principle, but of political judgment. But the objection indicates that the defense of this particular form should not itself be made a matter of principle.[10]

5. To qualify this idea of council democracy, however, is not at all to qualify the signal importance of workplace democracy for the democratic conception. Rather than serving as the organizational basis of a democratic order, however, worker-controlled enterprises are seen here as elements *within* that order, and their place and importance are interpreted in terms of the good of autonomy.

A minimal condition required for the satisfaction of mutual autonomy within the individual enterprise is the abolition of all positions which by their very definition preclude the exercise of self-governing capacities. This requirement of autonomy is not satisfied by the mere availability of choice of jobs, since that choice may range over alternatives which themselves involve subordination or the performance of relatively mechanical tasks. Rather, the principle requires the redefinition and reorganization of work in a way that offers to each participating individual the opportunity to exercise self-governing capacities. What this requires in detail would be expected to vary between different sorts of work. But at the level of general principle, autonomy within the workplace demands the elimination of traditional hierarchical forms of control of the labor process, most centrally the distinction between the planning and execution of production tasks. A structure of workplace democracy directly satisfies this requirement. It ensures that there are no positions which by their very specification deny the exercise of self-governing capacities, since all positions include participation in the functions of controlling the workplace itself. In such a structure of decision-making, the autonomy of some individuals is not realized at the expense of others. Workplace democracy thus extends the PDL's requirement of an order of mutually assured autonomy, and helps to satisfy the condition that such autonomy be expressed within important arenas of everyday life, as well as within the formal arenas of politics.[11]

Such an argument for the centrality of workplace democracy to a democratic conception should be distinguished from an argument that less hierarchical forms of work organization are desirable because they contribute to the material productivity of social systems. Such productivist claims have some plausibility. Less hierarchically organized work might be expected to generate greater enthusiasm among workers, and in any case would draw on the creative power of a broader pool of individuals than does traditionally organized and relatively mechanical work. But the importance of workplace democracy to the democratic conception does not depend on the truth of such speculations. It can freely acknowledge that as people shift among different types of work and spend time debating the problems facing a particular workplace and the relationship between that workplace and the democratic order, there may in fact be some loss of potential output (even if total output were growing). If there were such a loss, by conventional criteria workplace democracy could be regarded as "inefficient," but that is because those criteria apply only to losses or gains in material output, and not to losses or gains in human autonomy. The defense of workplace democracy provided by the democratic conception no more rests upon its being the most materially productive form of social order than the familiar defenses of capitalism as preferable to slavery depend for their force on judgments about the relative productivity of wage labor and slave labor.

The PDL's requirement of workplace democracy may be further clarified by noting its relation to received understandings of "meaningful work." It is sometimes said that work must be made "meaningful," but the idea is an ambiguous one, both because there are many grounds for finding meaning in work and because there is no final way of ensuring against alienation. Work may be regarded as meaningful in view of its contribution to some overall social good, or because it furthers the realization of divine purpose in the mundane world. The democratic conception respects these sources of meaning. Members of the democratic order may for example regard their work as contributing to the preservation of that order, and those who are religious may continue to see their activity as expressing a divine plan. But the conception also recognizes another source of meaningfulness, namely, that many find activities meaningful not because they contribute to a broader purpose, but because they draw on distinctively human capacities for thought, judgment, imagination, and reasoning. In its requirement of workplace democracy, the democratic conception is institutionally attentive to these other sources of meaning.

Finally it should be noted that the existence of workplace democracy does not violate the requirement of public control over investment decisions. Decisions at the level of the individual workplace are made *within* the framework provided by that broader social judgment, although they may of course contribute to the formation of that judgment. In a capitalist economy, decisions over the disposition of the social surplus and decisions about the organization of the production process are both subject to the control of capitalists. Property as control of the surplus and property as control of production are united in such systems. In the democratic order these two aspects of property are kept separate from one another. Investment decisions are subject to public debate and administration. Control over the organization of work is subject to workplace democracy.

6. Even when coupled with the requirements of distributive equity, the removal of institutional barriers to free deliberation within the polity or the economy does not ensure that individuals might not come to such arenas with clear prior disabilities resulting from material inequality. The democratic conception requires a commitment to a principle of "equal opportunity" in the sense that it requires commitment to the social removal of all such materially based disabilities. These commitments follow from the PDL's basic framework of equal freedom, a framework requiring that the absence of prior claims of advantage be manifest in the institutions of a democratic order.

This principle of equal opportunity has, at the minimum, two consequences.

The first is that education must be freely available under such conditions that residual material inequalities in the democratic order would not determine individual life chances. This not only means that free public education must be available up to a level sufficient to assure that the deliberative capacities of individuals can be exercised in public arenas. It requires as well that any sorts of special training that are a precondition for better paying jobs also be available without cost to the trainee.

The second consequence that follows is the required availability of child care. The conditions of the democratic order as an order of mutual autonomy are violated if the preparation or education of individuals for the free exercise of deliberative

capacities in public itself imposes special barriers to the autonomous activities of any select subgroup of adult members of
the order. Attention to the distribution of child-rearing costs is
required in view of the historic division of labor within the
household, where women have traditionally assumed the major
burden of child care and nurture.[12] Insofar as the household is
itself an arena for the exercise of autonomy, public authority
cannot be permitted to undermine or intrude directly in that
arena. But barriers to simultaneously raising children and
maintaining public autonomy must be removed so far as possible. To ensure against a double burden for women, the costs of
child care at a commonly determined level sufficient to assure
the minimal conditions of public life for responsible parents
would have to be collectively assumed. Equal opportunity for
all members of the political order to participate actively in the
order would thus be sought as a shared general social principle, but with due attention to the historical conditions that have
imposed de facto limits on women's participation. Such attention to the dangers that traditional constraints on women pose
to their status as equal members of the political order reflects
the general commitment of the democratic conception of equal
freedom to address informal noninstitutional barriers to the
exercise of that freedom, as well as formal institutional ones.

7. Thus far our account of the democratic conception has
been restricted to considering relations *within* a democratic
state, and indeed the PDL was itself characterized as a principle appealed to by members of a political order in the conduct
of their *internal* affairs. Nevertheless, the PDL does embody a
distinct conception of the members of a democratic order as
equally free and autonomous persons, and it would be natural
to extend that recognition of persons as equally free and autonomous to those who are not members of the domestic order,
and to reflect that recognition in decisions regarding foreign
policy.

The exact manner in which such an extension of recognition would be expressed within the conduct of foreign policy
cannot be specified here. The sheer complexity of considera-

tions bearing on the formulation of that policy precludes such specification, and again underscores the need for political prudence and judgment within the democratic conception. But there are three elementary principles that follow from recognizing the freedom and autonomy of those outside the democratic order, and in the conduct of foreign policy these principles would have to inform that political judgment. First, it is required that no democratic state unilaterally intervene in the affairs of another democratic state. Second, a democratic state can legitimately insist that no other state, democratic or otherwise, intervene in its own affairs, and it can legitimately defend itself against such intervention. It can, for example, use force to defend itself against force initiated against it by another state. Third, a democratic state cannot respect, *as a state*, any regime actively engaged in the suppression of movements aimed at the establishment of a democratic order. This means, among other things, that there is no bar in principle to public support of democratic movements within such orders, although it does not of course require such support as a matter of principle.

These seven main institutional requirements of the democratic order—civil rights and civil liberties, public subsidy for organized competitive political groups, egalitarian distributional measures, public control of investment, workplace democracy, equal opportunity, and a foreign policy informed by the principles of democratic legitimacy that underlie the domestic system—of course permit a variety of more specific institutional expressions. The more general principles and requirements of democratic order do not eliminate the need for prudence, politics, or institutional experimentation. They merely specify the framework within which more particular considerations have their legitimate and necessary place.

The democratic conception outlined here is, finally, not hostile to movements aimed at the partial "reform" of capitalist democracy. But it does yield two important grounds for skepticism about such reform struggles. Before leaving the discussion of the institutional requirements of the democratic order, those two grounds should be noted.

The first ground for skepticism returns to a point entered at the beginning of our outline of the institutional conditions for a democratic society, namely that those institutions are importantly interrelated within the democratic conception. Because they form a system, the failure to satisfy any one requirement seriously limits the force of satisfying any other. Within the democratic conception, neither a social order featuring civil liberties without public control of investment nor an order featuring public control of investment without civil liberties can properly be described as "democratic," because neither permits the members of the order a free and equal determination of the ends of social life. The same can be said of any other conjunction of the elements within the democratic conception. Public funding of political party competition is not sufficient in the absence of distributional equity. Distributional equity is not sufficient in the absence of workplace democracy. And so on.

The second ground for skepticism is that there is no particular reason to see even successful struggles for reform as steps in a progression toward a full realization of a democratic order. Because struggles for reform within capitalist democracy involve consent to capitalism itself, they may easily be undermined in ways that are beyond their control. If struggles over control of the workplace are transformed into purely wage-centered struggles, allegiance to those struggles can be undermined by a downturn in profits or disinvestment or massive levels of unemployment within the affected industry. If struggles to control the political arena are transformed into struggles merely to elect a certain candidate, then allegiance to those struggles can be undermined if that candidate makes little difference in the final distribution of power within the system, or is hopelessly outspent and then beaten "fairly" by well-heeled opponents preying on popular fears.

The logic of reform struggles is based on their need to provide some immediate tangible benefits within the constraints of the existing order.[13] Commonly a radical demand is made, is found to be "impractical" for a variety of reasons, and then is watered down and distorted in the hope that existing centers of power can unite in its satisfaction. A demand for racial equality may get watered down to a demand for affirmative action within labor markets, which may get further watered down to a requirement of publicity in hiring, which may get further watered down to a demand for equal pay for equal work, which may get further watered down to a demand for any work at all, or for the provision of occasional benefits during times of unemployment.

Reform struggles can lead to material gain and greater political power. They can equally lead to cynicism and fatalism. There is no sure path of progressive reform, and the uncertainty of the effects of reform demands is linked to their initial concession to the continued rule of capitalism.

The question of reform is important since the possibility of steadily progressing reform is commonly offered as a reason to defer considering more radical democratic challenge. But in view of the limits of reform strategies, no such deferral is possible. For its realization, democracy requires the abolition of capitalism. Again, this is not because of the materially unsatisfying character of life under capitalism, but because of its structural denial of freedom. To choose democracy is to choose against that denial.

Posing the question of choosing democracy brings us to the third and final aspect of our exploration of the democratic conception, the need to provide some account of how individuals in a capitalist democracy are or could be motivated to join the search and struggle for a democratic order. This is the question of "historical agency," or the question of who will contest capitalism and why they will do it. We order our discussion of agency by first considering some of the traditional answers to this question and the problems with those answers. We then consider how democratic principles can help coordinate political struggles of opposition. And finally we take up the question of initial motivation itself.

The historically most prominent solution to the problem of agency had many variants, but they all solved that problem by reference to the "iron laws" of capitalist development.[14] On such accounts, these iron laws were of two kinds. First there were the laws of capitalist motion, which predicted that through the progressive development of the capitalist accumulation process, an objective clarification of conflicting class interests would be achieved. This would occur because industrial workers would progressively approach a homogeneous condition of exploitation, characterized by miserable working conditions and the organization of workers into centralized units of production requiring huge amounts of unskilled labor. Within these centers of dehumanization, the common interests and identity of workers as a class would be made literally manifest in the structure and conditions of everyday working life.

The second sort of iron law saw this objective clarification of class interest as directly related to the expression of that interest. The working class would gradually emerge as the subject of history instead of its mere unwitting object. In the original argument, under conditions of objective class clarification workers would at first seek only to protect themselves from material deprivation. Their struggles would be "defensive" struggles aimed at protecting the threatened conditions of their own survival. But attempts at doing so would eventually lead to broader collective struggles by workers, and a new interest in their own free association. Workers would be led to make ever more radical demands, and finally they would demand the abolition of the chief constraint on their associational freedom, capitalism itself.

There is considerable dispute about the accuracy of the first sort of iron law, the increasing misery, concentration, homogenization, and deskilling of the workforce. Varying wage rates, heterogeneous working conditions, and the diversified and often decentralized structures of capitalist production do not correspond immediately to the picture just described. Nor does there seem to be any clear tendency toward the realization of these several conditions.

For our purposes, however, this dispute is irrelevant, because what is incontrovertible is that the second sort of iron law, the one bearing directly on agency, has proven to be false. The success of workers in struggling for material advantage has not led to ever more radical struggles against capitalism. On the contrary, it has, as we have attempted to argue at length, provided the material basis for consent to the continued rule of capitalist democracy. By providing the grounds for consent, the success of these more limited struggles has thus additionally contributed to the lack of "objective" clarification of the identity and shared interests of workers as a class. This lack of clarification does not derive from the laziness of the scientists of history, and greater clarification will not be achieved through the renewed dedication of their efforts to catalogue the objective determinants of political action and class identity. It reflects the vitality of political struggle as a determinant of that identity, and underscores the fact that history is not a science at all, but a record of political expression.

The promise of democracy thus cannot be advanced through the ever more careful listing of the objective conditions under which transformative political struggle will emerge. It is not that oppressive material conditions do not exist. It is merely that the existence of such conditions has no definite bearing on the willingness of members of the political order to contest them, and in any event provides no sure basis for the transformation of the social system which generates them. This observation cuts both ways on the agency issue. Although periods of crisis may increase popular willingness to consider alternatives to an existing social system, there is no point in the development of objective conditions which will guarantee a movement to democracy. But there is also no objective bar to the commencement of such a movement, and therefore no reason for waiting.

The second aspect of the question of agency concerns the relation between political struggles of opposition and the democratic ideal. We first explore this relation by distinguishing the principles of democratic coordination from other common strategies of opposition, and then give more substance to those principles by anticipating some objections to the framework of coordination they provide. This discussion does not constitute

an attempt to outline a specific strategy of transition or a particular program of action. We are skeptical about the usefulness
of producing such outlines during a period of low political
mobilization, and that skepticism informs the following account.
Such doubts about finding a single correct strategy at the present
time should not however be confused with doubts about the
value of acting at all. Implicit throughout the following discussion is the view that there are a variety of different actions
appropriate at this point, and that these different patterns of
action can be accommodated within a democratic vision of
alliance and transformation. Indeed, in responding to criticisms of democratic coordination, we are in effect attempting
to turn back the many temptations to political immobility.

The nature of democratic coordination can first be clarified
by distinguishing its principles from those of "vanguardism"
and "coalition politics."

"Vanguardism" refers generally to a strategy of political opposition that relies centrally upon the directing actions of a small
group of revolutionary leaders. This reliance is said to be necessary because, it is claimed, this small group is alone in correctly
understanding the overall pattern of historical dvelopment, and
therefore the current requirements of political action.
Vanguardism commonly claims to be directed toward the
achievement of some form of democratic order, but it also argues
that the objective conditions of political action under capitalism
preclude the development of a popular democratic framework
by which the vanguard leadership can itself be bound.[15]

The failure of workers' democratic agency has led to almost
infinite variations on such vanguardist themes. Common to all
these variations is the dual claim that during the transition to
a democratic order the interests of workers are best served by
leaders and actions not subordinated to clear democratic procedures, and that such procedures can and will be fully realized
once that order is achieved. But if those who participate in a
movement of radical social change do so under a certain set of
organizational principles, there is very little reason to believe
that an entirely different set of organizational principles will

come into force upon their seizure of power. The claim of vanguardism is therefore an improbable one, and practices associated with the claim have sometimes been world-historic crimes. The problems raised by vanguardism underscore the importance of achieving compatibility between the objects of political struggle and the organization of that struggle. While any movement toward a democratic order must be a coordinated one, if that order is truly to be democratic the movement should be coordinated democratically as well.

Vanguardism achieves coordination at the expense of mutual respect and democratic procedure. Sensitive to these failings of vanguardism, "coalition politics" makes the opposite mistake by effectively adopting fragmentation between resisting groups as the principle of their coordination. The practitioners of recent variants of coalition politics effectively assume that there is no broad basis of agreement which does or could animate the different movements of resistance that now exist, and indeed commonly imply that even to raise the question of possibly broader bases for the coordination of those movements is "divisive." Within the practice of coalition politics, the different movements of resistance are assumed to be competitive, and their coordination is limited to select points of convergent interest.

The problem with this form of coalition politics is that it provides no basis or momentum for continuing coordination among fragmented groups. Today, five groups may agree that it is important to resist welfare cutbacks, agreeing on the basis of very different agendas for action which tomorrow may again diverge. Tomorrow, another five groups may agree that it would be a good thing to organize a demonstration against nuclear war; but then the day after tomorrow, those five groups may also split into separate camps. Within such a form of coalition politics, coordination is only episodic, and political discussion is commonly limited to the arrangement and coordination of particular claims of advantage or gain. There is much discussion to ensure that the "community issue" is given proper notice alongside or in front of the "gay issue" or the "black issue" or the "woman issue" or the "nuclear issue" or any of the other particular issues which define the politics of resistance and its own self-understanding. But beyond points of limited convergence, setting a priority among those issues is baffled by the importance which each of their adherents attach to the particular claims.

Some believe that the failures of coalition politics can be remedied by specifying a "correct" hierarchy of particular claims. But this suggestion is implausible. Like claims about "correct" public policy outcomes, the notion of a "correct" hierarchy of political claims is a notion without any clear content. And when conceived as part of a strategy of political mobilization, an insistence on some particular hierarchy of claims seems particularly curious. The suppression of differences among people hardly seems a promising basis for forging a stable and growing coalition of opposition, especially when that suppression must in many cases take the form of denying the importance of what those people find most important at any particular point. But such suppression is, finally, also entirely unnecessary. Differences among people are not the problem. The pursuit of individual claims stands as a barrier to the achievement of a democratic society only if that pursuit takes the suicidal form of elevating one particular claim to the status of universality and rejecting all other claims as merely "divisive" issues. If those who are concerned with world peace claim that world peace is the only issue of any importance at this time, or if those who are concerned about racism and sexism claim that redressing racial and sexual inequalities is the only issue of importance at this time, then an unnecessary barrier to the achievement of a society of both peace and equality is unnecessarily erected. But that is not because either the demand for peace or the demand for equality is in some sense "unimportant." Nor is it because one of these demands is "secondary" to the other.

Democratic politics rejects the idea of distinguishing among people on the basis of the particular hierarchy of claims that they endorse, and it rejects the idea of imposing a priority upon such particular claims. In this rejection it shares the respect for particular claims of coalition politics. Democracy's commit-ment to mutually assured autonomy requires respect for partic-ular claims, just as it provides the basis for alliance among any number of groups or individuals who for different reasons are opposed to the existing structure of private advantage, but who have failed to achieve more than isolated political practice or episodic coordination. Its own framework of conditions provides a basis for judging the desired depth and duration of such alliances. And such alliances can be entered into within the democratic conception without sacrificing democratic ideals themselves. No subordination to a tiny cadre of unaccountable leaders is required.

But the basis of democratic alliance-building is also distin-guishable from the practice of coalition politics, since in offer-ing a way of coordinating individuals with different particular claims, democracy advances no such particular claims as its own central focus. The basis of democratic coalition-building is not the convergence of aims on any particular issue of advan-tage or gain, but the convergence of aims on securing a politi-cal order within which those particular claims can be addressed with mutual respect. To recognize such convergence is not merely to accede to another strategy of advertisement for the left, but the possibility of a strategy of principle. It is to accede to the principle of democracy itself.[16]

This general conception of democratic coordination can be made more concrete by considering some of the many objec-tions that might naturally be raised against it.

One objection is that in specifying no organization to join and proposing no particular agenda for action, the democratic conception is simply too vague to be useful. It might be asked: "But what should I do right now?" or "But what group should I join?" These are pressing questions, and they deserve a response. But that response must not provide yet another occasion for hoodwinking people. To be honest, it should start by recogniz-ing how very grim things now are in this country, and how decayed the arenas of mass politics have become. Despite all the discontent with conventional politics, there is very little overt resistance at the moment, and the organizational framework for such resistance is certainly not now in place. There is at present no mass party of democracy. There are therefore no straightforward ways of "signing up." And while there are any number of different movements of popular opposition, these movements have thus far notoriously failed to converge. Fragmentation remains the order of the day.

In face of such conditions, all that can be done now—although it is by no means a small "all"—is to pursue alliances within the current possibilities of action, and to try to forge new possibilities by extending those alliances, by raising basic questions about the justness of this political order, and by seeking to broaden political discussion by broadening both the content of the discussion and the range of its participants.

This can be done in many different ways, and through many different groups. It can be done in one's home or at one's job. It may have to begin in isolation, but it is the necessary precondition for breaking out of that isolation. Those who participate in the antinuclear movement can extend the concerns of that movement to include attention to the use of conventional military force and the relation between strategic weapons development and the more general aims of U.S. foreign policy. Those participating in the trade union movement can broaden the focus of that movement to include the needs and demands of the unemployed and unorganized. Those participating in the women's movement can attempt to forge alliances with those suffering from non-gender-based forms of oppression, be that oppression based on race or alienage or resistance to the projection of U.S. military power. Some who are participating in such movements are already engaging in just such actions or attempts. They can be joined by other participants. And those who are not participating in any movements of opposition at all might begin to do so. In suggesting such actions as part of a democratic strategy, we are again not recommending them as the most economically rational actions that can be undertaken at this time. Within the democratic conception of politics, the purpose served by such particular actions is not only the furtherance of particular aspirations per se, but the pursuit of those aspirations in democratic ways through the recognition of their affinity with other claims.

Such an answer may be unsatisfying because it may be unclear how such efforts at greater concerted action could lead to the massive mobilization that has not yet arrived. But honesty demands the recognition that no easy answer to the question of mobilization can be supplied. No one knows what particular action or set of political commitments will lead to mobilization. People become engaged in political action for a variety of reasons. Given low levels of mobilization, it might be argued that an organization should be formed to prompt broader activity. But while, everything else being equal, political organization is always better than political fragmentation, if only because it brings people together and makes their action more coordinated and forceful, no particular organization will of itself be able to produce high levels of political activity, even if such mobilization is the announced "purpose" of the organization. The history of the world is littered with the remains of "revolutionary" or "radical" organizations that steeled themselves for popular uprising, only to be rendered irrelevant once that uprising occurred. Wedded to one or another particular vision of political action or strategy of mobilization, these organizations were overtaken by the turmoil of actual events.

Or it may be that the answer to the question of what to do right now is unsatisfying because it does not seem ambitious enough. But if that is the case, then perhaps the question itself should be reframed. Perhaps the question to which an answer is desired is not exactly what one should do right now, given low levels of mobilization, but what one should do and what precise form coordination should take if a situation arises in which there are far higher levels of mobilization, and therefore broader possibilities for action, than those that are now present. But if that is the question then again no honest answer can be given in the abstract. Any mobilization of people that changes the possibilities of collective action, should it come, will be highly particular in time, in the space in which it unfolds, in the organizations which are party to it, in the personalities of the actors involved, and, above all, in the issues around which it is first crystallized. Despite the importance of leadership, mobilizations do not occur *because* of the existence of "great men" or "great women." They occur because ordinary people are outraged at something and see the possibilities of acting on that outrage. They see those possibilities because other people are similarly outraged and see the possibilities of *their* action if action is undertaken by others as well. There is no mystery here. But neither is there a "science" of social movements. Possibilities are read off events. If millions of people were taking to the streets in America, then some answer to the question of what to do during high levels of mobilization could be framed. But framing that answer would require knowing why it was that millions of people were taking to the streets, and that cannot be known before they decide to do so.

It might still be objected that even if the future cannot be anticipated organizationally, it can still be anticipated through the articulation of a program of action. But this is only to make the same mistake, removed to the level of ideas. Effective political programs arise out of action. They conserve and consolidate the focus of actually existing movements, and do not ordinarily produce such movements. It might be argued that programs can help make the ends of political action more imaginable, and thereby make action more imaginable as well. We agree, but then articulating a program is not articulating a set of conditions to be realized right now, but showing how action right now could be plausibly related to the achievement of such conditions in the future. This can be done in a variety of ways, and none of them is obviously more effective than any other. It can be done by writing novels, or writing political programs, or, as we have attempted to do, by indicating in outline the structure of an alternative social order.

More commonly, however, the question of articulating a program is a more demanding one in that it asks for a list of policies that can be enacted immediately. But this is a strange question if applied to popular politics, because if it is acknowledged that democratic mobilization levels are now low, then it follows that no comprehensive democratic program of action *can* be immediately enacted. What if we were to say, "Cut defense spending by $150 billion, shrink the work week to thirty hours, employ everybody who wants a job, and raise the minimum wage to $10 an hour." These might all be very good ideas, but given the current distribution of power in American society they are currently impossible to put into effect. For them to be realizable that distribution of power would itself have to be changed by people taking action. Then it might be declared that such an admission betrays the "impracticality" of democratic politics, but this objection amounts to claiming that for demands to be "practical" they have to be realizable within the current framework of power. The objection here is really an objection to any form of radical action, and the dispute over "practicality" is really a dispute over politics. When people say, "You're not being practical," they very often mean, "I don't agree with you." But saying something is "impractical" is better as a conversation stopper. Saying "I don't agree with you" might require clarifying the grounds of disagreement.

A final possible objection to democratic alliance and transition might take the form of declaring uncertainty over the future workings of the democratic order as a bar to present action. A declaration of basic agreement with the requirements of democracy might immediately be followed by the objection, "But I don't want to do anything until I know exactly how it will work." Like the dispute over "practicality," this objection is really a political one, and there is no way of elaborating a conception of democracy which can meet it. The final shape of the democratic order is importantly contingent, not only because it is generally impossible to predict exactly what will happen in the future, but because open-endedness is built into the democratic order itself. What the democratic order provides is an institutional framework within which people are free and equal in the making of social decisions. If one were able to specify those decisions precisely in advance, then one would not be describing a democratic order at all. Maybe a decision would be made to roll up GNP to stratospheric levels. Maybe it would be decided that such high levels of economic growth posed too great a threat to the environment. Maybe there would be a massive social commitment to subsidizing poetry. Maybe that commitment would be directed to the material infrastructure of bridges and roads and tunnels instead. Nobody knows exactly what would happen if people were free and equal and subject only to the principles of democracy itself. To say now what would happen within such an order of equal freedom is either to indicate that the order is not in fact a democratic one, or it is quite simply to lie.

To tell the truth is merely to accede to the possibilities now present, possibilities which are in some ways heightened by the current crisis, and to try to broaden those possibilities by taking different forms of concerted action. Such a pursuit of democratic coordination is no dismal undertaking, and the prospects for that undertaking are no mere pallid hopes. But of course all those hopes depend upon the existence of initial aspirations to democracy and the willingness of individuals to act upon them. This frames the question of initial motivation, the third and last element in our discussion of agency.

We have repeatedly insisted that the decision to pursue democracy is not a calculation but a choice. Who might make such a choice? Answering this question does not presume some process of moral reflection that proceeds in the absence of all known identity. If its answer can be found at all, it must be found in the identity and aspirations of ordinary persons as they ordinarily exist within the social order of capitalist democracy. The question can thus be posed in a direct and immediate fashion. Who might choose self-respect over work that seems meaningless? Who might choose autonomy over hierarchy and occupational disease? Who might choose a democratic foreign policy over the murder and torture of other individuals, scattered around the world, who under analogous circumstances have chosen to fight for their own freedom? We can imagine many doing so.

The choice for democracy is not only available to some structurally determined group of the ultraoppressed. It is not only available to the industrial proletariat, or to black or women workers in the industrial proletariat, or to black or Hispanic women, or to women generally, or to gay men or lesbians. Indeed it is not confined to any identifiable group at all, not to hetero-sexual men and women, or to those who raise families, or those who do not raise families, or the "universal class" of intellec-tuals, or those who live in the inner cities, or those who live in suburban enclaves, or those who are health food addicts, or those who like to smoke cigars. There is no vanguard of disgust or hope. While this choice is in the interest of a class, and cannot succeed without the active participation of members of that class, it need not even be made only by those who now identify themselves as members. As heretical as it may sound, there may be many people in America, indeed millions of Americans, who in one way or another participate in or benefit from the exploitation of others, but who do so not as a matter of free choice, but because they see no clear alternative that does not present even greater threats to their already distorted freedom.

We have argued that the structure and practice of democracy provide that alternative. One can imagine a situation in which many come to the same conclusion, not through coercion but through their own reflection, not because of a desire for confor-mity but because of a desire for individual freedom. These desires may be expressed or felt in many different ways, from material deprivation to moral outrage. The pluralism democ-racy promises reveals a plurality of motives for joining in its advance.

The question is whether these many motivations are acted upon in a way that is democratic. They very often are not. And this finally is the content of the choice to be made. One may suppress such motivations entirely, pleading the material exigencies of the present world. One may seek to join the exist-ing arrangements of authority. Or if that prospect seems too remote, one can uncritically accept continued subordination to those who wield social power. One may announce such moti-

vations as an article of private faith, but refuse to act upon that
faith in social arenas, preferring to use its articulation as a
source of "heroic" individual identity. One can opt for cynicism
or succumb to the many temptations of despair, fashioning a
persona of gadfly critic or bumblebee of the avant-garde. Even
during a period of crisis, the bare existence of aspirations to
democracy does not guarantee that those aspirations will be
acted upon as a source of democratic opposition.

But such an admission of contingency does not defeat our
account of democratic agency, for that account does not claim
to provide an assurance of opposition, and does not rest on
some "optimism of the intellect" that sees objective conditions
as ultimately and necessarily leading to a transformation of the
existing order. In our earlier discussion of motivation within
capitalist democracy, we argued that aspirations potentially
opposed to that order are commonly redefined or suppressed or
bent to accommodate the existing structure of social power.
The point bears repetition here. Moved by aspirations to democracy, one can always opt for a strategy of consent. All our account
of agency has insisted on, and all this book has argued for, is
that there is an alternative decision that can be made. Instead
of abandoning those aspirations, one can attempt to realize
them by joining with other people, recognizing the affinity of
such aspirations with the aspirations of others, recognizing
them therefore as particular, and as different impulses toward
an alternative political order whose achievement can provide a
unifying focus for action. One can make the democratic choice.

Once that choice is made, the consequences could be overpowering. Individual action could quickly be joined with the
actions of others, stretching the famous limits of the possible
as isolated practice is overtaken by a unified movement of
opposition and renewal. Such a movement would bring into
view a world quite different from the one we now inhabit, a
world in which obfuscation might give way to clarity as a
preferred method of public argument, in which humor might
replace posturing in the relation among equals, in which vast
stores of private wealth would no longer be taken as a mark of

inner distinction, and the refusal to oppress others would no longer be taken as a mark of weakness. The world of democracy.

Even to imagine such a social order is painfully difficult during the present period. Its realization seems so utterly improbable. All the leading social indicators point against it. The mind turns from the prospect, and seeks repose on the stability of received and dismal truth.

But the truth of things is not decided until the debates of history have been closed. There is simply no reliable way to "predict" resistance. There never has been a way, and there is none now. Who predicted the Lordstown strike? Who predicted the strange refusal of Rosa Parks to move to the back of the bus? Who predicted the upsurge of both black and white Americans who joined in that refusal? Who predicted that welfare mothers would rise against the humiliations of the state bureaucracy? Who predicted massive domestic opposition to the war in Vietnam? Who predicted that millions of women would suddenly demand the obvious, that they be treated with the respect accorded equal human beings? Who can now predict when resistance will emerge, or how it will emerge, or how one's own behavior may figure in that emergence?

What is most astonishing among those who identify with the ideal of freedom is their repeated astonishment that others share that improbable commitment. But past surprise and bewilderment are cause for present resolve and hope. Is it so improbable that the disasters of the present period may again prompt widespread reflection on the cause of human freedom? Is it so unlikely that the intrinsic merits of that cause might lead others to join in its pursuit? Is it so inconceivable that many might refuse the attacks upon their dignity which now define American public life? We think not. Even in these dark times, the restive dream of freedom may again be stirred to wakeful action. The future is open.

NOTES

CHAPTER 2

1. *New York Times,* 18 January 1983, p. D14, based on Federal Reserve Board report. The December rate of 67.3 percent was itself a record low. The previous yearly low was 72.9 percent in 1975.
2. *New York Times,* 20 January 1983, p. 41.
3. The 1941 rate of 9.9 percent is reported in *Economic Report of the President* (Washington, D.C.: U.S. Government Printing Office, 1982), Table B-29 (hereafter cited as *ER*). The 1982 figure is based on monthly reports of the Bureau of Labor Statistics, reported in issues of the *Daily Labor Report* (Washington, D.C.: Bureau of National Affairs), Table A.
4. Estimate based on yearly unemployment rate as compared to 1981, when roughly one out of every five workers reported unemployment at some point during the year. See *New York Times,* 21 July 1982, p. A19.
5. *Daily Labor Report,* 4 January 1983, Table A.
6. For discouraged workers, see ibid., Table A; for part-time workers, Table A-3.
7. *ER*, Table B-34.
8. Ibid.
9. *Daily Labor Report,* 4 January 1983, Table A-6.
10. Computed from *ER*, Table B-31.
11. In 1980 the rate was 7.1 percent; in 1981 it was 7.6 percent. See *ER*, Table B-31. For standard forecasts for the near-term, see the Organization for Economic Cooperation and Development's late 1982 semiannual forecast cited in *New York Times,*

23 December 1982, p. D1; and Conference Board, *Statistical Bulletin,* vol. 16, no. 1 (January 1983), pp. 8–9.

12. Dun and Bradstreet, author interview, 16 February 1983. For the first six weeks of 1983, failures ran at an annual level of more than 30,000.

13. *Business Week,* 27 December 1982, p. 16.

14. *ER,* Table B-93 for historical rates; Dun and Bradstreet, author interview, for 1982 rate.

15. Ibid.

16. *Business Week,* 26 July 1982, p. 44.

17. James Cooper and Gelvin Stevenson, "What the Fed Says Is Not What It Does," *Business Week,* 7 June 1982, p. 29.

18. For 1981 data, see *Business Week,* 3 May 1982, p. 119, quoting Gary M. Wenglowski, chief economist for Goldman Sachs. For 1982 finding, author interview with Wenglowski, 11 February 1983.

19. *Time,* 2 August 1982, p. 50; *New York Times,* 23 August 1982, p. A14.

20. Ibid.

21. *New York Times,* 21 May 1982, p. D1. The amount lost was $6.4 billion.

22. For general discussion, see William R. Cline, "External Debt, System Vulnerability, and Development," unpublished manuscript; Robert Solomon, "The International Debt Problem" (Washington, D.C.: Center for National Policy, 1982).

23. *Business Week,* 17 January 1983, p. 37. The total debt for developing countries reached $626 billion at the end of 1982. See *Wall Street Journal,* 17 December 1982, p. 31.

24. *Business Week,* 17 January 1983, p. 37.

25. Solomon, "The International Debt Problem," pp. 10–11.

26. Ibid.

27. *Time,* 2 August 1982, p. 50.

28. American Iron and Steel Institute, *Pig Iron and Raw Steel Production,* December 1982.

29. *New York Times,* 25 December 1982, p. 29.

30. *New York Times,* 26 November 1982, p. D4.

31. *New York Times,* 31 January 1982, p. D1.

32. *New York Times,* 19 January 1983, p. D1.

33. U.S. Department of Labor, Bureau of Labor Statistics, *Employment and Earnings,* January 1983, Table 12.

34. *New York Times,* 16 December 1982, p. D1.
35. U.S. Department of Defense, *Report of the Secretary of Defense on the FY 1983 Budget* (Washington, D.C.: U.S. Government Printing Office, 1982), pp. 1–25.
36. *New York Times,* 13 October 1982, p. A1.
37. *New York Times,* 21 January 1983, p. A15, reporting excerpts from a White House midterm report on the Reagan presidency.
38. Ira Magaziner and Robert Reich, *Minding America's Business* (New York: Harcourt Brace Jovanovich, 1982), p. 2.
39. *Wall Street Journal,* 27 January 1983, p. 4.
40. Figures (from 1979) for cutlery, textile machinery, and machine tools are taken from Magaziner and Reich, *Minding America's Business,* p. 33. In 1982 imported steel took a record 22.3 percent of the U.S market. *Wall Street Journal,* 10 February 1983, p. 4.
41. Magaziner and Reich, *Minding America's Business,* p. 2.
42. *New York Times,* 28 February 1982, p. F1; *Wall Street Journal,* 2 March 1982, p. 35.
43. U.S. Department of Commerce, *1983 U.S. Industrial Outlook* (Washington, D.C.: U.S. Government Printing Office, 1983), Table 5.
44. On the drop in capital spending, see *New York Times,* 14 December 1982, p. D1. For figures on foreign investment, see *The Economist,* 16 October 1982, p. 97.
45. For general discussion, see Pat Choate and Susan Walter, *America in Ruins* (Washington, D.C.: Council of State Planning Agencies, 1982); *Congressional Quarterly Weekly Report,* 20 November 1982, pp. 2871–78; *Economist,* 4 December 1982, pp. 25–26.
46. Reported in *Congressional Quarterly Weekly Report,* 20 November 1982, p. 2876.
47. Ibid., pp. 2875–76.
48. Thomas Weisskopf, "The Current Economic Crisis," *Socialist Review,* vol. 11, no. 3 (May–June 1981), p. 10.
49. Ibid.
50. *ER,* Table B-2; *New York Times,* 20 January 1983, p. A20.
51. Organization for Economic Cooperation and Development, *National Accounts 1951–1980* (Paris: OECD, 1982), vol. I, p. 88. The ranking is based on 1980 prices and exchange rates.

With 1975 prices and exchange rates, the United States is sixth. See ibid.

52. Ibid.

53. *New York Times*, 28 March 1982, p. 1. In fiscal 1981, 9.6 percent of GNP went to health care, up from 5.3 percent in 1960 and 7.5 percent in 1970.

54. For comparative inflation rates, see *ER*, Table B-52.

55. Ibid.

56. *New York Times*, 24 January 1983, p. A8. The 1982 rate was the third highest on record, lower only than 1974 and 1981.

57. *Democratic Fact Book: Issues for 1982* (Washington, D.C.: Democrats for the 80's, 1982), p. 111.

58. See United Nations, *Demographic Yearbook 1980* (New York: United Nations, 1982), Tables 20 and 34. The comparisons are for 1980. In ranking the United States, we have of course eliminated all cases with incomplete data (e.g. Fiji and Syria). In those cases (e.g. Canada) with no rate for 1980, we have compared the rate in the last reported year (for Canada, 1978) with the U.S. rate in that year. Finally, we have calculated rates for Luxembourg and Iceland from the absolute number of infant deaths (in Table 20) and the number of live births (in Table 9).

59. For international rates, see ibid., Table 20. For the Washington, D.C., rate, see U.S. Bureau of the Census, *State and Metropolitan Area Data Book, 1982* (Washington, D.C.: U.S. Government Printing Office, 1982), p. 293.

60. Michael H. Brown, "Love Canal, U.S.A.," *New York Times Magazine*, 21 January 1979, p. 23, cited in Institute for Labor Education and Reseach, *What's Wrong with the U.S. Economy?* (Boston: South End Press, 1982), p. 186.

61. See Magaziner and Reich, *Minding America's Business*, p. 21.

62. *New York Times*, 30 June 1980, p. A1, based on EPA report.

63. Federal Home Loan Bank Board, press release, 7 December 1982, Table 2.

64. Ibid.

65. Walter Dean Burnham, "The Eclipse of the Democratic Party," *Democracy*, vol. 2, no. 3 (July 1982), p. 11.

66. Harris Poll reported in *Newsweek*, 17 January 1983, p. 12.

67. Federal Home Loan Bank Board, "Mortgage Foreclosures by FSLIC Insured Savings and Loan Associations First Half 1982"

(Washington, D.C., 1982), Table 1; idem, "Monthly Press Release of Savings and Loan Activity," 28 January 1983; idem, *Savings and Home Financing Sourcebook*, 1981, Table 26.

68. Conference on Alternative State and Local Policies, *The Issues of 1982: A Briefing Book* (Washington, D.C.: Conference on Alternative State and Local Policies, 1982), p. 91.

69. For the range of projections, see *U.S. News and World Report*, 17 January 1983, p. 23. Cf. also Mary Ellen Hombs and Mitch Snyder, *Homelessness in America* (Washington, D.C.: The Community for Creative Non-Violence, 1982).

70. See Magaziner and Reich, *Minding America's Business*, pp. 14–18.

71. For discussion, see David Gordon and Michele Naples, "More Injuries on the Job," *New York Times*, 13 December 1981, p. E29. The rate cited is the "injury frequency rate" and is the number of manufacturing accidents resulting in lost workdays per worker hours of employment.

72. U.S. President, *President's Report on Occupational Safety and Health* (Washington, D.C., 1978), p. 58. The report indicates 5.3 million injuries and 160,000 illnesses for 1977, up from a total of 5.16 million injuries and illnesses for 1976.

73. National Safety Council, *Accident Facts* (Chicago, 1981), p. 25; U.S. Department of Health and Human Services, *Promoting Health/Preventing Disease* (Washington, D.C.: U.S. Government Printing Office, 1980), p. 39.

74. Ibid. There were 13,000 deaths on the job in 1980, equal to the 1975–80 annual average.

75. U.S. Department of Health and Human Services, *Promoting Health*, p. 39. For higher estimates, see figures from the National Institute of Health Study cited in Leslie Boden, "The Economic Impact of Environmental Health on Health Care Delivery," *Journal of Occupational Medicine*, vol. 18, no. 7 (July 1976), Table 6.

76. U.S. Department of Health and Human Services, *Promoting Health*, p. 31, for the number of toxic chemicals. For a complete list of regulated substances, see U.S. Department of Labor, *Occupational Safety and Health: General Industry Standards* (Washington, D.C.: U.S. Government Printing Office, 1976), pp. 505–10.

77. *Wall Street Journal,* 20 December 1982, p. 1.

78. Ibid. For general discussion, see Peter S. Barth and H. Allan Hunt, *Worker's Compensation and Work-Related Illnesses and Diseases* (Cambridge, Mass.: M.I.T. Press, 1980).

79. U.S. Government, Interagency Task Force on Workplace Safety and Health, *First Recommendations Report,* 1 August 1978, pp. 1–3.

80. Ibid.

81. Sierra Club, *Poisons on the Job: The Reagan Administration and American Workers* (San Francisco: Sierra Club, 1982), p. 18.

82. Taken from a 5 June 1980 interview with the *Washington Post,* cited in ibid., p. 21.

83. *New York Times,* 29 December 1982, p. A1, reporting on drafts of an EPA report released by Congressman Toby Moffett.

84. The figure comes from a General Accounting Office report, cited in Friends of the Earth, *Ronald Reagan and the American Environment* (San Francisco: Friends of the Earth Books, 1982), p. 11. For general discussion of water pollution, see *Environment and Health* (Washington, D.C.: Congressional Quarterly Inc., 1981), ch. 4.

85. The lower figure comes from a recent EPA report cited in *New York Times,* 21 December 1982, p. A1. The 50,000 estimate comes from *Preliminary Assessment of Cleanup Costs for National Hazardous Waste Problems,* consultant report to the EPA Office of Solid Waste, 1979, p. 24. This report also indicated that 1,200 of the dumps posed "significant dangers."

86. U.S. Environmental Protection Agency, *Everybody's Problem: Hazardous Wastes* (Washington, D.C.: U.S. Government Printing Office, 1980), pp. 1, 15.

87. Estimates reported in *Democratic Fact Book,* p. 275.

88. Irving J. Selikoff, *Disability Compensation for Asbestos-Associated Disease in the United States* (New York: Environmental Sciences Laboratory, Mount Sinai School of Medicine, 1981). We are combining Table 2-25 with the estimates for asbestosis on pp. 67–69. The estimates of mortality in this study are only for past occupational exposures, and not for past or future environmental exposures, or exposures from use of asbestos products by consumers.

89. Irving J. Selikoff, "Asbestos-Associated Disease," *Public Health and Preventive Medicine,* ed. John Last, 11th ed. (Englewood Cliffs, N.J.: Prentice-Hall, 1980), p. 597.

90. *New York Times,* 7 September 1982, p. A22. For further discussion and documents, see Linda Walker-Hill and Betsey Weltner, "Fifty Years of Deception: An Overview of the Manville Corporation's Efforts to Avoid Responsibility for Asbestos-Related Diseases," unpublished manuscript.

91. Magaziner and Reich, *Minding America's Business,* p. 16. For comparisons of transfer payments as a percentage of GDP, see Morris Beck, *Government Spending: Issues and Trends* (New York: Praeger, 1981), Table 7-4.

92. Beck, *Government Spending,* Table 7-3.

93. For analysis of budgets for fiscal 1982 and 1983, see John L. Palmer and Isabel Sawhill, eds., *The Reagan Experiment* (Washington, D.C.: Urban Institute Press, 1982), especially chapters 1, 12, and 16; Frances Fox Piven and Richard Cloward, *The New Class War* (New York: Pantheon Books, 1982), especially pp. 13–19; Tom Joe, "Profile of Families in Poverty: Effects of the FY1983 Budget Proposals on the Poor" (Washington, D.C.: Center for the Study of Social Policy, 1982). For discussion of the budget proposals for fiscal 1984, see *New York Times,* 1 February 1983, p. A17.

94. See Magaziner and Reich, *Minding America's Business,* p. 22.

95. Ibid.

96. U.S. Department of Justice, *Uniform Crime Reports for the United States* (Washington, D.C.: U.S. Government Printing Office, 1982), Appendix 5. In 1981 the murder rate for nonwhite 30-year-old men was 12.5 times the rate for the population in general.

97. Ibid., p. 36.

98. Ibid.

99. Ibid.

100. Ibid., p. 39.

101. Ibid., pp. 15–17.

102. *Democratic Fact Book,* p. 173.

103. Elliott Currie, "Crime and Ideology," *Working Papers* (May–June 1982), p. 29.

104. *Los Angeles Times,* 3 May 1982; and Timothy J. Flanagan, David J. van Alstyne, and Michael Gottfredson, eds., *Source-*

book of Criminal Justice Statistics—1982, U.S. Department of Justice, Bureau of Justice Statistics (Washington, D.C.: U.S. Government Printing Office, 1982), Table 6.22.

105. *New York Times*, 8 November 1982, p. A12, based on a report from the Bureau of Justice Statistics.

106. Ibid.

107. *Democratic Fact Book*, p. 175.

108. U.S. Department of Justice, *Uniform Crime Reports*, p. 10.

109. Conference on Alternative State and Local Policies, *The Issues of 1982*, p. 183.

110. For discussion, see George O'Toole, *The Private Sector: Private Spies, Rent-a-Cops, and the Police-Industrial Complex* (New York: Norton, 1978), p. xii.

111. Ibid, p. 5.

112. Ibid, p. 4.

113. The estimate on the suicide rate is reported in the *Wall Street Journal*, 21 October 1982, p. 1. All other correlates are reported in the *New York Times*, 23 October 1982, p. A20, based on a study by Dr. Harvey Brenner of Johns Hopkins University. For a study of job loss and child abuse, see Lawrence D. Steinberg, Ralph Catalano, and David Dooley, "Economic Antecedents of Child Abuse and Neglect," *Child Development*, 52 (1981), pp. 975–85.

114. *New York Times*, 15 June 1982, p. B1, based on a study directed by Joseph A. Califano, Jr., for New York State.

115. Massachusetts Advocacy Center, *Massachusetts: The State of the Child* (Boston, 1982), p. 52.

116. Gallup Poll reported in *New York Times*, 16 November 1982, p. A16. The *Times* report adds, "Mr. Gallup said it was rare for 81 percent of people to agree on anything."

117. *New York Times*, 15 June 1982, p. B1 (see note 114, sup.).

118. Ibid.

119. Ibid.

120. U.S. Department of Health and Human Services, *Monthly Vital Statistics Report*, National Center for Health Statistics, vol. 29, no. 13, 17 September 1981, Table 10.

121. U.S. Bureau of the Census, Current Population Reports, ser. P-23, no. 114, *Characteristics of American Children and Youth: 1980* (Washington, D.C.: U.S. Government Printing Office, 1982), Table 31.

122. U.S. Department of Health and Human Services, *Monthly Vital Statistics Report*, Table E (for 1980).

123. See U.S. Bureau of the Census, Current Population Reports, ser. P-60, no. 134, *Money Income and Poverty Status of Families and Persons in the United States: 1981 (Advance Data from the March 1982 Current Population Survey)* (Washington, D.C.: U.S. Government Printing Office, 1982), Tables 1 and 3; and U.S. Bureau of the Census, Current Population Reports, ser. P-60, no. 132, *Money Income of Households, Families, and Persons in the United States: 1980* (Washington, D.C.: U.S. Government Printing Office, 1982), Table 17.

124. Institute for Labor Education and Research, *What's Wrong with the U.S. Economy?*, p. 2.

125. Ibid., p. 3.

126. Ibid.

127. Magaziner and Reich, *Minding America's Business*, p. 23.

128. For 1951, see Current Population Reports, ser. P-60, no. 132, Table 19; for 1981, Current Population Reports, ser. P-60, no. 134, Table 4.

129. Magaziner and Reich, *Minding America's Business*, p. 23.

130. Current Population Reports, ser. P-60, no. 134, Table 19.

131. Ibid., Table 4. The top 20 percent had family income above $37,457, the bottom 20 percent had income less than $10,918.

132. Magaziner and Reich, *Minding America's Business*, p. 25.

133. U.S. Bureau of the Census, *Statistical Abstract of the United States: 1980*, 101st ed. (Washington, D.C.: U.S. Government Printing Office, 1980), p. 471.

134. Jeffrey G. Williamson and Peter H. Lindert, "Long-Term Trends in American Wealth Inequality," in *Modeling the Distribution and Intergenerational Transmission of Wealth*, ed. James D. Smith (Chicago: University of Chicago Press, 1980), p. 65; U.S. Bureau of the Census, *Statistical Abstract*, p. 471. The 1972 figures are the most recent ones available.

135. The poverty line for a family of four in 1981 was $9287. See U.S. Bureau of the Census, Current Population Reports, ser. P-60, no. 136, *Characteristics of Households and Persons Receiving Selected Non-Cash Benefits: 1981* (Washington, D.C.: U.S. Government Printing Office, 1983).

136. Ibid., Table 1. Fully 19 percent of households earn less than

125 percent of poverty-level income, that is, under $11,609. See Table 1.

137. *New York Times,* 27 July 1982, p. D22.
138. U.S. Bureau of the Census, Current Population Reports, ser. P-60, no. 136, Table 3.
139. Ibid.
140. Ibid.
141. Ibid., Table 2 and Table A.
142. Ibid.
143. Mollie Orshansky, "Counting the Poor," *Social Security Bulletin,* January 1965, p. 12, cited in Institute for Labor Education and Research, *What's Wrong with the U.S. Economy?,* p. 4.
144. Current Population Reports, ser. P-60, no. 136, Table 4. The median full-time income for women in 1981 was $10,352, for men $17,395.
145. Current Population Reports, ser. P-60, no. 132, Table 59. Comparisons are of median incomes.
146. Ibid., Table 52.
147. Ibid., Table 59.
148. Current Population Reports, ser. P-60, no. 136, Table 1. Some 15.4 percent of all families are headed by women.
149. Ibid.
150. U.S. Bureau of the Census, Current Population Reports, ser. P-60, no. 133, *Characteristics of the Population Below the Poverty Level: 1980* (Washington, D.C.: U.S. Government Printing Office, 1982), Table 3.
151. The census classification here is "black, female, unrelated individuals, 65 years and over." See ibid., Table 41. The comparable figure for white women is 46.7 percent.
152. Institute for Labor Education and Research, *What's Wrong with the U.S. Economy?,* p. 267.
153. Ibid., p. 266.
154. Samuel Bowles and Herbert Gintis, "The Crisis of Liberal Democratic Capitalism: The Case of the United States," *Politics and Society,* vol. 11, no. 1 (1982), p. 83. Bowles and Gintis derive their measure by summing the differences in the four unemployment rates of white males, black males, white females, and black females. Recalculated by the authors for 1951 and 1981. Data from *ER,* Table B-33.

155. *Daily Labor Report,* 4 January 1983, Table A.

156. Ibid., Tables A and A-2.

157. *Newsweek,* 17 January 1983, p. 29, based on Census Bureau report.

158. Institute for Labor Education and Research, *What's Wrong with the U.S. Economy?,* p. 216.

159. For sustained discussion of this issue in historical and comparative perspective, see Walter Dean Burnham, *The Current Crisis in American Politics* (New York: Oxford University Press, 1982), especially chs. 4 and 5.

160. See Thomas Mackie and Richard Rose, *The International Almanac of Electoral History* (New York: Free Press, 1974). More recent data on France, West Germany, Great Britain, Italy, and Sweden can be found in Burnham, *The Current Crisis,* p. 183.

161. The last presidential election turnout above 60 percent was in 1968. Not since 1900 has the turnout surpassed 70 percent. See Walter Dean Burnham, "The 1980 Earthquake: Realignment, Reaction, or What?," in Thomas Ferguson and Joel Rogers, eds., *The Hidden Election: Politics and Economics in the 1980 Presidential Campaign* (New York: Pantheon, 1981), p. 101.

162. Ibid., pp. 100–102.

163. Burnham notes this striking comparison in ibid., p. 102. Willkie received support from 28.2 percent of the eligible voters.

164. Reported in *Congressional Quarterly Weekly Report,* 13 November 1982, vol. 40, no. 46, p. 2850.

165. U.S. Bureau of the Census, *Statistical Abstract of the United States: 1980,* 101st ed. (Washington, D.C.: U.S. Government Printing Office, 1980), p. 513.

166. U.S. Bureau of the Census, *Statistical Abstract of the United States 1965,* 86th ed. (Washington, D.C.: U.S. Government Printing Office, 1965), p. 384.

167. For the 1980 election, see U.S. Bureau of the Census, Current Population Reports, ser. P-20, no. 370, *Voting and Registration in the Election of November 1980* (Washington, D.C.: U.S. Government Printing Office, 1982), Table 12; for 1978 see U.S. Bureau of the Census, Current Population Reports, ser. P-20, no. 344, *Voting and Registration in the Election of November 1978* (Washington, D.C.: U.S. Government Printing Office,

1982), Table 13. We are combining, from these and other surveys, the categories of "professional, technical, and kindred workers" with "managers and administrators" and comparing their turnouts with the combined categories of "blue collar workers" and "service workers." For a contrast between class and age skews in American voting and their general absence in Western Europe, see Burnham, *The Current Crisis,* pp. 183–89.

168. See U.S. Census Bureau Reports cited in footnote 167, Table A.

169. Harris Polls, discussed in John C. Pierce, Kathleen M. Beatty, and Paul R. Hagner, *The Dynamics of American Public Opinion: Patterns and Processes* (Glenview, Ill.: Scott, Foresman, 1982), p. 214.

170. Ibid.

171. Poll by Center for Political Studies, cited in ibid., p. 212.

172. Warren E. Miller and the National Election Studies, *American National Election Study, 1980* (Ann Arbor: Inter-University Consortium for Political and Social Research, 1982), vol. 1, pp. 220–21.

173. Harris Poll, reported in Pierce, et al., *Dynamics of American Public Opinion,* p. 211.

174. Ibid.

175. Ibid., p. 212.

176. Miller and the National Election Studies, *American National Election Study, 1980,* p. 220.

177. Poll by Patrick Caddell, reported in Conference on Alternative State and Local Policies, *The Issues of 1982,* p. 211.

178. From a Gallup Poll in March 1980, in *The Gallup Poll: Public Opinion 1980* (Wilmington: Scholarly Resources, 1981), pp. 65–66.

179. Ibid., p. 65.

180. See S. Prakash Sethi, "Grassroots Lobbying and the Corporation," *Business and Society Review,* no. 29 (Spring 1979), p. 8, cited in Edward S. Herman, *Corporate Control, Corporate Power* (New York: Cambridge University Press, 1981), pp. 384–85.

181. Ibid.

182. *New York Times,* 29 April 1983, p. A16.

183. Elizabeth Drew, "Politics and Money," *New Yorker,* 6 December 1982, p. 60.

184. *New York Times,* 29 April 1983, p. A16.
185. *New York Times,* 29 September 1982, p. A25, reporting on a study by the Citizen-Labor Energy Coalition.
186. Ibid.
187. Drew, "Politics and Money," p. 122.
188. *New York Times,* 18 January 1979, p. A19.
189. Steven D. Lydenberg and Alice Tepper Marlin, "Business and Votes," *New York Times,* 27 October 1982, p. 27. Cf. also Steven D. Lydenberg and Susan Young, "Business Bankrolls for Local Ballots," *Business and Society Review,* no. 33 (Spring 1980), pp. 51–55.
190. Drew, "Politics and Money," p. 68. Cf. also *New York Times,* 5 November 1982, p. A1; *Washington Post,* 12 September 1982, p. H1; and *Business Week,* 8 November 1982, p. 49, for discussion of money and close races.
191. Between 1958 and 1978, union membership as a percentage of total labor force dropped from 24.2 percent to 19.7 percent. See AFL-CIO Department of Research, *Union Membership and Employment 1959–1979,* February 1980, p. I-11.
192. See ibid., and Magaziner and Reich, *Minding America's Business,* p. 146.
193. *Union Membership and Employment,* pp. I-5, I-11.
194. National Labor Relations Board, *Thirty-Fifth Annual Report for the Fiscal Year Ended June 30, 1970* (Washington, D.C.: U.S. Government Printing Office, 1970), Table 3A; and idem, *Forty-Fifth Annual Report for the Year Ended September 30, 1980* (Washington, D.C.: U.S. Government Printing Office, 1980), Table 3A.
195. See George Ruben, "Collective Bargaining in 1982: Results Dictated by Economy," *Monthly Labor Review,* vol. 66, no. 1 (January 1983), p. 28.
196. "Current Labor Statistics," in ibid., Table 35.
197. *Report of the Secretary of Defense on the FY 1984 Budget* (Washington, D.C.: U.S. Government Printing Office, 1983), Table II.A.4. The five-year program calls for $1.768 trillion in obligational authority, $1.553 trillion in outlays.
198. Unfortunately, the 1984 Department of Defense Report does not contain any estimates of price inflation for the years after 1985. We have, therefore, simply assumed a constant rate of 3.6 percent, the figure used in the report for 1984 (see ibid.,

Appendix B, Table 1). On the figure for 1987, see the FY 1983 report cited in note 35, Table I.A.1.

199. *Report of the Secretary of Defense on the FY 1984 Budget,* Chart II.A.2, Table II.A.4; *Report of the Secretary of Defense on the FY 1983 Budget,* Table IV.E.1.

200. *Wall Street Journal,* 31 January 1983, p. 3; and *Report of the Secretary of Defense on the FY 1983 Budget,* Table IV.G.1.

201. *Boston Globe,* 24 May 1981.

202. Seymour Melman, "Looting the Means of Production," *New York Times,* 26 July 1981, p. E21.

203. In 1980 the "income deficit," or amount of money required to bring all American families and unrelated individuals up to the poverty line, was $19.3 billion. See U.S. Bureau of the Census, Current Population Reports, ser. P-60, no. 133, Table 6.

204. Here we follow estimates by William Kaufmann, "The Defense Budget," in *Setting National Priorities: The 1983 Budget,* ed. Joseph Pechman (Washington, D.C.: The Brookings Institution, 1982), Table 3-7.

205. The calculation here has several aspects: (1) We are assuming that the yield of the Hiroshima bomb was 12.5 kilotons, following calculations by L. Penny, D.E.J. Samuels, and G. C. Scorgie, "The Nuclear Explosive Yields at Hiroshima and Nagasaki," *Philosophical Transactions of the Royal Society of London,* 1970, A266, p. 357; (2) the figure of 3,000 warheads is a slightly low, rounded estimate, based on the assumption that 55 percent of U.S. submarines are on "day-to-day alert," and that all submarine-launched ballistic missiles have a 0.8 probability of penetrating to their targets. Thus, 6,880 warheads would deliver an attack of 3,050 warheads; (3) we are assuming that all 3,000 warheads have 125 kiloton yields; (4) for yields (y) below one metagon, the rule of thumb is to take $(y^{2/3})$ to find the "megaton equivalent." Each 125-kiloton warhead is equivalent to 0.25 megatons, and 3,000 warheads are therefore equivalent to 750 megatons. Each Hiroshima bomb, by contrast, is equivalent to 0.054 megatons, and 1,000 such bombs are equivalent to 54 megatons.

206. *Report of the Secretary of Defense on the FY 1984 Budget,* Appendix B, Table 2, Comparing General Purpose and Strategic Forces.

207. For discussion of the details of the fiscal 1983 proposals, see

Kaufmann, "The Defense Budget"; and Michael Klare, "The Weinberger Revolution," *Inquiry*, September 1982, reprinted by the Institute for Policy Studies, Washington, D.C.

208. On Iran, see recollections by Kermit Roosevelt, *Countercoup* (New York: McGraw-Hill, 1979); and the brief account by Ervand Abrahamian, *Iran Between the Two Revolutions* (Princeton: Princeton University Press, 1982), pp. 279–80. On Guatemala, see Steven Schlesinger and Steven Kinzer, *Bitter Fruit* (Garden City: Doubleday, 1982). On Brazil, see Gayle Hudsons Watson, "Our Monster in Brazil: It All Began with Brother Sam," *Nation* 224, 15 January 1977, pp. 51–54; Jan Knippers Black, *United States Penetration of Brazil* (Philadelphia: University of Pennsylvania Press, 1977); and A. J. Langguth, *Hidden Terrors* (New York: Pantheon, 1978). On Chile, see U.S. Senate, *Hearings Before the Select Committee to Study Governmental Operations with Respect to Intelligence Activities,* 94th Congress, vol. 7, 4 and 5 December 1975 (Washington, D.C.: U.S. Government Printing Office, 1976), p. 96; and Seymour Hersh, "The Price of Power," *Atlantic Monthly*, December 1982, pp. 41–43. On Nicaragua and other current operations, see *Newsweek,* 8 November 1982, pp. 42–55.

209. See U.S. Senate, *Alleged Assassination Plots Involving Foreign Leaders,* Report No. 94-465, Select Committee to Study Government Intelligence Activities, 84th Congress, 1st Session, November 1975, (Washington, D.C.: U.S. Government Printing Office, 1975), p. 75.

210. Barry M. Blechman and Steven S. Kaplan, *Force Without War* (Washington, D.C.: Brookings Institution, 1978). For a discussion of the incidents involving strategic nuclear forces, see pp. 47 ff. Blechman and Kaplan define "force without war" as follows: "A political use of the armed forces occurs when physical actions are taken by one or more components of the uniformed military services as part of a deliberate attempt by national authorities to influence, or be prepared to influence, specific behavior of individuals in another nation without engaging in a continuing contest of violence" (p. 12).

211. See William Shawcross, *Sideshow* (New York: Simon & Schuster, 1979), pp. 211, 272, 297; *Boston Globe,* 23 March 1973, p. 1.

212. The list is taken from Noam Chomsky and Edward S. Herman,

The Political Economy of Human Rights (Boston: South End Press, 1979), vol. 1, frontispiece, and p. 361, notes 1 and 2. See also Michael Klare, *Supplying Repression* (New York: Field Foundation, 1977); Penny Lernoux, *Cry of the People* (New York: Penguin, 1982); Lars Schoultz, *Human Rights and United States Policy towards Latin America* (Princeton: Princeton University Press, 1981); Langguth, *Hidden Terrors;* and, in general, individual country reports and the annual reports of Amnesty International.

213. Americas Watch, Helsinki Watch, Lawyers Committee for International Human Rights, *The Reagan Administration's Human Rights Policy: A Mid-Term Review,* New York, 10 December 1982, p. 1.

214. On U.S. aid, see ibid., pp. 33–34; and U.S. Senate, *Fiscal Year 1983 Security Assistance,* Hearings Before the Committee on Foreign Relations, 97th Congress, Second Session, 14, 15, and 16 April 1982 (Washington, D.C.: U.S. Government Printing Office, 1982), pp. 61 ff.

215. Amnesty International, *Pakistan: Human Rights Violations and the Decline of the Rule of Law* (London: Amnesty International Publications, 1982), p. 1; see also pp. 32 ff. on "Torture, Flogging, Amputation, and Stoning to Death."

216. "Openness and warmth" was the phrase used by administration officials. See Americas Watch et al., *The Reagan Administration's Human Rights Policy,* p. 34. The remark on torture is made in Amnesty International, *Pakistan,* p. 32.

217. U.S. Senate, *Fiscal Year 1983 Security Assistance,* pp. 61–63, 123.

218. Americas Watch et al., *The Reagan Administration's Human Rights Policy,* p. 50; Amnesty International, *Amnesty International Report 1982* (London: Amnesty International Publications, 1982), pp. 294–96.

219. For a discussion of the new constitution, see *Times* (London), 15 September 1982, p. 7.

220. Amnesty International, *Report 1982,* p. 295.

221. This is noted in Americas Watch et al., *The Reagan Administration's Human Rights Policy,* p. 50.

222. On the purchase of equipment, see Flora Montealegre and Cynthia Aronson, "Background Information on Guatemala, Human Rights, and U.S. Military Assistance," Institute for Policy

Studies Resource, Update No. 1, July 1982, Charts I, II. The report also considers U.S. AID assistance and economic assistance from multilateral lending institutions in which the United States plays a central role. Also see *New York Times,* 19 December 1982, p. A1. On the government program of torture and murder, see Amnesty International, *Guatemala: A Government Program of Political Murder* (London: Amnesty International Publications, 1981). In considering the more recent history of Guatemala, it is important to be attentive to the background discussed in Schlesinger and Kinzer, *Bitter Fruit,* especially ch. 15, and Lernoux, *Cry of the People,* pp. 185 ff.

223. Amnesty International, *Report 1982,* pp. 142–43. For more recent material, see Americas Watch, *Human Rights in Guatemala: No Neutrals Allowed* (New York, 1982), pp. 38–39, where it is said that as of September 1982, "torture, multilation, rape and burning of Indians, including burning alive, are methods commonly used by the army."

224. For a full discussion, see Americas Watch, *Human Rights in Guatemala:* "Our close examination of the decrees promulgated by President Rios Montt since the March 23 coup persuades us that the Guatemalan Government has overtly abandoned the rule of law and that it has overtly substituted a system of government that is both despotic and totalitarian" (p. 3). They add that "the decrees of the government abolish virtually all the rights of Guatemalans." For criticism of U.S. government reporting on human rights in Guatemala, see ibid., ch. 5.

225. Amnesty International, press release, 11 October 1982. The Guatemalan Commission for Human Rights puts the number at 8,000, according to Americas Watch, *Human Rights in Guatemala,* p. 13.

226. Americas Watch, *Human Rights in Guatemala,* pp. 49–53.

227. Americas Watch et al., *The Reagan Administration's Human Rights Policy,* pp. 2, 25; *Boston Globe,* 6 December 1982; Anthony Lewis, "Howdy, Genghis," *New York Times,* 6 December 1982, p. A23.

228. Quoted in Walden Bello, David Kinley, and Elaine Elinson, *Development Debacle: The World Bank in the Philippines* (San Francisco: Institute for Food and Development Policy), pp. 1–2.

229. Amnesty International, *Report 1982,* pp. 118–22; Americas

Watch et al., *The Reagan Administration's Human Rights Policy,* pp. 17–19; *New York Times,* 6 December 1982, p. A1.

230.   Americas Watch et al., *The Reagan Administration's Human Rights Policy,* pp. 2, 17–19.

231.   For sources and discussion see *New York Times,* 30 May 1982, p. 1; Michael Klare, "The Weinberger Revolution"; idem, "Reviving the American Century," *Inquiry,* May 1982, reprinted by the Institute for Policy Studies, Washington, D.C.; Theodore Draper, "Dear Mr. Weinberger," *New York Review of Books,* 4 November 1982, p. 26 ff.

232.   Harris Poll reported in Conference on Alternative State and Local Policies, *The Issues of 1982,* p. 211.

233.   U.S. Department of Justice, Criminal Division, *Report to Congress on the Activities and Operations of the Public Integrity Section for 1981* (Washington, D.C.: U.S. Government Printing Office, 1982), Table 11.

234.   Ibid.

235.   For a complete list of individuals and corporations found guilty of criminal violations for the Watergate coverup, the Fielding break-in, campaign violations, President Nixon's tax returns, and the Watergate break-in itself, see *The Final Report of the Watergate Special Prosecution Force* (Washington, D.C.: U.S. Government Printing Office, 1977), pp. 43 ff.

236.   In many of the cases cited in the next few paragraphs, the disclosure came through requests under the Freedom of Information Act. A study of 500 disclosures is provided in Evan Hendricks, *Former Secrets* (Washington, D.C.: Campaign for Political Rights, 1982). In the compilation, Hendricks indicates who made the request and where the disclosed information was first published. We will cite the Hendricks study (hereafter abbreviated as *FS*) rather than the places of publication themselves.

237.   Frank J. Donner, *The Age of Surveillance: The Aims and Methods of America's Political Intelligence System* (New York: Alfred A. Knopf, 1980), p. 169.

238.   Ibid., p. 127.

239.   Ibid.

240.   Ibid., p. 137.

241.   Ibid., pp. 270 ff. In a recent case (September 1982) concerning Operation CHAOS (Halkin v. Helms), the U.S. Court of Appeals

for the District of Columbia held that targets of CHAOS are not entitled to learn the specifics of the operation. Thus, much about this operation will probably remain unknown. For a brief discussion, see Campaign for Political Rights, *Organizing Notes*, vol. 7, no. 1 (January–February 1983), p. 6.

242. Donner, *Age of Surveillance*, p. 153.

243. *FS*, pp. 157, 172, 185. Joan Baez was an object of National Security Agency (NSA) surveillance. For an account of the NSA, see James Bamford, *The Puzzle Palace: A Report on America's Most Secret Agency* (Boston: Houghton Mifflin, 1982), especially ch. 6. It should not go unmentioned that another popular entertainer, Elvis Presley, volunteered to become an FBI informant in 1970. He was turned down. See *FS*, p. 173.

244. For Hoover's memo, see Christy Macy and Susan Kaplan, *Documents* (New York: Penguin, 1980), p. 80. Other documents concerning FBI worries about the "Exploitation of the women's movement by Socialist Worker's Party," are also in ibid., pp. 30–33. For further FBI material, see U.S. Senate, *Intelligence Activities*, Hearings Before the Select Committee to Study Governmental Operations with Respect to Intelligence Activities, 94th Congress, 1st Session, vol. 6, November–December 1975 (Washington, D.C.: U.S. Government Printing Office, 1976), Exhibits 7, 54-1, 54-2, 54-3.

245. Donner, *Age of Surveillance*, p. 131; *Intelligence Activities*, Senate Hearings, p. 23, and Exhibit 13.

246. Donner, *Age of Surveillance*, p. 212; *Intelligence Activities*, Senate Hearings, Exhibit 11.

247. Donner, *Age of Surveillance*, pp. 222–23. For typical documents, see Macy and Kaplan, *Documents*, pp. 116, 183.

248. See *Intelligence Activities*, Exhibit 10. These operations were together called "factionalization."

249. For several examples, see Macy and Kaplan, *Documents*, ch. 7.

250. *Intelligence Activities*, Senate Hearings, Exhibit 19-1.

251. Ibid.

252. Ibid., Exhibit 19-2.

253. Donner, *Age of Surveillance*, p. 217.

254. Macy and Kaplan, p. 180.

255. Ibid.

256. On the FBI's planned role for Samuel Pierce, see Victor Navasky, "The FBI's Wildest Dream," *Nation*, 17 June 1978. On the

accusation of racism, see *Boston Globe,* 12 July 1982, p. 7.

257. For a full treatment of the "missile gap," see Desmond Ball, *Politics and Force Levels* (Berkeley: University of California Press, 1980); Fred Kaplan, *The Wizards of Armageddon* (New York: Simon & Schuster, 1983), chs. 10 and 19.

258. These figures, published by journalist Joseph Alsop, are reported in Ball, *Politics and Force Levels,* p. 7.

259. Kaplan, *Wizards of Armageddon,* ch. 19.

260. Ibid.

261. For discussion, see Ball, *Politics and Force Levels,* pp. 91 ff. McNamara gave a press briefing on 6 February 1961 which indicated that there was no missile gap, but the administration subsequently retracted the admission, and it was not until the fall of 1961 that it was officially acknowledged that no gap existed.

262. On the Gulf of Tonkin incident, see Eugene G. Windchy, *Tonkin Gulf* (New York: Doubleday, 1971); Joseph C. Goulden, *Truth Is the First Casualty: The Gulf of Tonkin Affair—Illusion and Reality* (New York: Rand McNally, 1969). Early skepticism about the "incident" was expressed in I. F. Stone's 24 August 1964 newsletter story, "What Few People Know About the Gulf of Tonkin Incidents," reprinted in I. F. Stone, *In a Time of Torment* (New York: Random House, 1967), pp. 195–203. Leslie Gelb notes that drafts of the resolution were prepared before the events in the Gulf of Tonkin. See Leslie H. Gelb, *The Irony of Vietnam: The System Worked* (Washington, D.C.: The Brookings Institution, 1979), pp. 103–4.

263. Reported in David Halberstam, *The Best and the Brightest* (New York: Random House, 1969), p. 503.

264. Ibid.

265. For discussion of administration views on escalation, see *The Pentagon Papers: The Defense Department History of United States Decisionmaking on Vietnam,* Senator Gravel, ed. (Boston: Beacon Press, 1971), vol. 3, pp. 107–8, 149–206. For discussion of February 1964 escalation of covert action against North Vietnam under so-called OPLAN-34A, see ibid., pp. 149–52.

266. U.S. Senate, *Hearing Before the Select Committee to Study Governmental Operations with Respect to Intelligence Activities,* vol. 7, p. 96. The remarks quoted are from Richard Helms's "handwritten notes" from a meeting with President Nixon on

15 September 1970. For discussion of these "notes," see Hersh, "The Price of Power," pp. 41–43. Hersh offers powerful evidence that Helms in fact was ordered to "get rid of Allende" (p. 43).

267. U.S. Senate, *Alleged Assassination Plots,* p. 228, citing Cable 236 from CIA Headquarters to the Santiago station of the CIA, 21 September 1970.

268. See U.S. Senate, *Hearings Before the Select Committee to Study Governmental Operations with Respect to Intelligence Activities,* vol. 7, Appendix A; and Hersh, "The Price of Power," p. 57. The quotations are from National Security Decision Memorandum 93 (NSDM-93), cited by Hersh. U.S. economic assistance from the Agency for International Development and Food for Peace totaled $50.4 million in 1969, dropped to an average of $6 million per year between 1971 and 1973, and then increased 15-fold, to $93.7 million in 1975 after the successful coup. See Schoultz, *Human Rights and United States Policy towards Latin America,* p. 172.

269. Hersh, "The Price of Power," p. 58. The quotation comes from material deleted from the Church Committee's public report, as does the discussion of the CIA role in collecting information needed for a coup.

270. Quotation from NSDM-93, cited in Hersh, p. 57.

271. William Greider, *The Education of David Stockman and Other Americans* (New York: E. P. Dutton, 1982), p. 33.

272. See Campaign for Political Rights, *Organizing Notes,* vol. 6, no. 4 (May 1982), p. 3.

273. *New York Times,* 10 August 1982, p. A13.

274. Campaign for Political Rights, *Organizing Notes,* vol. 6, no. 2 (March 1982), pp. 6–7; Working Committee on the CIA/FBI Order, "Suspending the Constitution" (Washington, D.C.: General Board of Church and Society, 1982).

275. See Campaign for Political Rights, *Organizing Notes,* vol. 6, no. 5 (June–July 1982), p. 3 for analysis.

276. All the cases cited here can be found in *FS.*

CHAPTER 3

1. Throughout the following discussion of capitalist democracy, we draw on the work of Adam Przeworksi. See especially Adam Przeworski, "Proletariat into a Class: The Process of Class Formation from Karl Kautsky's *The Class Struggle* to Recent Controversies," *Politics and Society*, vol. 7 (1977), pp. 343–403; idem, "Material Bases of Consent: Economics and Politics in a Hegemonic System," *Political Power and Social Theory*, vol. 1 (1980), pp. 21–66; and Adam Przeworski and Michael Waller-stein, "The Structure of Class Conflict in Democratic Capitalist Societies," *American Political Science Review*, vol. 76 (1982), pp. 215–38.

2. The point of course was first made forcefully by Marx. See Karl Marx and Frederick Engels, *The German Ideology*, in Karl Marx and Frederick Engels, *Collected Works*, vol. 5 (New York: International Publishers, 1976). See as well Antonio Gramsci, *Selections from the Prison Notebooks*, ed. and trans. Quintin Hoare and Geoffrey Nowell Smith (New York: International Publishers, 1971). Gramsci notes: "But the development and expansion of the particular group are conceived of, and presented, as being the motor force of universal expansion, of a development of all the 'national' energies" (p. 182). The point has been under-scored more recently by Charles Lindblom in remarks on the "privileged position of business." See Charles E. Lindblom, *Politics and Markets: The World's Political-Economic Systems* (New York: Basic Books, 1977), especially ch. 13.

3. See Claus Offe and Helmut Wiesenthal, "Two Logics of Collective Action: Theoretical Notes on Social Class and Organizational Form," *Political Power and Social Theory*, vol. 1 (1980), pp. 67–116.

4. The generation of such compromises within capitalist democracy is usefully explored in Antonio Gramsci, *Selections from the Prison Notebooks*. He remarks there, for example: "[T]he dominant group is coordinated concretely with the general interests

of the subordinate groups, and the life of the State is conceived of as a continuous process of formation and superseding of unstable equilibria (on the juridical plane) between the interests of the fundamental group and the interests of the subordinate groups—equilibria in which the interests of the dominant group prevail, but only up to a certain point, i.e. stopping short of narrowly corporate economic interest" (p. 182). See as well Przeworski, "The Material Bases of Consent," and Przeworski and Wallerstein, "The Structure of Class Conflict." In the text we will commonly refer to such compromises as "accords." We take the term from Samuel Bowles and Herbert Gintis, "The Crisis of Liberal Democratic Capitalism: The Case of the United States," *Politics and Society,* vol. 11 (1982), pp. 51–94.

5. In the discussion of the resource constraint, different parts of the argument draw on Randall Bartlett, *Economic Foundations of Political Power* (New York: The Free Press, 1973); Anthony Downs, *An Economic Theory of Democracy* (New York: Harper & Row, 1957); Lindblom, *Politics and Markets;* and Mancur Olson, *The Logic of Collective Action: Public Goods and the Theory of Groups* (Cambridge: Harvard University Press, 1965). For a short treatment of problems of information and collective action similar to the one developed here, see Hans Peter Widmaier, Jürgen Frank, and Otto Roloff, "Public Expenditure and Private Consumption," in European Cultural Foundation, *The Future Is Tomorrow* (The Hague: Martinus Nijhoff, 1975), pp. 348–68.

6. The term is associated with Marx. See Karl Marx, *Capital,* vol. 1, trans. Ben Fowkes (Middlesex: Penguin, 1976), pp. 159–63.

7. Recent philosophical discussion of deliberation about ends has often been tied to consideration of Aristotle's views on practical reasoning. For a useful account of such deliberation which is attentive to the problem of specifying the ends of action, see David Wiggins, "Deliberation and Practical Reason," in Amélie Oksenberg Rorty, ed., *Essays on Aristotle's Ethics* (Berkeley: University of California Press, 1980), pp. 221–40.

8. On a notorious case of regime instability in a capitalist democracy, analyzed within a framework similar to that developed here, see David Abraham, *The Collapse of the Weimar Republic: Political Economy and Crisis* (Princeton: Princeton University Press, 1981).

9. Lester Thurow has recently argued for the partial applicability

of these conditions to the United States. See Lester C. Thurow, *The Zero Sum Society: Distribution and the Possibilities for Economic Change* (New York: Basic Books, 1980).

CHAPTER 4

1. In developing the overall line of argument of this section, we found several books and articles particularly helpful, even in those cases where we disagreed with them both in general and in detail. See Michel Aglietta, *A Theory of Capitalist Regulation,* trans. David Fernbach (London: New Left Books, 1979); Samuel Bowles and Herbert Gintis, "The Crisis of Liberal-Democratic Capitalism"; Robert Boyer and J. Mistral, *Accumulation, Inflation, Crises* (Paris: P.U.F., 1978); David M. Gordon, "Stages of Accumulation and Long Economic Cycles," in Terence Hopkins and Immanuel Wallerstein, eds., *Processes of the World System* (Beverly Hills: Sage Publications, 1980); Ernest Mandel, *Late Capitalism,* trans. Joris De Bres (London: New Left Books, 1975); and more immediately, Thomas Weisskopf, "The Current Economic Crisis in Historical Perspective," *Socialist Review,* vol. 11, no. 3 (May–June 1981), pp. 9–53.

2. There are any number of general accounts of the Bretton Woods system. For useful discussions, see Richard Gardner, *Sterling-Dollar Diplomacy* (New York: McGraw-Hill, 1969), and Fred L. Block, *The Origins of International Economic Disorder: A Study of United States International Monetary Policy from World War II to the Present* (Berkeley: University of California Press, 1977).

3. There is an enormous literature on the post–New Deal labor movement. For useful accounts, see Stanley Aronowitz, *False Promises: The Shaping of American Working-Class Consciousness* (New York: McGraw-Hill, 1973); Irving Bernstein, *Turbulent Years: A History of the American Worker, 1933–1941* (Boston: Houghton Mifflin, 1971); Richard Edwards, *Contested Terrain: The Transformation of the Workplace in the Twentieth Century* (New York: Basic Books, 1979); James R. Green, *The World of the Worker: Labor in Twentieth-Century America* (New York: Hill & Wang, 1980); Clark Kerr, *Labor Markets and Wage Determination: The Balkanization of Labor Markets and Other Essays*

(Berkeley: University of California Press, 1977); David Mont-gomery, *Workers' Control in America: Studies in the History of Work, Technology, and Labor Struggles* (Cambridge: Cambridge University Press, 1979); Albert G. Rees, *The Economics of Trade Unions* (Chicago: University of Chicago Press, 1962); and Sumner H. Slichter, *Union Policies and Industrial Management* (Washington, D.C.: The Brookings Institution, 1941). A particularly illuminating discussion is offered by David M. Gordon, Richard Edwards, and Michael Reich, *Segmented Work, Divided Workers: The Historical Transformation of Labor in the United States* (Cambridge: Cambridge University Press, 1982). For an excellent recent overview especially attentive to the declining political power of labor, see Mike Davis, "Why the U.S. Working Class is Different," *New Left Review*, no. 123 (September–October 1980), pp. 3–46; and idem, "The Barren Marriage of American Labour and the Democratic Party," *New Left Review*, no. 124 (November–December 1980), pp. 43–84.

4. All quotations are from NSC-68, published in U.S. Department of State, *Foreign Relations of the United States 1950* (Washington, D.C.: U.S. Government Printing Office, 1977), vol. 1, pp. 235–92. See p. 285 for recommendations, including the call for a "substantial increase" in military spending.

5. Calculated from *ER*, Table B-1.

6. For further discussion, see Herman, *Corporate Control, Corporate Power*, ch. 5; Theodore J. Lowi and Alan Stone, eds., *Nationalizing Government* (Beverly Hills: Sage Publications, 1978); George Stigler, *The Citizen and the State* (Chicago: University of Chicago Press, 1978); Alan Stone, *Economic Regulation and the Public Interest* (Ithaca: Cornell University Press, 1977); and James Q. Wilson, ed., *The Politics of Regulation* (New York: Basic Books, 1980).

7. Gabriel Kolko, *Main Currents in Modern American History* (New York: Harper & Row, 1976), p. 317.

8. Federal Reserve Board, *Flow of Funds Accounts,* various issues, cited in Harry Magdoff and Paul Sweezy, "Financial Stability: Where Will It All End?" *Monthly Review*, vol. 34, no. 6 (November 1982), p. 19.

9. U.S. Bureau of the Census, *Historical Statistics of the United States, Colonial Times to 1970* (Washington, D.C.: Government

Printing Office, 1975), ser. P-119, W-22, F-25, cited in Gordon, Edwards, and Reich, *Segmented Work,* p. 168.

10. Bowles and Gintis, "The Crisis of Liberal-Democratic Capitalism," p. 78.

11. Calculated from *ER,* Table B-29.

12. For data on unemployment rates and levels of output through the century, see *The Statistical History of the United States: From Colonial Times to the Present* (New York: Basic Books, 1976), Table D85-86, ser. F1-5.

13. Ernest Mandel, *Late Capitalism,* p. 142.

14. U.S. Bureau of the Census, *Statistical Abstract of the United States,* 101st ed. (Washington, D.C.: U.S. Government Printing Office, 1982), p. 796.

15. On the automobile industry, see Emma Rothschild, *Paradise Lost: The Decline of the Auto-Industrial Age* (New York: Random House, 1973).

16. Harry Magdoff and Paul M. Sweezy, "The Deepening Crisis of U.S. Capitalism," *Monthly Review,* vol. 33, no. 5 (October 1981), p. 12.

17. Walt Whitman Rostow, *The World Economy: History and Prospect* (Austin: University of Texas Press, 1978), pp. 248–49, Table III-53.

18. Riccardo Parboni, *The Dollar and Its Rivals,* trans. Jon Rothschild (London: New Left Books, 1981), p. 110.

19. For our account of the dynamics of U.S. decline and monetary response, we are especially indebted to Gerald Epstein, "Domestic Stagflation and Monetary Policy: The Federal Reserve and the Hidden Election," in Thomas Ferguson and Joel Rogers, eds., *The Hidden Election* (New York: Pantheon, 1981), pp. 141–95; and to Riccardo Parboni, *The Dollar and Its Rivals.*

20. Epstein, "Domestic Stagflation," p. 144.

21. Parboni, *The Dollar and Its Rivals,* pp. 92–93, Tables 9, 10, 11.

22. Ibid., p. 93, Table 12.

23. See William H. Branson and Helen B. Junz, "Trends in U.S. Trade and Comparative Advantage," *Brookings Papers on Economic Activity,* 2 (Washington, D.C.: The Brookings Institution, 1971), pp. 285–338.

24. See Robert Triffin, *Gold and the Dollar Crisis: The Future of Convertibility* (New Haven: Yale University Press, 1961).

25. On the declining gold stock and other problems in the U.S. position, see generally Stephen V. O. Clarke, "Perspective on the United States External Position since World War II," *Federal Reserve Bank of New York Quarterly Review* 5 (Summer 1980), cited in Epstein, "Domestic Stagflation," p. 148.

26. Clarke, "Perspective on the United States External Position," p. 23, cited in Epstein, "Domestic Stagflation," p. 152.

27. Ibid.

28. For a useful general discussion of employment policy in the United States, see Richard B. DuBoff, "Full Employment: The History of the Receding Target," *Politics and Society,* vol. 7, no. 1 (1977), pp. 1–25.

29. *ER,* Table B-29.

30. Kenneth Flamm, "Explaining U.S. Multinationals in the Postwar Era," unpublished manuscript, Table 2.

31. Ibid., Table 3.

32. See generally U.S. Senate, Foreign Relations Committee, Subcommittee on Foreign Economic Policy Staff Report, *International Debt, the Banks and U.S. Foreign Policy* (Washington, D.C. Government Printing Office, 1977).

33. For a broadly parallel account, see Mary Kaldor, *Baroque Arsenal* (New York: Hill & Wang, 1981), especially pp. 65–78.

34. For discussions of strategy, see William W. Kaufman, *The McNamara Strategy* (New York: Harper & Row, 1964); Jerome Kahan, *Security in the Nuclear Age* (Washington, D.C.: The Brookings Institution, 1975), ch. 2; and Kaplan, *The Wizards of Armageddon.* In the period 1957–66, U.S. manufacturing investment in Latin America grew 213 percent; in Asia, 563 percent. See Flamm, "Explaining U.S. Multinationals," Table 4.

35. *ER,* Table B-1.

36. U.S. Senate, Foreign Relations Committee, "Security Agreements and Commitments Abroad," 91st Congress, Second Session, 21 December 1970, p. 3, cited in Edward S. Herman, "Military Spending: The Last Externality?," unpublished manuscript.

37. The material in this paragraph is based on Blechman and Kaplan, *Force Without War.* See Appendix B for a list of all incidents of "force without war," p. 103 on Venezuela, and pp. 47 ff. for a discussion of cases involving "nuclear threats."

38. Bureau of the Budget, *U.S. Budget in Brief Fiscal Year 1970* (Washington, D.C.: Government Printing Office, 1969), p. 23.

39. In 1970 the United States spent 7.9 percent of its GNP on defense, while Germany spent 3.3 percent and Japan 0.8 percent. See U.S. Bureau of the Census, *Statistical Abstract of the United States 1980,* 101st ed., p. 924. On U.S. expenditures on research and development, see U.S. Senate, *Research and Development in the United States: The Role of the Public and Private Sectors,* Hearings before the Subcommittee on Energy, Nuclear Proliferation, and Government Processes, 97th Congress, Second Session, 9 March 1982 (Washington, D.C.: U.S. Government Printing Office, 1982), pp. 51–65. In 1971 the U.S. government spent 0.73 percent of U.S. GDP on defense research and development, while West Germany spent 0.16 percent and Japan spent no public money. See Organization for Economic Cooperation and Development, *Science and Technology Indicators* (Paris: OECD, 1981).

40. For a general discussion, see Seymour Melman, *Pentagon Capitalism: The Political Economy of War* (New York: McGraw-Hill, 1970); idem, *The Permanent War Economy: American Capitalism in Decline* (New York: Simon & Schuster, 1974).

41. On the structure and performance of the defense sector, see Jacques Gansler, *The Defense Industry* (Cambridge: M.I.T. Press, 1980). According to Gansler, "less than 8 percent [of defense contract money] is awarded solely on the basis of price-competition" (p. 2).

42. See ibid., pp. 15 ff. on rising unit costs; Kaldor, *Baroque Arsenal* for general discussion; and James Fallows, *National Defense* (New York: Random House, 1981) for some useful illustrations.

43. U.S. Bureau of the Census, *Statistical Abstract of the United States 1974,* 95th ed. (Washington, D.C.: U.S. Government Printing Office, 1975), p. 246.

44. U.S. Office of Management and Budget, *Special Analyses, Budget of the United States Government, Fiscal Year 1970* (Washington, D.C.: U.S. Government Printing Office, 1969), Part II; idem, *Special Analyses, Budget of the United States Government, Fiscal Year 1975* (Washington, D.C.: U.S. Government Printing Office, 1974), Part II.

45. *ER,* Table B-29.

46. Ibid., Table B-34.

47. On increases in unit labor costs, see *ER,* Table B-41, figures for private business sector. For increasing strike levels in the late

1960s, see U.S. Bureau of the Census, *Statistical Abstract of the United States 1980,* p. 431. On particular wildcat strikes and labor militancy, see Samuel Friedman, *Teamster Rank and File* (New York: Columbia University Press, 1982), ch. 7; James A. Geschwender, *Class, Race, and Worker Insurgency* (Cambridge: Cambridge University Press, 1977); and Aronowitz, *False Promises,* for a discussion of Lordstown.

48. See Harvard Sitkoff, *The Struggle for Black Equality 1954–1980* (New York: Hill & Wang, 1981), pp. 197–204.

49. See Helen M. Ingram and Dean E. Mann, "Environmental Policy: From Innovation to Implementation," in Lowi and Stone, *Nationalizing Government,* pp. 131–62.

50. James E. Anderson, "Economic Regulatory and Consumer Protection Policies," in ibid., pp. 61–84.

51. Andrew B. Dunham and Theodore Marmor, "Federal Policy and Health: Recent Trends and Differing Perspectives," in ibid., pp. 263–98.

52. List provided by Walter Dean Burnham.

53. Samuel Bowles and Herbert Gintis, "The Crisis of Liberal Democratic Capitalism," manuscript version (1980), p. 48.

54. Ibid., p. 51.

55. Ibid.

56. Ibid.

57. On wage share of income in manufacturing, see Jeffrey Sachs, "Wages, Profits and Macroeconomic Adjustment: A Comparative Study," *Brookings Papers on Economic Activity* 2 (1979), pp. 269–332, cited in Epstein, "Domestic Stagflation."

58. On the Kennedy Round, see Thomas Bradford Curtis, *The Kennedy Round and the Future of American Trade* (New York: Praeger, 1967).

59. U.S. Department of Commerce, *Survey of Current Business,* for various years.

60. *ER,* Table B-39. The movement is more complicated than indicated in the text, but the point remains. Gross weekly earnings increased sharply between 1970 and 1972, but fell in 1975 back to 1966 levels. In the following upswing they did not quite regain 1969 levels, and by the end of 1982 were below 1962 levels.

61. For a summary of the relevant facts, see Institute for Labor Education and Research, *What's Wrong with the U.S. Economy?,* pp. 339–47.

62. On tax incidence generally, see Joseph A. Pechman and Benjamin A. Okner, *Who Bears The Tax Burden?* (Washington, D.C.: The Brookings Institution, 1974) and Benjamin A. Okner, "Total U.S. Taxes and Their Effect on the Distribution of Family Income in 1966 and 1970," in Henry J. Aaron and Michael J. Boskin, eds., *The Economics of Taxation* (Washington, D.C.: The Brookings Institution, 1980). On the regressive features of social spending financing in general, see Richard A. Musgrave and Peggy B. Musgrave, *Public Finance in Theory and Practice*, 3rd ed. (New York: McGraw-Hill, 1980).

63. Jeffrey Sachs, "Wages, Profits, and Macroeconomic Adjustment," pp. 269–332, cited in Epstein, "Domestic Stagflation," p. 160.

64. Bowles and Gintis, "The Crisis of Liberal-Democratic Capitalism," *Politics and Society,* p. 81.

65. *ER*, Table B-2.

66. See Parboni, *The Dollar and Its Rivals,* p. 126, Table 14.

67. *ER*, Table B-105.

68. James Tobin, "Stabilization Policy Ten Years After," *Brookings Papers on Economic Activity,* 1 (1980), p. 32, cited in Epstein, "Domestic Stagflation," p. 168.

69. International Monetary Fund, *Direction of Trade Statistics 1982* (Washington, D.C.: IMF, 1982), pp. 167, 224.

70. David Gisselquist, *Oil Prices and Trade Deficits: U.S. Conflicts with Japan and West Germany* (New York: Praeger, 1979), pp. 3, 5.

71. William R. Cline, "External Debt, System Vulnerability, and Development," unpublished manuscript, p. 29, Table 1.

72. Ibid.

73. Ibid., p. 22.

74. *ER*, Table B-101.

75. *ER*, Table B-101; *ER*, Table B-29. In the seven years between 1968 and 1975, for example, nonagricultural employment grew by 14.3 percent, 10 percent less than in the four years between 1975 and 1979.

76. Lester Thurow, "Solving the Productivity Problem," in *Strengthening the Economy: Studies in Productivity* (Washington, D.C.: Center for Democratic Policy, 1982), Report No. 2 in the "Alternatives for the 1980's" series, p. 13.

77. Epstein, "Domestic Stagflation," p. 176.

78. On growth of the Eurocurrency market, see *World Financial Markets,* Morgan Guaranty Trust Company, April 1981, p. 13. On the trade and growth averages, see International Monetary Fund, *Annual Report, 1980* (Washington, D.C.: IMF, 1980).
79. Paul Volcker, "The Recycling Problem Revisited," *Challenge* (July–August, 1980), cited in Epstein, "Domestic Stagflation," p. 182.
80. The facts on banking competition are all reported in Epstein, "Domestic Stagflation," pp. 179, 181.
81. Cline, "External Debt," p. 15a, Table 3.
82. Epstein, "Domestic Stagflation," p. 161.

CHAPTER 6

1. The conception of democratic order outlined in this chapter is significantly influenced by the work of John Rawls. Even where we disagree with Rawls's views, they have commonly provided a point of reference and departure in the development of our own. See in particular John Rawls, *A Theory of Justice* (Cambridge: Harvard University Press, 1971), and his more recent Dewey Lectures, "Kantian Constructivism in Moral Theory," *Journal of Philosophy,* vol. 57, no. 9 (September 1980), pp. 515–72. Always in the background, and also influencing our discussion, are the views of Rousseau, Hegel, and Marx. See Jean-Jacques Rousseau, *The Social Contract,* ed. Roger D. Masters, trans. Judith R. Masters (New York: St. Martin's Press, 1978); Rousseau, *The First and Second Discourses,* ed. Roger D. Masters, trans. Roger D. Masters and Judith R. Masters (New York: St. Martin's Press, 1964); G.W.F. Hegel, *The Philosophy of Right,* trans. T. M. Knox (Oxford: Oxford University Press, 1952); and Karl Marx, *Capital,* vol. 1, trans. Ben Fowkes (Middlesex: Penguin, 1976).
2. For particularly clear expression of concern about this issue within the socialist tradition, see Rosa Luxemburg, *The Russian Revolution* (Ann Arbor: University of Michigan Press, 1961). Luxemburg comments that "it is a well-known and indisputable fact that without a free and untrammelled press, without the unlimited right of association and assemblage, the rule of the broad mass of the people is entirely unthinkable" (pp. 66–67). She adds: "Freedom only for the supporters of the government, only

for the members of one party—however numerous they may be—is no freedom at all. Freedom is always and exclusively freedom for the one who thinks differently. Not because of any fanatical concept of 'justice' but because all that is instructive, wholesome and purifying in political freedom depends on this essential characteristic, and its effectiveness vanishes when 'freedom' becomes a special privilege" (p. 69). Recognizing the institutional conditions for this, Luxemburg concludes: "Without general elections, without unrestricted freedom of the press and assembly, without a free struggle of opinion, life dies out in every public institution, becomes a mere semblance of life, in which only the bureaucracy remains as the active element. Public life gradually falls asleep, a few dozen party leaders of inexhaustible energy and boundless experience direct and rule. Among them, in reality only a dozen outstanding heads do the leading and an elite of the working class is invited from time to time to meetings where they are to applaud the speeches of the leaders, and to approve proposed resolutions unanimously—at bottom then, a clique affair—a dictatorship, to be sure, not the dictatorship of the proletariat, however, but only the dictatorship of a handful of politicians, that is a dictatorship in the bourgeois sense, in the sense of the rule of the Jacobins. . . . Yes, we can go further: such conditions must inevitably cause a brutalization of public life: attempted assassinations, shooting of hostages, etc." (pp. 71–72). For more recent commentary in the same vein by another prominent socialist theoretician, see Nicos Poulantzas, *State, Power, Socialism,* trans. Patrick Camiller (London: New Left Books, 1978), especially Part 5.

3. On the idea of democratic legitimacy see Rousseau, *Social Contract,* Book 1, chs. 6 and 7; Book 2, chs. 1–4; and Book 4, chs. 1–2; Jürgen Habermas, *Legitimation Crisis,* trans. Thomas McCarthy (Boston: Beacon Press, 1975), Part 3, ch. 2; and idem, *Communication and the Evolution of Society,* trans. Thomas McCarthy (Boston: Beacon Press, 1979), pp. 184–88.

4. The idea of manifestness and its relation to stability has been expressed in many different ways. See Rawls, *Theory of Justice,* §29 (on publicity and stability); idem, "Kantian Constructivism," pp. 537–49; Habermas, *Communication and the Evolution of Society,* p. 186 (on "finding arrangements which can ground the presumption"); Hegel, *Philosophy of Right,* especially paras. 142–

56 (on the role of self-consciousness in Ethical Life); paras. 211–28 (on the right of self-consciousness and the rule of law); and paras. 298–320 (on the role of the legislative body in relation to "the subjective moment in universal freedom"); and Marx, *Capital*, p. 173 (on the removal of the "veil . . . from the countenance of the social life-process"). Rousseau does not expressly state a requirement of manifestness or publicity, though it is natural to interpret his conception of the "general will" and his views about direct (nonrepresentative) democracy as presupposing this idea. On the relationship between the general will, direct democracy, and stability, see Rousseau, *Social Contract*, Book 3, chs. 12–15.

5. For a classic treatment, see John Stuart Mill's *On Liberty* in John Stuart Mill, *Utilitarianism, On Liberty, and Considerations on Representative Government,* ed. H. B. Acton (New York: E.P. Dutton, 1972), especially chs. 2–3. For more recent consideration of the scope and rationale of individual liberties, see John Hart Ely, *Democracy and Distrust: A Theory of Judicial Review* (Cambridge: Harvard University Press, 1980); and especially Ronald Dworkin, *Taking Rights Seriously* (Cambridge: Harvard University Press, 1977), in particular ch. 12.

6. The point about the relationship between diversity and reasoned judgment is made powerfully in Mill's *On Liberty:* "But it is not the minds of heretics that are deteriorated most by the ban placed on all inquiry which does not end in the orthodox conclusions. The greatest harm done is to those who are not heretics, and whose whole mental development is cramped, and their reason cowed, by fear of heresy. Who can compute what the world loses in the multitude of promising intellects combined with timid characters, who dare not follow out any bold, vigorous, independent train of thought, lest it should land them in something which would admit of being considered irreligious or immoral? . . . Not that it is solely, or chiefly, to form great thinkers, that free thinking is required. On the contrary, it is as much and even more indispensable to enable average human beings to attain the mental stature which they are capable of. There have been, and may again be, great individual thinkers in a general atmosphere of mental slavery. But there never has been, nor ever will be, in that atmosphere an intellectually active people" (p. 94). For more recent discussion specifically attentive to the function

of parties, see Ernest Mandel, *From Stalinism to Eurocommunism: The Bitter Fruits of "Socialism in One Country,"* trans. Jon Rothschild (London: New Left Books, 1978). Mandel comments: "But under these conditions, the essential function of the state in post-capitalist society is to determine *which* priorities and preferences should orient the plan. There are only two possible institutional variants. Either the selection of these priorities is *imposed* on the producer-consumers by forces outside themselves . . . or else they are made democratically by the mass of citizens, the producer-consumers themselves. Since there is no material possibility for this mass to choose among 10,000 variants of the plan (nor, for that matter, is there any possibility of their elaborating 10,000 different and coherent general plans each year), the real content of socialist democracy is indissolubly linked to the possibility of their choosing among *certain* coherent alternatives for the general plan. . . . The formulation of such alternatives presupposes precisely a multi-party system, with free access to the mass media and free debate by the mass of the population. It is only under these conditions that the enormous potential for creative initiative that exists among a highly skilled and cultivated proletariat can be fully liberated" (pp. 123–24).

7. See Karl Marx, *Capital,* vol. 3 (Moscow: Progress Publishers, 1971). Marx comments: "In fact, the realm of freedom actually begins only where labour which is determined by necessity and mundane considerations ceases; thus in the very nature of things it lies beyond the sphere of actual material production. . . . Beyond it [the sphere of material production] begins that development of human energy which is an end in itself, the true realm of freedom, which, however, can blossom forth only with this realm of necessity as its basis. The shortening of the working-day is its basic prerequisite" (p. 820).

8. As stated, our second principle of distributional equity is very nearly identical to Rawls's "Difference Principle." Rawls states this principle as follows: "Social and economic inequalities are to be arranged so that they are . . . to the greatest benefit of the least advantaged." Rawls, *Theory of Justice,* p. 302. Our use of the principle is constrained by conditions 4 and 5 of the democratic order (i.e. public control of investment and workplace democracy). It is also limited in its application to material goods.

9. See remarks of Ernest Mandel cited in note 6 above.

10. A similar point is made in Rudolf Bahro, *The Alternative in Eastern Europe*, trans. David Fernbach (London: New Left Books, 1978), p. 441. See as well related discussion in Poulantzas, *State, Power, Socialism*, Part 5. For an opposing view, see Mandel, *From Stalinism to Eurocommunism*, particularly pp. 158–78. For a summary of debate on this point, see Perry Anderson, *Arguments Within English Marxism* (London: New Left Books, 1980), ch. 7.

11. The need for producer control of the instruments of production is associated most squarely with Marx. See Karl Marx, *Grundrisse: Foundations of the Critique of Political Economy*, trans. Martin Nicolaus (New York: Random House, 1973), pp. 611–12 and 705–12 for particularly important statements of the argument that express concerns close to those we note. For a more recent Marxist view on the subject also analogous to our own, see Mihailo Marković, *The Contemporary Marx: Essays on Humanist Communism* (Bristol: Spokesman Books, 1974), especially ch. 12. For a version of the point as made within the liberal tradition, see John Stuart Mill, *Principles of Political Economy* (London and Toronto: University of Toronto Press, 1965). Mill comments: "The form of association, however, which if mankind continue to improve, must be expected in the end to predominate, is not that which can exist between a capitalist as chief, and workpeople without a voice in the management, but the association of the labourers themselves on terms of equality, collectively owning the capital with which they carry on their operations, and working under managers elected and removable by themselves." See generally Book 4, ch. 7, §6.

12. For useful recent discussions of this problem see Michèle Barrett, *Women's Oppression Today: Problems in Marxist Feminist Analysis* (London: New Left Books, 1980); and Maxine Molyneux, "Socialist Societies Old and New: Progress Toward Women's Emancipation?," *Monthly Review*, vol. 34, no. 3 (July–August 1982), pp. 56–100.

13. For an illuminating recent discussion of the logic and constraints on reform struggles within capitalist democracy, see Adam Przeworski, "Social Democracy as a Historical Phenomenon," *New Left Review*, no. 122 (July–August 1980), pp. 27–58.

14. For the first sort of iron law, see Marx, *Capital*, vol. 1, chs. 12–

15. On the second sort, see Karl Marx and Frederick Engels, *Collected Works,* vol. 6 (New York: International Publishers, 1976), pp. 210–12 and 492–94. For a general statement, see Marx's remark in *Capital,* vol. 1: "Along with the constant decrease in the number of capitalist magnates, who usurp and monopolize all the advantages of this process of transformation, the mass of misery, oppression, slavery, degradation and exploitation grows; but with this there also grows the revolt of the working class, a class constantly increasing in numbers, and trained, united and organized by the very mechanism of the capitalist process of production. The monopoly of capital becomes a fetter upon the mode of production which has flourished alongside and under it. The centralization of the means of production and the socialization of labour reach a point at which they become incompatible with their capitalist integument. This integument is burst asunder. The knell of capitalist private property sounds. The expropriators are expropriated. . . . [C]apitalist production begets, with the inexorability of a natural process, its own negation" (p. 929).

15. See V. I. Lenin, *The State and Revolution,* in Lenin, *Selected Works in Three Volumes* (Moscow: Progress Publishers, 1970), vol. 2. Lenin notes: "And so in capitalist society we have a democracy that is curtailed, wretched, false, a democracy for the rich, for the minority. The dictatorship of the proletariat, the period of transition to communism, will for the first time create democracy for the people, for the majority, along with the necessary suppression of the exploiters, of the minority. Communism alone is capable of providing really complete democracy, and the more complete it is, the sooner it will become unnecessary and wither away of its own accord" (p. 352).

16. For a similar discussion of problems of vanguardism and coalition building, see Sheila Rowbotham, Lynne Segal, and Hilary Wainwright, *Beyond the Fragments: Feminism and the Making of Socialism* (Boston: Alyson Publications, 1981).

BIBLIOGRAPHY

Abraham, David, *The Collapse of the Weimar Republic: Political Economy and Crisis* (Princeton: Princeton University Press, 1981).

Abrahamian, Ervand, *Iran Between the Two Revolutions* (Princeton: Princeton University Press, 1982).

AFL-CIO Department of Research, *Union Membership and Employment 1959–1979*, February 1980.

Aglietta, Michel, *A Theory of Capitalist Regulation,* trans. David Fernbach (London: New Left Books, 1979).

American Iron and Steel Institute, *Pig Iron and Raw Steel Production,* December 1982.

Americas Watch, *Human Rights in Guatemala: No Neutrals Allowed* (New York, 1982).

Americas Watch, Helsinki Watch, Lawyers Committee for International Human Rights, *The Reagan Administration's Human Rights Policy: A Mid-Term Review,* New York, 10 December 1982.

Amnesty International, *Amnesty International Report 1982* (London: Amnesty International Publications, 1982).

——, *Guatemala: A Government Program of Political Murder* (London: Amnesty International Publications, 1981).

——, *Pakistan: Human Rights Violations and the Decline of the Rule of Law* (London: Amnesty International Publications, 1982).

——, Press Release, 11 October 1982.

Anderson, Perry, *Arguments Within English Marxism* (London: New Left Books, 1980).

Aronowitz, Stanley, *False Promises: The Shaping of American Working-Class Consciousness* (New York: McGraw-Hill, 1973).

Bahro, Rudolf, *The Alternative in Eastern Europe,* trans. David Fernbach (London: New Left Books, 1978).

Ball, Desmond, *Politics and Force Levels* (Berkeley: University of California Press, 1980).

Bamford, James, *The Puzzle Palace: A Report on America's Most Secret Agency* (Boston: Houghton Mifflin Co., 1982).

Barrett, Michèle, *Women's Oppression Today: Problems in Marxist Feminist Analysis* (London: New Left Books, 1980).

Barth, Peter S., and H. Allan Hunt, *Worker's Compensation and Work-Related Illnesses and Diseases* (Cambridge: M.I.T. Press, 1980).

Bartlett, Randall, *Economic Foundations of Political Power* (New York: The Free Press, 1973).

Beck, Morris, *Government Spending: Issues and Trends* (New York: Praeger, 1981).

Bello, Walden, David Kinley, and Elaine Elinson, *Development Debacle: The World Bank in the Philippines* (San Francisco: Institute for Food and Development Policy, 1982).

Bernstein, Irving, *Turbulent Years: A History of the American Worker, 1933–1941* (Boston: Houghton Mifflin, 1971).

Black, Jan Knippers, *United States Penetration of Brazil* (Philadelphia: University of Pennsylvania Press, 1977).

Blechman, Barry M., and Steven S. Kaplan, *Force Without War* (Washington, D.C.: The Brookings Institution, 1978).

Block, Fred L., *The Origins of International Economic Disorder: A Study of United States International Monetary Policy from World War II to the Present* (Berkeley: University of California Press, 1977).

Boden, Leslie, "The Economic Impact of Environmental Health on Health Care Delivery," *Journal of Occupational Medicine*, vol. 18, no. 7 (July 1976).

Bowles, Samuel, and Herbert Gintis, "The Crisis of Liberal-Democratic Capitalism: The Case of the United States," *Politics and Society*, vol. 11, no. 1 (1982).

_____ , "The Crisis of Liberal Democratic Capitalism," manuscript version (1980).

Boyer, Robert, and J. Mistral, *Accumulation, Inflation, Crises* (Paris: P.U.F., 1978).

Branson, William H., and Helen B. Junz, "Trends in U.S. Trade and Comparative Advantage," *Brookings Papers on Economic Activity*, 2 (Washington, D.C.: The Brookings Institution, 1971).

Brown, Michael H., "Love Canal, U.S.A.," *New York Times Magazine*, 21 January 1979.

Bureau of the Budget, *U.S. Budget in Brief Fiscal Year 1970* (Washington, D.C.: U.S. Government Printing Office, 1969).

Burnham, Walter Dean, "The Eclipse of the Democratic Party," *Democracy*, vol. 2, no. 3 (July 1982).

————— , *The Current Crisis in American Politics* (New York: Oxford University Press, 1982).

————— , "The 1980 Earthquake: Realignment, Reaction, or What?," in Thomas Ferguson and Joel Rogers, eds., *The Hidden Election: Politics and Economics in the 1980 Presidential Campaign* (New York: Pantheon Books, 1981).

Choate, Pat, and Susan Walter, *America in Ruins* (Washington, D.C.: Council of State Planning Agencies, 1982).

Chomsky, Noam, and Edward S. Herman, *The Political Economy of Human Rights* (Boston: South End Press, 1979).

Clarke, Stephen V. O., "Perspective on the United States External Position since World War II," *Federal Reserve Bank of New York Quarterly Review* 5 (Summer 1980).

Cline, William R., "External Debt, System Vulnerability, and Development," unpublished manuscript.

Conference Board, *Statistical Bulletin*, vol. 16, no. 1 (January 1983).

Conference on Alternative State and Local Policies, *The Issues of 1982: A Briefing Book* (Washington, D.C.: Conference on Alternative State and Local Policies, 1982).

Cooper, James, and Gelvin Stevenson, "What the Fed Says Is Not What It Does," *Business Week*, 7 June 1982.

Currie, Elliott, "Crime and Ideology," *Working Papers* (May–June 1982).

Curtis, Thomas Bradford, *The Kennedy Round and the Future of American Trade* (New York: Praeger, 1967).

Davis, Mike, "The Barren Marriage of American Labour and the Democratic Party," *New Left Review*, no. 124 (November–December 1980).

————— , "Why the U.S. Working Class is Different," *New Left Review*, no. 123 (September–October 1980).

Democratic Fact Book: Issues for 1982 (Washington, D.C.: Democrats for the 80's, 1982).

Donner, Frank J., *The Age of Surveillance: The Aims and Methods of America's Political Intelligence System* (New York: Alfred A. Knopf, 1980).

Downs, Anthony, *An Economic Theory of Democracy* (New York: Harper & Row, 1957).

Draper, Theodore, "Dear Mr. Weinberger," *New York Review of Books*, 4 November 1982.

Drew, Elizabeth, "Politics and Money," *New Yorker*, 6 December 1982.

DuBoff, Richard B., "Full Employment: The History of a Receding Target," *Politics and Society*, vol. 7, no. 1 (1977).

Dworkin, Ronald, *Taking Rights Seriously* (Cambridge: Harvard University Press, 1977).

Edwards, Richard, *Contested Terrain: The Transformation of the Workplace in the Twentieth Century* (New York: Basic Books, 1979).

Ely, John Hart, *Democracy and Distrust: A Theory of Judicial Review* (Cambridge: Harvard University Press, 1980).

Environment and Health (Washington, D.C.: Congressional Quarterly, 1981).

Epstein, Gerald, "Domestic Stagflation and Monetary Policy: The Federal Reserve and the Hidden Election," in Thomas Ferguson and Joel Rogers, eds., *The Hidden Election: Politics and Economics in the 1980 Presidential Campaign* (New York: Pantheon Books, 1981).

Fallows, James, *National Defense* (New York: Random House, 1981).

Federal Home Loan Bank Board, "Mortgage Foreclosures by FSLIC Insured Savings and Loan Associations First Half 1982" (Washington, D.C., 1982).

————, Press Release, 7 December 1982.

————, *Savings and Home Financing Sourcebook,* 1981.

Ferguson, Thomas, and Joel Rogers, eds., *The Hidden Election: Politics and Economics in the 1980 Presidential Campaign* (New York: Pantheon Books, 1981).

Final Report of the Watergate Special Prosecution Force (Washington, D.C.: U.S. Government Printing Office, 1977).

Flamm, Kenneth, "Explaining U.S. Multinationals in the Postwar Era," unpublished manuscript.

Flanagan, Timothy J., David J. van Alstyne, and Michael Gottfredson, eds., *Sourcebook of Criminal Justice Statistics—1982*, U.S. Department of Justice, Bureau of Justice Statistics (Washington, D.C.: U.S. Government Printing Office, 1982).

Friedman, Samuel, *Teamster Rank and File* (New York: Columbia University Press, 1982).

Friends of the Earth, *Ronald Reagan and the American Environment* (San Francisco: Friends of the Earth Books, 1982).

Gallup Poll: Public Opinion 1980 (Wilmington: Scholarly Resources, 1981).

Gansler, Jacques, *The Defense Industry* (Cambridge: M.I.T. Press, 1980).

Gardner, Richard, *Sterling-Dollar Diplomacy* (New York: McGraw-Hill, 1969).

Gelb, Leslie H., *The Irony of Vietnam: The System Worked* (Washington, D.C.: The Brookings Institution, 1979).

Geschwender, James A., *Class, Race, and Worker Insurgency* (Cambridge: Cambridge University Press, 1977).

Gisselquist, David, *Oil Prices and Trade Deficits: U.S. Conflicts with Japan and West Germany* (New York: Praeger, 1979).

Gordon, David M., "Stages of Accumulation and Long Economic Cycles," in *Processes of the World System,* ed. Terence Hopkins and Immanuel Wallerstein (Beverly Hills: Sage Publications, 1980).

————, and Michele Naples, "More Injuries on the Job," *New York Times,* 13 December 1981.

————, Richard Edwards, and Michael Reich, *Segmented Work, Divided Workers: The Historical Transformation of Labor in the United States* (Cambridge: Cambridge University Press, 1982).

Goulden, Joseph C., *Truth Is the First Casualty: The Gulf of Tonkin Affair—Illusion and Reality* (New York: Rand McNally, 1969).

Gramsci, Antonio, *Selections from the Prison Notebooks,* ed. and trans. Quintin Hoare and Geoffrey Nowell Smith (New York: International Publishers, 1971).

Green, James R., *The World of the Worker: Labor in Twentieth-Century America* (New York: Hill & Wang, 1980).

Greider, William, *The Education of David Stockman and Other Americans* (New York: E. P. Dutton, 1982).

Habermas, Jürgen, *Communication and the Evolution of Society,* trans. Thomas McCarthy (Boston: Beacon Press, 1979).

————, *Legitimation Crisis,* trans. Thomas McCarthy (Boston: Beacon Press, 1975).

Halberstam, David, *The Best and the Brightest* (New York: Random House, 1969).

Hegel, G.W.F., *The Philosophy of Right,* trans. T. M. Knox (Oxford: Oxford University Press, 1952).

Hendricks, Evan, *Former Secrets* (Washington, D.C.: Campaign for Political Rights, 1982).

Herman, Edward S., *Corporate Control, Corporate Power* (New York: Cambridge University Press, 1981).

————, "Military Spending: The Last Externality?," unpublished manuscript.

Hersh, Seymour, "The Price of Power," *Atlantic Monthly,* December 1982.

Hombs, Mary Ellen, and Mitch Snyder, *Homelessness in America* (Washington, D.C.: The Community for Creative Non-Violence, 1982).

Institute for Labor Education and Research, *What's Wrong with the U.S. Economy?* (Boston: South End Press, 1982).

International Monetary Fund, *Annual Report, 1980* (Washington, D.C.: IMF, 1980).

———, *Direction of Trade Statistics 1982* (Washington, D.C.: IMF, 1982).

Joe, Tom, "Profile of Families in Poverty: Effects of the FY1983 Budget Proposals on the Poor" (Washington, D.C.: Center for the Study of Social Policy, 1982).

Kahan, Jerome, *Security in the Nuclear Age* (Washington, D.C.: The Brookings Institution, 1975).

Kaldor, Mary, *Baroque Arsenal* (New York: Hill & Wang, 1981).

Kaplan, Fred, *The Wizards of Armageddon* (New York: Simon & Schuster, 1983).

Kaufman, William W., *The McNamara Strategy* (New York: Harper & Row, 1964).

Kaufmann, William, "The Defense Budget," in *Setting National Priorities: The 1983 Budget,* ed. Joseph Pechman (Washington, D.C.: The Brookings Institution, 1982).

Kerr, Clark, *Labor Markets and Wage Determination: The Balkanization of Labor Markets and Other Essays* (Berkeley: University of California Press, 1977).

Klare, Michael, *Supplying Repression* (New York. Field Foundation, 1977).

———, "Reviving the American Century," *Inquiry,* May 1982, reprinted by the Institute for Policy Studies, Washington, D.C.

———, "The Weinberger Revolution," *Inquiry,* September 1982, reprinted by the Institute for Policy Studies, Washington, D.C.

Kolko, Gabriel, *Main Currents in Modern American History* (New York: Harper & Row, 1976).

Langguth, A. J., *Hidden Terrors* (New York: Pantheon Books, 1978).

Lenin, V. I., *Selected Works in Three Volumes* (Moscow: Progress Publishers, 1970).

Lernoux, Penny, *Cry of the People* (New York: Penguin, 1982).

Lewis, Anthony, "Howdy, Genghis," *New York Times,* 6 December 1982.

Lindblom, Charles E., *Politics and Markets: The World's Political-Economic Systems* (New York: Basic Books, 1977).

Lowi, Theodore J., and Alan Stone, eds., *Nationalizing Government* (Beverly Hills: Sage Publications, 1978).

Luxemburg, Rosa, *The Russian Revolution* (Ann Arbor: University of Michigan Press, 1961).

Lydenberg, Steven D., and Alice Tepper Marlin, "Business and Votes," *New York Times,* 27 October 1982.

Lydenberg, Steven D., and Susan Young, "Business Bankrolls for Local Ballots," *Business and Society Review,* no. 33 (Spring 1980).

Mackie, Thomas, and Richard Rose, *The International Almanac of Electoral History* (New York: Free Press, 1974).

Macy, Christy, and Susan Kaplan, *Documents* (New York: Penguin Books, 1980).

Magaziner, Ira, and Robert Reich, *Minding America's Business* (New York: Harcourt Brace Jovanovich, 1982).

Magdoff, Harry, and Paul Sweezy, "Financial Stability: Where Will It All End?," *Monthly Review,* vol. 34, no. 6 (November 1982).

——— , "The Deepening Crisis of U.S. Capitalism," *Monthly Review,* vol. 33, no. 5 (October 1981).

Mandel, Ernest, *From Stalinism to Eurocommunism: The Bitter Fruits of "Socialism in One Country,"* trans. Jon Rothschild (London: New Left Books, 1978).

——— , *Late Capitalism,* trans. Joris De Bres (London: New Left Books, 1975).

Marković, Mihailo, *The Contemporary Marx: Essays on Humanist Communism* (Bristol: Spokesman Books, 1974).

Marx, Karl, *Capital,* vol. 1, trans. Ben Fowkes (Middlesex: Penguin, 1976).

——— , *Capital,* vol. 3 (Moscow: Progress Publishers, 1971).

——— , *Grundrisse: Foundations of the Critique of Political Economy,* trans. Martin Nicolaus (New York: Random House, 1973).

——— and Frederick Engels, *Collected Works,* vol. 5 (New York: International Publishers, 1976).

——— and Frederick Engels, *Collected Works,* vol. 6 (New York: International Publishers, 1976).

Massachusetts Advocacy Center, *Massachusetts: The State of the Child* (Boston, 1982).

Melman, Seymour, "Looting the Means of Production," *New York Times,* 26 July 1981.

——— , *Pentagon Capitalism: The Political Economy of War* (New York: McGraw-Hill, 1970).

——— , *The Permanent War Economy: American Capitalism in Decline* (New York: Simon & Schuster, 1974).

Mill, John Stuart, *Principles of Political Economy* (London and Toronto: University of Toronto Press, 1965).

——— , *Utilitarianism, On Liberty, and Considerations on Representative Government,* ed. H. B. Acton (New York: E. P. Dutton, 1972).

Miller, Warren E., and the National Election Studies, *American National Election Study, 1980* (Ann Arbor: Inter-University Consortium for Political and Social Research, 1982).

Molyneux, Maxine, "Socialist Societies Old and New: Progress Toward Women's Emancipation?," *Monthly Review,* vol. 34, no. 3 (July–August 1982).

Montealegre, Flora, and Cynthia Aronson, "Background Information on Guatemala, Human Rights, and U.S. Military Assistance," Institute for Policy Studies Resource, Update No. 1, July 1982.

Montgomery, David, *Workers' Control in America: Studies in the History of Work, Technology, and Labor Struggles* (Cambridge: Cambridge University Press, 1979).

Musgrave, Richard A., and Peggy B. Musgrave, *Public Finance in Theory and Practice,* 3rd ed. (New York: McGraw-Hill, 1980).

National Labor Relations Board, *Thirty-fifth Annual Report for the Fiscal Year Ended June 30, 1970* (Washington, D.C.: U.S. Government Printing Office, 1970).

————, *Forty-fifth Annual Report for the Year Ended September 30, 1980* (Washington, D.C.: U.S. Government Printing Office, 1980).

National Safety Council, *Accident Facts* (Chicago, 1981).

Navasky, Victor, "The FBI's Wildest Dream," *Nation,* 17 June 1978.

Offe, Claus, and Helmut Wiesenthal, "Two Logics of Collective Action: Theoretical Notes on Social Class and Organizational Form," *Political Power and Social Theory,* vol. 1 (1980).

Okner, Benjamin A., "Total U.S. Taxes and Their Effect on the Distribution of Family Income in 1966 and 1970," in Henry J. Aaron and Michael J. Boskin, eds., *The Economics of Taxation* (Washington, D.C.: The Brookings Institution, 1980).

Olson, Mancur, *The Logic of Collective Action: Public Goods and the Theory of Groups* (Cambridge: Harvard University Press, 1965).

Organization for Economic Cooperation and Development, *National Accounts 1951–1980* (Paris: OECD, 1982).

————, *Science and Technology Indicators* (Paris: OECD, 1981).

Orshansky, Mollie, "Counting the Poor," *Social Security Bulletin,* January 1965.

O'Toole, George, *The Private Sector: Private Spies, Rent-a-Cops, and the Police-Industrial Complex* (New York: Norton, 1978).

Palmer, John L., and Isabel Sawhill, eds., *The Reagan Experiment* (Washington, D.C.: Urban Institute Press, 1982).

Parboni, Riccardo, *The Dollar and Its Rivals,* trans. Jon Rothschild (London: New Left Books, 1981).

Pechman, Joseph A., and Benjamin A. Okner, *Who Bears the Tax*

Burden? (Washington, D.C.: The Brookings Institution, 1974).

Penny, L., D. E. J. Samuels, and G. C. Scorgie, "The Nuclear Explosive Yields at Hiroshima and Nagasaki," *Philosophical Transactions of the Royal Society of London,* 1970.

The Pentagon Papers: The Defense Department History of United States Decisionmaking on Vietnam, Senator Gravel, ed. (Boston: Beacon Press, 1971).

Pierce, John C., Kathleen M. Beatty, and Paul R. Hagner, *The Dynamics of American Public Opinion: Patterns and Processes* (Glenview, Ill.: Scott, Foresman, 1982).

Piven, Frances Fox, and Richard Cloward, *The New Class War* (New York: Pantheon Books, 1982).

Poulantzas, Nicos, *State, Power, Socialism,* trans. Patrick Camiller (London: New Left Books, 1978).

Preliminary Assessment of Cleanup Costs for National Hazardous Waste Problems, consultant report to the EPA Office of Solid Waste, 1979.

Przeworski, Adam, "Material Bases of Consent: Economics and Politics in a Hegemonic System," *Political Power and Social Theory,* vol. 1 (1980).

————, "Proletariat into a Class: The Process of Class Formation from Karl Kautsky's *The Class Struggle* to Recent Controversies," *Politics and Society,* vol. 7 (1977).

————, "Social Democracy as a Historical Phenomenon," *New Left Review,* no. 122 (July–August 1980).

————, and Michael Wallerstein, "The Structure of Class Conflict in Democratic Capitalist Societies," *American Political Science Review,* vol. 76 (1982).

Rawls, John, *A Theory of Justice* (Cambridge: Harvard University Press, 1971).

————, Dewey Lectures, "Kantian Constructivism in Moral Theory," *Journal of Philosophy,* vol. 57, no. 9 (September 1980).

Rees, Albert G., *The Economics of Trade Unions* (Chicago: University of Chicago Press, 1962).

Roosevelt, Kermit, *Countercoup* (New York: McGraw-Hill, 1979).

Rostow, Walt Whitman, *The World Economy: History and Prospect* (Austin: University of Texas Press, 1978).

Rothschild, Emma, *Paradise Lost: The Decline of the Auto-Industrial Age* (New York: Random House, 1973).

Rousseau, Jean-Jacques, *The First and Second Discourses,* ed. Roger D. Masters, trans. Roger D. Masters and Judith R. Masters (New York: St. Martin's Press, 1964).

——, *The Social Contract*, ed. Roger D. Masters, trans. Judith R. Masters (New York: St. Martin's Press, 1978).

Rowbotham, Sheila, Lynne Segal, and Hilary Wainwright, *Beyond the Fragments: Feminism and the Making of Socialism* (Boston: Alyson Publications, 1981).

Ruben, George, "Collective Bargaining in 1982: Results Dictated by Economy," *Monthly Labor Review*, vol. 66, no. 1 (January 1983).

Sachs, Jeffrey, "Wages, Profits and Macroeconomic Adjustment: A Comparative Study," *Brookings Papers on Economic Activity* 2 (Washington, D.C.: The Brookings Institution, 1979).

Schlesinger, Steven, and Steven Kinzer, *Bitter Fruit* (Garden City: Doubleday, 1982).

Schoultz, Lars, *Human Rights and United States Policy towards Latin America* (Princeton: Princeton University Press, 1981).

Selikoff, Irving J., "Asbestos-Associated Disease," *Public Health and Preventive Medicine*, ed. John Last, 11th ed. (Englewood Cliffs, N.J.: Prentice-Hall, 1980).

——, *Disability Compensation for Asbestos-Associated Disease in the United States* (New York: Environmental Sciences Laboratory, Mount Sinai School of Medicine, 1981).

Sethi, S. Prakash, "Grassroots Lobbying and the Corporation," *Business and Society Review*, no. 29 (Spring 1979).

Shawcross, William, *Sideshow* (New York: Simon & Schuster, 1979).

Sierra Club, *Poisons on the Job: The Reagan Administration and American Workers* (San Francisco: Sierra Club, 1982).

Sitkoff, Harvard, *The Struggle for Black Equality 1954–1980* (New York: Hill & Wang, 1981).

Slichter, Sumner H., *Union Policies and Industrial Management* (Washington, D.C.: The Brookings Institution, 1941).

Solomon, Robert, "The International Debt Problem" (Washington, D.C.: Center for National Policy, 1982).

The Statistical History of the United States: From Colonial Times to the Present (New York: Basic Books, 1976).

Steinberg, Lawrence D., Ralph Catalano, and David Dooley, "Economic Antecedents of Child Abuse and Neglect," *Child Development*, 52 (1981).

Stigler, George, *The Citizen and the State* (Chicago: University of Chicago Press, 1978).

Stone, Alan, *Economic Regulation and the Public Interest* (Ithaca: Cornell University Press, 1977).

Stone, I. F., *In a Time of Torment* (New York: Random House, 1967).

Thurow, Lester, "Solving the Productivity Problem," in *Strengthening* the Economy: Studies in Productivity (Washington, D.C.: Center for Democratic Policy, 1982).

———, The Zero Sum Society: Distribution and the Possibilities for Economic Change (New York: Basic Books, 1980).

Tobin, James, "Stabilization Policy Ten Years After," Brookings Papers on Economic Activity, 1 (Washington, D.C.: The Brookings Institution, 1980).

Triffin, Robert, Gold and the Dollar Crisis: The Future of Convertibility (New Haven: Yale University Press, 1961).

U.S. Bureau of the Census, Current Population Reports, ser. P-20, no. 344, Voting and Registration in the Election of November 1978 (Washington, D.C.: U.S. Government Printing Office, 1982).

———, Current Population Reports, ser. P-20, no. 370, Voting and Registration in the Election of November 1980 (Washington, D.C.: U.S. Government Printing Office, 1982).

———, Current Population Reports, ser. P-23, no. 114, Characteristics of American Children and Youth: 1980 (Washington, D.C.: U.S. Government Printing Office, 1982).

———, Current Population Reports, ser. P-60, no. 132, Money Income of Households, Families, and Persons in the United States: 1980 (Washington, D.C.: U.S. Government Printing Office, 1982).

———, Current Population Reports, ser. P-60, no. 133, Characteristics of the Population Below the Poverty Level: 1980 (Washington, D.C.: U.S. Government Printing Office, 1982).

———, Current Population Reports, ser. P-60, no. 134, Money Income and Poverty Status of Families and Persons in the United States: 1981 (Advance Data from the March 1982 Current Population Survey) (Washington, D.C.: U.S. Government Printing Office, 1982).

———, Current Population Reports, ser. P-60, no. 136, Characteristics of Households and Persons Receiving Selected Non-Cash Benefits: 1981 (Washington, D.C.: U.S. Government Printing Office, 1983).

———, State and Metropolitan Area Data Book, 1982 (Washington, D.C.: U.S. Government Printing Office, 1982).

———, Statistical Abstract of the United States 1965, 86th ed. (Washington, D.C.: U.S. Government Printing Office, 1965).

———, Statistical Abstract of the United States 1974, 95th ed. (Washington, D.C.: U.S. Government Printing Office, 1975).

———, Statistical Abstract of the United States: 1980, 101st ed. (Washington, D.C.: U.S. Government Printing Office, 1982).

U.S. Department of Commerce, 1983 U.S. Industrial Outlook (Washington, D.C.: U.S. Government Printing Office, 1983).

U.S. Department of Defense, *Report of the Secretary of Defense on the FY 1983 Budget* (Washington, D.C.: U.S. Government Printing Office, 1982).

———, *Report of the Secretary of Defense on the FY 1984 Budget* (Washington, D.C.: U.S. Government Printing Office, 1983).

U.S. Department of Health and Human Services, *Monthly Vital Statistics Report,* National Center for Health Statistics, vol. 29, no. 13, 17 September 1981.

———, *Promoting Health/Preventing Disease* (Washington, D.C.: U.S. Government Printing Office, 1980).

U.S. Department of Justice, *Uniform Crime Reports for the United States* (Washington, D.C.: U.S. Government Printing Office, 1982).

———, Criminal Division, *Report to Congress on the Activities and Operations of the Public Integrity Section for 1981* (Washington, D.C.: U.S. Government Printing Office, 1982).

U.S. Department of Labor, Bureau of Labor Statistics, *Employment and Earnings,* January 1983.

U.S. Department of Labor, *Occupational Safety and Health: General Industry Standards* (Washington, D.C.: U.S. Government Printing Office, 1976).

U.S. Department of State, *Foreign Relations of the United States 1950* (Washington, D.C.: U.S. Government Printing Office, 1977).

U.S. Environmental Protection Agency, *Everybody's Problem: Hazardous Wastes* (Washington, D.C.: U.S. Government Printing Office, 1980).

U.S. Government, Interagency Task Force on Workplace Safety and Health, *First Recommendations Report,* 1 August 1978.

U.S. Office of Management and Budget, *Special Analyses, Budget of the United States Government, Fiscal Year 1970* (Washington, D.C.: U.S. Government Printing Office, 1969).

———, *Special Analyses, Budget of the United States Government, Fiscal Year 1975* (Washington, D.C.: U.S. Government Printing Office, 1974).

U.S. President, *Economic Report of the President* (Washington, D.C.: U.S. Government Printing Office, 1982).

———, *President's Report on Occupational Safety and Health* (Washington, D.C.: U.S. Government Printing Office, 1978).

U.S. Senate, *Alleged Assassination Plots Involving Foreign Leaders,* Report No. 94-465, Select Committee to Study Government Intelligence Activities, 84th Congress, 1st Session, November 1975 (Washington, D.C.: U.S. Government Printing Office, 1975).

———, *Fiscal Year 1983 Security Assistance,* Hearings Before the

Committee on Foreign Relations, 97th Congress, Second Session, 14, 15, 16 April 1982 (Washington, D.C.: U.S. Government Printing Office, 1982).

———, *Hearings Before the Select Committee to Study Governmental Operations with Respect to Intelligence Activities*, 94th Congress, vol. 7; 4, 5 December 1975 (Washington, D.C.: U.S. Government Printing Office, 1976).

———, *Intelligence Activities*, Hearings Before the Select Committee to Study Governmental Operations with Respect to Intelligence Activities, 94th Congress, 1st Session, vol. 6, November–December 1975 (Washington, D.C.: U.S. Government Printing Office, 1976).

———, *International Debt, the Banks and U.S. Foreign Policy*, Foreign Relations Committee (Washington, D.C.: U.S. Government Printing Office, 1977).

———, *Research and Development in the United States: The Role of the Public and Private Sectors*, Hearings before the Subcommittee on Energy, Nuclear Proliferation, and Government Processes, 97th Congress, Second Session, 9 March 1982 (Washington, D.C.: U.S. Government Printing Office, 1982).

———, "Security Agreements and Commitments Abroad," Foreign Relations Committee, 91st Congress, Second Session, 21 December 1970 (Washington, D.C.: U.S. Government Printing Office, 1971).

United Nations, *Demographic Yearbook 1980* (New York: United Nations, 1982).

Volcker, Paul, "The Recycling Problem Revisited," *Challenge* (July–August 1980).

Walker-Hill, Linda, and Betsey Weltner, "Fifty Years of Deception: An Overview of the Manville Corporation's Efforts to Avoid Responsibility for Asbestos-Related Diseases," unpublished manuscript.

Watson, Gayle Hudsons, "Our Monster in Brazil: It All Began with Brother Sam," *Nation* 224, 15 January 1977.

Weisskopf, Thomas, "The Current Economic Crisis in Historical Perspective," *Socialist Review*, vol. 11, no. 3 (May–June 1981).

Widmaier, Hans Peter, Jürgen Frank, and Otto Roloff, "Public Expenditure and Private Consumption," in European Cultural Foundation, *The Future Is Tomorrow* (The Hague: Martinus Nijhoff, 1975).

Wiggins, David, "Deliberation and Practical Reason," in Amélie Oksenberg Rorty, ed., *Essays on Aristotle's Ethics* (Berkeley: University of California Press, 1980).

Williamson, Jeffrey G., and Peter H. Lindert, "Long-Term Trends in

American Wealth Inequality," in *Modeling the Distribution and Intergenerational Transmission of Wealth,* ed. James D. Smith (Chicago: University of Chicago Press, 1980).

Wilson, James Q., ed., *The Politics of Regulation* (New York: Basic Books, 1980).

Windchy, Eugene G., *Tonkin Gulf* (New York: Doubleday, 1971).

Working Committee on the CIA/FBI Order, "Suspending the Constitution " (Washington, D.C.: General Board of Church and Society, 1982).

World Financial Markets, Morgan Guaranty Trust Company, April 1981.

INDEX

ACTION (civil rights group), 42
advertising, by corporate and trade
associations, 34–35
Agent Identities Law, 45–46
aircraft industry, 90, 96
air pollution, 24–25
alcohol abuse, 29
Allende, Salvador, 44
Americas Watch, 37
Amnesty International, 38
antinuclear movement, 175
asbestos exposure, 27
authoritarianism, in protectionist
strategy, 142–43
automobile industry, 22, 23, 90, 92,
95, 98, 137
autonomy, in democracy, 151, 153,
155, 157–58, 162–64, 165–67

Baez, Joan, 41
balance of payments, 102, 105, 121
bank failures, 21–22
banking system, international, 22, 90,
101, 102, 104, 124, 125–28, 131–
32
bankruptcy, 84; increase of, 21, 119
Black Panther Party, 42
black population: civil rights movement and, 42, 111, 112; FBI activities directed against, 41–43;
poverty of, 31–32; unemployment
of, 32; voting turnouts in, 33
Brazil, 22, 36, 132
Bretton Woods monetary system, 89–
90, 97, 100, 117; advantages vs.

disadvantages of, 101–106; collapse
of, 121, 140
Bush, George, 39
business: failures of, 21, 85, 119;
political role of, 15–16, 129–30. *See
also* capitalism; capitalist democracy

Cambodia, 36–37, 45
capitalism: capitalist democracy vs.,
49–50, 146, 164–65; in domestic
vs. international markets, 74–76,
78–80; iron laws of development of,
169–72; material uncertainty in,
53–55; "people's," 30–31; profits
and investment in, 52–54, 72, 73,
79, 84–85, 148; shared vs. varied
interests in, 74–76; threat of exit
in, 79–80; uneven development of,
74–75
capitalist democracy, 47–145; alternatives to, 146–83; bargaining and
coordination problem in, 60, 61–62,
64–67; 76; breakdown of, 81–87;
compatibility of economic rationality and diverse motivations in, 67–
71; demand constraint in, 51–59,
61–62, 83; democracy vs., 49, 50–
67, 146, 150–51, 167–69, 180–81;
domestic-international interdependence in, 73–77, 81–129; domestic politics in, 47, 71–72, 81–87;
foreign policy in, 73–77; hypothet-
ical case of collective action in, 58–
60; legitimacy of state in, 71–73,
76–77, 82–83, 133; money as